Your Kid Has ADHD, Now What?

A Handbook for Parents, Educators and Practitioners

Janette M. Schaub, Ph.D.

Beaver's Pond Press

ISBN: 1-890676-22-5

Library of Congress Catalog Number 98-85609

Interior Design: Mori Studio
Cover Design: Don Popelka
Production Editor: Milt Adams

For information about additional books and workshops, please contact the author:

7400 Metro Blvd, Suite 417
Minneapolis, Minnesota 55439
Telephone 612 835-4466
Fax 612 820-0113

Printed in the United States of America.

J   I   H   G   F   E   D   C   B   A

Beaver's Pond Press

Edina, Minnesota

*To those people who have greatly influenced my life:
my parents, Dr. August and Helen Schaub;
my children, Kate, Matthew and Sarah;
and my husband Ken.*

Contents

Author's Note 1
Preface 3
Acknowledgments 9

INTRODUCTION
    Parents' Trials and Tribulations 11

PART ONE: WHAT WE NOW KNOW ABOUT ADHD
    1. The Evolution of ADHD 21
    2. ADHD Through the Lifespan 29
    3. Causes: Fiction and Fact 47
    4. ADHD Affects Motivation 59
    5. ADHD Affects the Ability to Follow Rules 61

PART TWO: WHAT ADHD LOOKS LIKE IN REAL LIFE
    6. Twelve Common Behavioral Patterns 67
       • Inattention 67
       • Impulsivity 72
       • Hyperactivity 73
       • Poor Response to Consequences 74
       • Excessive Noncompliance 76
       • Inconsistency 77
       • Difficulty Delaying Gratification 80
       • Emotional Overarousal 81
       • Poor Persistence 82
       • Difficulty with Change and Transitions 83
       • Disorganization 84
       • Social Problems 85

PART THREE: PARENTING PRINCIPLES
    7. Form Realistic Expectations 91
    8. Distinguish Between ADHD-Related
       Behavior and Willful Noncompliance 99

9. Consider How Your
   Temperament "Fits" with Your Child 103
10. Parent Proactively 113
11. Avoid Over-Punishing 131
12. Give Positive Redirections and Specific Feedback 143

**PART FOUR: BEHAVIOR MANAGEMENT
STRATEGIES AND METHODS**
13. Structuring Your Home 149
14. Structuring Your Child 157
15. Teaching Your Child to Structure Himself 165
16. "Catching Him Being Good" 171
17. Devising Behavior Modification Systems 179
18. Breaking the Cycle of Willful Noncompliance 207
19. Using Active Listening 223

PART FIVE: MEDICATION MANAGEMENT
20. Stimulants. 245
21. Other Medications Used to Manage ADHD 261

**PART SIX: HOW TO BE AN EFFECTIVE ADVOCATE
FOR YOUR CHILD AT SCHOOL**
22. Understanding the Effects of
   ADHD in the Classroom 271
23. Understanding Appropriate
   Classroom Modifications 281
24. Knowing the Laws and Your Rights 303
25. Keeping Records of Your Child 319
26. Preparing for the IEP or Section 504 Meeting 323
27. Providing Input Into the
   Selection of Your Child's Teacher....................... 333
28. Communicating with the School 341

Concluding Remarks for Parents 345

APPENDICES
A. Where to Get Information 349
B. Home Charts 359
   Let's Get Ready 361
   Home Behavior Charts (2) 362
   Self-Control Contract 364
   Reward Menus (3) 365

C. School Charts 369
   Daily Progress Reports (2) 371
   Daily Student Rating Cards (2) 373
   504 Plan: Student Progress Report 375
D. Behavior Rating Scales for
   Medication Monitoring... 377

REFERENCES AND SUBJECT INDEX
   References 383
   Subject Index 391

About the Author 397

Author's Notes

Both boys and girls have ADHD, and both are dramatically affected by it. However, it is currently diagnosed most often in boys. As a reflection of this fact, and for purposes of simplification, I have used "he" throughout most of this book when referring to an individual with ADHD.

All the stories and profiles included in this book were drawn from clients with whom I have worked over the years. In some cases, stories are composites of more than one individual. All identifying information has been changed to protect people's privacy.

This book deals with what to do once a child is diagnosed with ADHD. If you are still struggling with the question of whether your child has an attention deficit, please refer to other references that provide more discussion of assessment, such as *Taking Charge of ADHD*, by Russell Barkley, (New York: Guilford Press, 1995).

Preface

Your Kid Has ADHD: Now What? is a book for parents who are struggling with managing the behavior of their child with ADHD. Parenting a child with ADHD may be one of the most demanding challenges of your life. You have likely asked yourself a hundred times, "What am I doing wrong?" "Why doesn't anything work with my child?" "Will my child ever outgrow this?" or "Why did this happen to me?"

You wonder if you'll be able to control your child's behavior without sacrificing his self-esteem in the process. You're puzzled because your child seems to do well in some situations but not in others. You're frustrated because your child seems so easily upset, and he continually argues with you. You may ask yourself, "Can my child really not keep up with his homework, or is he just lazy?" You may wonder which of his behaviors are related to his ADHD and which are just stubborn refusal or a stage he is going through. This book answers these and many other questions.

Your Kid Has ADHD: Now What? is also for teachers, who struggle with the same questions, challenges and self-doubts from their own perspectives. Teachers want to see their students learn and succeed. They want to be able to handle the challenging situations, and they are looking for better tools. This book gives them the needed tools as well as the underlying principles to use these tools effectively with their students with ADHD.

Your Kid Has ADHD: Now What? is a valuable reference for practitioners as well. It can be used as a guide for conducting parent training sessions, developing behavior modification programs and providing educational consultation to schools and parents.

Your Kid Has ADHD: Now What? helps you to understand that ADHD is much more than an attention deficit. It is an all-encompassing problem in self-regulation and self-control that has far-reaching effects on many aspects of an individual's life, not just paying attention and ignoring distractions. To simply view ADHD as an attention problem downplays the significance of the disorder and leads parents down the wrong road for effective parenting strategies.

This book is based on the latest scientific research, which shows that ADHD is fundamentally a biochemically-based disorder of self-control — the child is unable to put the "brakes" on his behavior and emotions to effectively control himself. This problem is technically termed **dis-inhibition**. We now have a better understanding that the fundamental behavior problems associated with ADHD are a result of the child's biological make-up, not the result of poor parenting, childhood laziness or character flaws.

Understanding that ADHD is fundamentally a disorder of inhibition or poor self-control has profound meaning for the way that parents and teachers manage the behavior of these children. A disorder of inhibition means that children with ADHD are governed by their impulses *at the moment* rather than by consequences in the future (even if the future is 10 minutes from now). Since children with ADHD are "managed by the moment," consequences have less influence over their behavior. Yet parents tend to discipline by consequences, reacting after the fact and imposing punishments after the "crime" has occurred.

Despite the fact that consequence-driven discipline doesn't work with ADHD, parents continue to use it repeatedly, often lamenting, "No matter how many times I get angry and punish my child for doing something, he continues to do it!" Like their child with ADHD, parents get caught in a cycle of reacting impulsively and engaging in the same counterproductive behavior over and over again in attempts to change their child's behavior. Simply put, because ADHD renders consequences less effective in controlling behavior, parents should not rely on consequences as their main tool in controlling the behavior of their child with ADHD. *Your Kid Has ADHD: Now What?* teaches parents how to use other, more effective concepts, tools and methods.

The methods in this book are built around the principle that to parent a child with ADHD effectively, parents must parent proactively, not reactively. They can no longer rely on the ineffective use of consequences, which is disciplining "after the fact." Instead, they must be proactively thinking ahead, structuring situations and making important changes. This is parenting "before the fact."

I first began working with children with ADHD and their families more than 24 years ago, a time when this disorder was called hyperactivity, and the cause was believed to be brain dysfunction or inept parenting. As I worked with parents, I experienced their frustration and discouragement as they tried in vain to use conventional methods to control their children's behavior. If common discipline and logical consequences regulated the behavior of other children, why did these traditional methods fail with hyperactive children? In order to answer this fundamental question and to better understand this complex and frustrating disorder, I delved into the research. The more I researched this disorder, the more I appreciated its complexities and the challenges facing parents of children with ADHD.

I eventually channeled my curiosity and my confusion in a return to graduate school to earn my Ph.D. at the University of Minnesota. My research focused on ADHD, culminating in a doctoral dissertation entitled, *An Investigation of Diagnostic Procedures for Identifying Attention Deficit Disorders In Children.*

I studied under Dr. Philip Kendall, a leader in cognitive-behavioral interventions for impulsive children. My work has also been greatly influenced by Dr. Russell Barkley, a prominent researcher of ADHD and the main proponent of the concept that ADHD is fundamentally a disorder of self-regulation. Other parenting specialists and child developmentalists who have influenced my work include Erik Erickson, Mel Levine, Lawrence Balter, Gerald Patterson, Matthew McKay, Thomas Gordon, Tom Phalen, Stanley Turecki, and Donald Dinkmeyer.

Your Kid Has ADHD: Now What? is an outgrowth of the years of research on this disorder coupled with the knowledge and experience I have gained working with well over a thousand children with ADHD and their families. My experience as a parent of three young children has also vastly contributed to my knowledge and abilities, helping me to understand that as parents we need practical and sound parenting methods that actually work. We don't need strategies that may be good in theory but have no effect in real life.

Finally, I have gained insight as well as hope from my husband, who also happens to have an attention deficit disorder. A successful businessman who earned an undergraduate degree from Yale and an MBA and a Ph.D. from Stanford, he would surprise most people with the news that he has ADHD. Hopefully his example can provide a ray of hope for parents reading this book. He is a daily reminder to me that despite the profound effect that ADHD may have on one's life, it does not relegate one to a life of dysfunction and failure.

Your Kid Has ADHD: Now What? has six parts.

PART ONE *What We Now Know About ADHD*, profiles the evolution of our understanding of this disorder. ADHD is described in detail from infancy through adulthood. Parents are helped to understand how ADHD expresses itself at each stage of their child's development. We also discuss what does and does not cause ADHD. Myths are debunked and facts are explained. A working model of ADHD, based on the neurology of this disorder, is presented, providing parents with a practical blueprint from which to operate as they develop more effective parenting strategies. Part One concludes with detailed explanations why these children struggle with poor motivation and frequent rule-breaking.

PART TWO *What ADHD Looks Like in Real Life*, takes ADHD out of the theoretical realm and describes it in a down-to-earth way that helps parents understand what this disorder is all about. ADHD is described not as a list of clinical symptoms, but as a constellation of 12 common behavioral patterns. As parents read about these patterns, it will seem as though they are watching ADHD on a videotape. They will come to understand why their child continually breaks rules, does not respond to consequences, has difficulty making and keeping friends, overreacts to even the simplest things, can't keep track of his belongings, gives up too early, and argues too long. Parents will also learn that they are not alone in their daily trials and tribulations.

PART THREE *Parenting Principles*, teaches parents to realize that they must understand the fundamental principles of ADHD before they can effectively and proactively parent their child. Six critical parenting principles are explained, grounded in current scientific research. Principle 1 guides parents in forming realistic expectations for their child's behavior (which ultimately helps parents calm down and control their own impulsivity). Principle 2 teaches parents the importance of determining whether their child's behavior is related to ADHD or is just willful stubbornness. Principles 3 and 4 help parents understand that their actions and reactions may actually be contributing to their child's problems. Principles 5 and 6 provide the rationale and guidance for engaging in positive parenting.

PART FOUR *Behavior Management Strategies and Methods*, teaches parents practical ways to put the six management principles into practice. Seven important management areas are described in detail with step-by-step procedures for managing the behavior of ADHD. Parents are taught how to properly structure the home, structure their child, and teach their child to eventually structure himself. Concrete methods for improving the climate in the household and increasing positive attention are detailed. Parents are also given step-by-step procedures for setting up practical behavior modification programs within the home. An effective method to stop the arguing and increase compliance is presented. Finally, parents are taught how to talk to their child in such a way that they avoid defensiveness and the emotional overreactions so common with ADHD.

PART FIVE *Medication Management*, demystifies medication and provides parents with the information they need to know to make informed decisions about whether to use medication. The medications most commonly used to manage the symptoms of ADHD are explained as well as other medications that are considered second- and third-tier alternatives. Common side effects, benefits, and dosage levels are detailed. Guidelines for parents to follow once medication is initiated are also included.

PART SIX *How to be an Effective Advocate for Your Child at School*, presents specific steps parents should follow to advocate for their child's well-being at school. These steps include helping parents understand how and why ADHD affects their child in the classroom, knowing what to look for in a classroom and a teacher, learning how to gain appropriate services for their child at school, and understanding the services and adaptations that would best meet their child's needs. This chapter will make parents more knowledgeable about ADHD in the classroom and will increase their confidence in advocating for their child's educational needs.

Ultimately, *Your Kid Has ADHD: Now What?* teaches parents how to put the "brakes" on themselves and on their child, steering everyone down a new road that includes a calmer household, fewer arguments, better compliance, and a more confident and successful child.

Janette M. Schaub, Ph.D.
April 27, 1998

Acknowledgments

I have many people to thank.

First, I must thank all of the individuals and families I have seen throughout the years. They have been my most valuable teachers, offering their experiences, their insights, their frustrations, and their successes. I am grateful for the confidence they gave me and the lessons I learned.

My sincere thanks is extended to Milt Adams, my publisher. His boundless enthusiasm for this book and his heart-felt insight as a parent of a child with ADHD were inspirational. Milt gave generously of his time, always willing to meet any hour of the day. He had the gift of allowing me to feel that this project was the most important on his "full plate."

I am grateful for the intelligence and talents of my editor Pat Morris. Her suggestions were clear, wise and helpful. Time and again, she impressed me with her ability to thoroughly grasp a subject and offer new and creative insights that made complex ideas come to life.

A special thanks goes to my friend and colleague Dr. Jim Moore for graciously taking the time to review the chapters on medication. I have great respect for Jim's experience and wisdom, and I was eager to hear his comments and add his thoughtful suggestions.

I also wish to thank Jack Caravela and Jaana Bykonich for their creativity and artistic talents. They transformed my charts and diagrams from amateur drawings to professional exhibits. Also on the artistic front, special thanks go to Don Popelka, who created a cover design and color scheme that captured the emotional impact of ADHD.

I cannot adequately express my gratitude to my parents Dr. August and Helen Schaub, for the inspiration and direction they have given me. Through their example, I learned the value of hard work and the drive to accept no other option but success. I thank my mother for her wonderful humor and irreverence, her remarkable spirit of survival, and her unfailing generosity. I thank my father for his awe-inspiring self-discipline, his constant striving for learning, and his deep sense of responsibility.

I want to express my appreciation to my brother Jim Schaub for his technical expertise and time. Every team should have its own computer genius!

My warmest gratitude goes to my three children, Kate, Sarah and Matthew. They are my constant reminders of the value of proactive parenting and the benefits of active listening. Throughout this project, especially during those times when it seemed overwhelming, I took much strength from my children, knowing that they were proud of their mom for writing a book. And at those times when I allowed myself to shut out the world and obsess on "the book," they were always there to remind me of my true priorities.

Finally, and most significantly, my deep thanks and appreciation go to my husband Ken. My gratitude for his unfailing support and pride cannot be measured. Every step of the way, he was my most ardent advocate and my wisest advisor. His clarity of thought and suggestions about both content and flow helped transform this book from a dream into a reality. His patience throughout was more than I deserved but just what I needed. His proddings to keep going, his irrepressible optimism, and his business common sense gave me the will, the strength and the sanity to stick with this project and make it the best possible. He renews my appreciation of the fact that I am truly blessed.

Introduction

PARENTS' TRIALS AND TRIBULATIONS

As a parent of a child with ADHD you may feel frustrated, demoralized, defensive, depressed, angry and ... misunderstood. There are good reasons for this array of emotions. Some of the comments you may have heard about your child include:

> An in-law saying, *"Well, if you'd just give him a good spanking now and then, he'd be just fine."*

or

> Your child's teacher asking, *"Are there problems at home we should know about?"*

or

> A neighbor overheard saying, *"I don't want my son to play with their child anymore. It's always trouble when he's around."*

or

> Your family physician proclaiming, *"Give him time; he'll out-grow it. Just go home and take an aspirin."*

or

> Your husband stating, *"You give in too easily with him."*

or

> Your wife exclaiming, *"Sure, that's easy for you to say. You come home and play with him. I'm the one who has to keep after him to do his homework, pick up his socks, wash his face, brush his teeth, put his toys away, stop hitting his sister... And then I have to take the weekly phone calls from his teacher telling me what he did wrong today. I'm at the point where I hate to answer the phone."*

You and your spouse have probably argued about whose way of handling your child is better, especially since he seems to respond better to Dad. Babysitters often won't come back to babysit again. As a result, you don't get out much. Running necessary errands with your child is always a battle, and you dread asking a relative to watch him one more time because you don't want to hear what you're doing wrong or what you could be doing better. Other parents stop inviting your child over to play. You may feel isolated in your own neighborhood. Teachers are constantly calling about what your child did wrong today or that his assignments are still missing. Your spouse starts coming home from work later and later. You see other children responding to rules and consequences, but your child never seems to change his behavior despite all of the time-outs, loss of privileges, punishments and even yelling. You may now be depressed, especially if you're the mom, and feel that maybe you *are* a bad parent.

To add to the confusion and frustration, you probably often hear contradictory and incorrect information from magazines, radio, television, grandma, and your neighbors:

"He can't be ADD. He can play Nintendo® for an hour!"

"Ritalin causes drug addiction and turns your kid into a zombie."

"Children outgrow ADHD by the time they're adolescents."

"ADHD is the result of poor parenting."

"You need a neurologist to make the diagnosis."

"A child has to be really hyperactive to be ADHD."

"Diet, and especially sugar, cause ADHD."

"Ritalin causes Tourette's syndrome."

"There's no such thing as ADD. It's just a fad."

"Tough love is the answer."

Parents have revealed to me their frustration and confusion by the following comments:

"I think this diagnosis is wrong. Jason can sit and play with his Legos® or watch TV for hours. And he is not bouncing off the walls. Sure he gets revved up sometimes and gets into mischief, but I think he's just a normal kid. In fact, he reminds me of myself when I was a kid. I think his teacher just doesn't like him."

"Nothing I do seems to work with him. I keep telling him and telling him to stop, but he keeps doing the same things over and over again."

"He runs our household."

"I must be crazy! This child is impossible to handle. But when he goes over to his grandparents, they say he acts just fine, no problems. So there must be something wrong with me."

"I'm afraid to let him go to birthday parties because I'm embarrassed about how he'll act. You'd think that by this age, he'd know how to act."

If you are confused, angry, fed up, worn down or desperate, you are not alone in your feelings! Millions of parents are struggling with the frustrations and exasperations of raising a child with ADHD. You pray that he will outgrow this "thing." You find yourself looking for that cure or miracle method that will make this disorder go away so that you and your family can live your lives like other families.

Although ADHD is a disorder that cannot be "cured" or "fixed," it can be managed. Using multiple methods, which include parent training, behavior management, classroom interventions and/or special education, medication, and individual or family therapy, you can learn how to manage and cope with ADHD-related behaviors.

Since the disorder is complicated, your child will exhibit a vast array of problems over the years. Just knowing some techniques will not be enough to help you manage the numerous and unending behavioral difficulties which arise. You must first develop an understanding of ADHD and how it affects behavior. Then you will be better able to intuitively devise appropriate behavior management and coping strategies for each situation as it arises.

As you begin the demanding process of dealing with the problems associated with ADHD, it is important that you consider the many rewards and benefits that can be part of this disorder as well. Although many parents report that they go through a grieving process upon learning their child's diagnosis (i.e., grieving the loss of a dream and what life could have been had their child been "normal"), ADHD does not extinguish all chances for a happy and fulfilling life. Consider the true story of young Al.

The townspeople gathered and stared as the 6-year-old boy received a number of harsh blows from his father's birch switch. Young Al was in trouble again. He was a mischievous child and considered difficult to handle. This latest offense was a bit more serious than the others — he accidentally burned down his father's barn. He innocently explained that he had set a little fire inside the barn "just to see what it would do."

His father had grown weary of young Al's countless scrapes and had resorted to physical punishment as a way to teach him a lesson and curb his behavior. He often lamented that this boy seemed to lack ordinary common sense. The harsh corporal punishment, however, did not serve to change Al's behavior or keep him from playing tricks on others. While his parents tried to rear him properly (and his mother seemed to exert extraordinary patience in this endeavor) Al seemed to march to his own drummer.

Al was a curious child, and from the moment he could talk, he seemed to ask countless questions. The unending "whys," "wheres," and "whats" are said to have driven his father to exhaustion. His inquisitive nature often landed him in misadventures. Besides the barn incident, he once fell into a canal and had to be fished out before he drowned. On another occasion, he fell into a grain elevator, almost smothering to death.

Although Al was considered to be basically a good child, he was very strong-willed and stubborn, particularly when he could not have his way. His parents believed in "spare the rod, spoil the child," and it has been said that the bark was worn off the birch switch used to punish him.

By eight years of age, young Al was considered a challenge in the classroom. Corporal punishment was allowed at that time, and Al was often on the receiving end because of his "refusal" to take in the lessons or follow the ways of the classroom. He irritated his teacher by asking so many questions and failing to pay proper attention. His teacher said that Al's mind was "addled." Al complained that the lessons were boring, that his teacher talked too long, and that it was hard for him to learn everything through memory. He wanted to learn by "seeing, doing and making." He later said:

I remember I used to never be able to get along at school. I was always at the foot of the class. I used to feel that the teach-

ers did not sympathize with me, and that my father thought I was stupid..."

Al's mother could see that this was a bad situation for her son and removed him from the school after three months. She knew that her son's mind was not "addled" but that he responded to "hands on" learning. Rather than forcing and prodding him to engage in lessons that were tortuous for him, she approached him with sympathetic understanding that nurtured his confidence.

Unusual for the times, his mother had the notion that learning could be fun. She made a game out of teaching him and called it "exploring." She responded to his likes and interests and built her lesson plans around that which truly ignited him and captured his attention. She knew that her son had a florid imagination and that he expressed his ideas through creative and inventive images rather than through writings. She realized his interests were more in the direction of science, so when Al was nine, she bought him an elementary book on physical science full of illustrated scientific experiments. Young Al's desire for learning caught fire, and he developed a passion for chemistry and conducting experiments. His mother had accomplished what only great educators can do; she brought her son to the stage of learning for the love of learning.

Al's bedroom soon became an endless collection of chemicals in jars. His laboratory was very messy with chemicals spilled on the floor and wet-cell batteries leaking sulfuric acid on furniture. His mother complained to no avail, and he was ordered to set up shop in the basement. From this subterranean level, occasional rattlings could be felt and explosions could be heard, causing his father to lament that Al would blow them all up one day!

Al's unconventional and busy mind led him down many inventive and, at times, mischievous paths. One day Al learned that balloons could fly when filled with gas. His unbridled curiosity caused him to convince a boyhood friend to swallow a triple dose of Seidlitz powders. Al was convinced that once his friend's stomach was filled with gas, he would start flying. Instead, his friend became terribly sick to his stomach. On another occasion, Al was intrigued by Benjamin Franklin's discoveries in static electricity. He attempted to create his own version of static electricity by tying the tails of two big tomcats together with wire and vigorously rubbing their fur together. The end result was a good clawing by two perturbed cats.

Al's experiments progressed and matured from these early days of curiosity. By the age of 23 he had earned over $ 40,000 for one of his first inventions, an improved stock ticker. From there he went on to improve the typewriter. He improved the telephone by adding a carbon transmitter, which eliminated the need to shout into the mouthpiece. His invention of the phonograph ranks as one of the world's most original inventions. Other inventions included the storage battery, a cement mixer, the dictaphone, a duplicating machine and synthetic rubber.

Perhaps the invention that Al is best known for, however, is the electric light bulb. Yes, Thomas Alva Edison grew from a mischievous young boy who was considered "addled," uncontrollable and unteachable by conventional standards, to one of the most revered and respected scientists in American history.

Although we cannot confirm a diagnosis, Thomas Edison showed all the classic characteristics of ADHD. His ADHD was a "disorder" only to the extent that he (and his mother) would allow it to be. In fact, he was driven by the spirit and energy of his ADHD throughout his life. He channeled and used it to his (and society's) advantage.

His creativity sparked the rich ideas that drove him. His curiosity caused him to investigate that which most of us never consider. His stubbornness fortified him through difficult and demeaning times. His willfulness would not allow his spirit to be broken when the conventional minds around him tried to tame him. His energy propelled him to turn into reality those ideas that most of us only contemplate. His willingness to take risks allowed him to travel down paths that bore fruit for all of us. His refusal to consider the possibility of failure guaranteed his success. His refusal to bow to stifling and extra-punitive consequences helped him to overcome barriers that would halt most of us in our tracks.

We can all take a lesson from Thomas Alva Edison and his mother. Accept your child for who and what he is. Nurture his strengths and downplay his weaknesses. But realize that what may be viewed as his weaknesses by conventional minds may actually be his strengths. Be your child's strongest advocate, and he will learn that he is worth advocating for. Value your child's strengths, and he will learn to value himself.

Set up your child for success, and he will learn to succeed. Have confidence in your child, and he will learn to have confidence in himself. Accept your child, and he will learn to accept himself.

Before you read this book and resume your challenge of dealing with your child's problematic behaviors, discover the "young Al" in your child. Take time to do an important inventory, compiling a list of all of your child's positive qualities, such as his humor, his energy, his creativity, his spontaneity, his sociability, his sensitivity, etc. Post this list in a place where you can read it every day and remind yourself that your child is not defined by his ADHD. Yes, there will be bad days and bad weeks when you will feel totally exasperated and worn out. It is especially important that you read this list on those trying days. Make an effort to redirect your focus on what is good about your child, not what is bad. Take heart in your child's strengths and protect and nurture them. Realize that with your guidance and structure, your child has the potential to use his strengths to not only succeed in this world but also to make a contribution that is unique to him.

Part One

What We Now Know About ADHD

Although **ADHD** is one of the most common childhood disorders, it is perhaps the most misunderstood. It has been called many names throughout the years, and there have been even more theories about its cause. Our understanding of this disorder has grown considerably because of improved research methods and hundreds of controlled studies.

The Evolution of ADHD

ADHD, the most common childhood disorder, is the number one reason children are referred to child guidance clinics. ADHD affects 3-5 percent of the school-age population, approximately 2.5 to 3 million children. This is equivalent to about two children in every classroom. It is believed that boys manifest the disorder more than girls by a ratio of approximately 4:1 to 9:1, but we are now realizing that it is likely many girls with this disorder are undiagnosed.

Despite the fact that ADHD is so common, researchers have been baffled by this disorder for some time. To illustrate the long-standing confusion of the experts, just take a look at the many different names this disorder has been called throughout the years:

- Defect of Moral Character in 1900

- Minimal Brain Damage in 1950

- Hyperkinetic Reaction of Childhood in 1968

- Hyperactivity in 1970

- Attention Deficit Disorder with Hyperactivity and Attention Deficit Disorder without Hyperactivity in 1982

- Attention-deficit Hyperactivity Disorder and Undifferentiated Attention-deficit Disorder in 1987

- Attention-Deficit/Hyperactivity Disorder (Combined Type, Predominantly Inattentive Type, or Predominantly Hyperactive-Impulsive Type) in 1994 with the publication of the *Diagnostic and Statistical Manual of Mental Disorders, Fourth Edition* (DSM-IV).[1]

The name changes over the years reflect the evolution of our understanding of this disorder and its symptoms.

A major shift in how researchers thought about this disorder was reflected in a dramatic name change in 1982 to Attention Deficit Disorder with Hyperactivity (ADD/H) and Attention Deficit Disorder without Hyperactivity (ADD-H).

This new thinking was an outgrowth of more stringent research methods and long-term studies that suggested hyperactivity was not as central to this disorder as once believed. Although many individuals seemed to "outgrow" their hyperactivity, they continued to have various other problems. Researchers began to direct their focus away from hyperactivity and found that the primary problem with these children was not that they were overstimulated or had excessive amounts of energy, but rather they had short attention spans and were impulsive. They would go from one thing to another without thinking about the consequences of their behavior until after the fact, if then.

Three primary deficits were considered to underlie ADD with and without Hyperactivity:

1. Difficulty **sustaining attention** to tasks, particularly if the tasks were long, monotonous, or boring
2. Difficulty **controlling impulses**
3. Difficulty **controlling activity level** to fit the situation

The name for this disorder was changed again in 1987 to Attention-deficit Hyperactivity Disorder (ADHD) and Undifferentiated Attention-deficit Disorder (UADD) because research indicated that there were significant differences between those children who were hyperactive (ADHD) and those who were not (UADD). Certainly there was the group of children who had attention problems coupled with their "hyperactivity." However, there were also children who had attention and concentration difficulties who were not "hyperactive" or disruptive at all. In fact, these children seemed to bring little attention to themselves and often "fell through the cracks." Researchers began to understand that those children without hyperactivity may represent a very distinct disorder, different from ADD with Hyperactivity.

THE LATEST RECONCEPTUALIZATION OF ADHD
The Three Types of ADHD

In 1994, this complex disorder got yet another set of names. The disorder is still called Attention-Deficit/Hyperactivity Disorder (ADHD), but symptoms fall into two basic categories, *inattention* and *hyperactivity-impulsivity*. There are now three classifications of ADHD:

- ADHD, Predominantly Inattentive Type
- ADHD, Predominantly Hyperactive-Impulsive Type
- ADHD, Combined Type

An individual who shows *mostly* symptoms of inattention is **ADHD, Predominantly Inattentive Type.** If an individual displays *mostly* symptoms of hyperactivity and impulsivity, he is considered **ADHD, Predominantly Hyperactive-Impulsive Type**. This second category is especially useful for preschoolers because they may manifest a number of problematic hyperactive-impulsive behaviors at this age, but they are not yet expected at this age to demonstrate much concentration or sustained attention. An individual who manifests inattention as well as hyperactivity-impulsivity symptoms is considered **ADHD, Combined Type.**

Most parents as well as clinicians find these new diagnostic labels to be even more confusing. But these three categories were meant to stress the fact that individuals with ADHD do not fit exclusively into one category because they do not show symptoms from only one category. A child is not totally Hyperactive-Impulsive or totally Inattentive. The important diagnostic point is to determine under which category most of the child's symptoms fall. For example, your child may be diagnosed ADHD, Predominantly Hyperactive-Impulsive Type because most of his symptoms are of this nature, but he may also show some symptoms of inattention such as daydreaming, disorganization, and forgetfulness. The same is true if your child is diagnosed with ADHD, Predominantly Inattentive Type. Although most of his symptoms are related to inattention, he may also show some hyperactive-impulsive symptoms such as restlessness, impatience, or excessive talking.

CURRENT DIAGNOSTIC GUIDELINES
The Necessary Symptoms

Specific criteria must be met before an individual can be diagnosed with ADHD. The current guidelines which professionals follow in making a diagnosis are in the American Psychiatric Association's *Diagnostic and Statistical Manual of Mental Disorders, Fourth Edition* (DSM-IV). The diagnostic criteria are:

Attention-Deficit/Hyperactivity Disorder

A. Either (1) or (2):

(1) six (or more) of the following symptoms of **inattention** have persisted for at least 6 months to a degree that is maladaptive and inconsistent with developmental level:

Inattention

(a) often fails to give close attention to details or makes careless mistakes in schoolwork, work or other activities

(b) often has difficulty sustaining attention in tasks or play activities

(c) often does not seem to listen when spoken to directly

(d) often does not follow through on instructions and fails to finish schoolwork, chores, or duties in the workplace (not due to oppositional behavior or failure to understand instructions)

(e) often has difficulty organizing tasks and activities

(f) often avoids, dislikes, or is reluctant to engage in tasks that require sustained mental effort (such as schoolwork or homework)

(g) often loses things necessary for tasks or activities (e.g., toys, school assignments, pencils, books or tools)

(h) is often easily distracted by extraneous stimuli

(i) is often forgetful in daily activities

(2) six (or more) of the following symptoms of **hyperactivity-impulsivity** have persisted for at least 6 months to a degree that is maladaptive and inconsistent with developmental level:

Hyperactivity

(a) often fidgets with hands or feet or squirms in seat

(b) often leaves seat in classroom or in other situations in which remaining seated is expected

(c) often runs about or climbs excessively in situations in which it is inappropriate (in adolescents or adults, may be limited to subjective feelings of restlessness)

(d) often has difficulty playing or engaging in leisure activities quietly

(e)   is often "on the go" or acts as if "driven by a motor"

(f)   often talks excessively

Impulsivity

(g)   often blurts out answers before questions have been completed

(h)   often has difficulty awaiting turn

(i)   often interrupts or intrudes on others (e.g., butts into conversations or games)

From the *Diagnostic and Statistical Manual of Mental Disorders,* fourth edition. Copyright © 1994 by the American Psychiatric Association. Reprinted by permission of the publisher.

Dis-inhibition

This latest renaming of ADHD attempts to make a more pronounced distinction between problems with attention and problems with hyperactivity. The notion of *pure* hyperactivity is now underplayed. Hyperactivity is viewed as coexisting with impulsivity. In fact, researchers believe that impulsivity, rather than hyperactivity, is the more problematic or dominant feature of ADHD.[2] Now ADHD is viewed as primarily a disorder of impulsivity, or what is more broadly termed **dis-inhibition**.

Dis-inhibition is the inability to put the brakes on impulses and self-regulate one's behavior and emotions. Dis-inhibition causes your child to be *managed by the moment,* rather than by rules, consequences or previous learning experiences.[3] Dis-inhibition interferes with your child's ability to put the brakes on his urges so that he can:

• think more reflectively,

• plan what he should do,

• stay on course and do it,

• consider rules of behavior,

• consider consequences to his behavior *before* he engages in the behavior, and

• use the good social and behavior skills he has been taught.

Dis-inhibition leads your child to act first and think later, if he takes the time to think at all.

More About ADHD, Predominantly Inattentive Type

Children with **ADHD, Predominantly Inattentive Type** are notably different from those children who are hyperactive and impulsive. Their main problems are with focused and selective attention, that is, day-dreaming and paying attention to the wrong thing. These children are more easily bored and appear to be somewhat lethargic and sluggish, almost drowsy in some cases. They tend to have more difficulty getting started with tasks that require sustained concentration and mental effort (such as classwork or homework) and often avoid such tasks. They are generally slower when completing paper and pencil tasks. They have greater difficulties with short-term memory and are forgetful, often losing things — including their train of thought. They are often "spacey" or preoccupied, are easily disorganized, are confused in their thinking, and appear apathetic or unmotivated. They do not do well with keeping track of time and seem to move at their own, slow pace.

The predominantly inattentive individuals are more prone to anxiety and depression. They may not have the negative temperament that is more common with the Hyperactive-Impulsive or Combined Types, and they are less likely to be disruptive or defiant. Although they are not socially outgoing, they tend to be less rejected by peers than their hyperactive-impulsive counterparts.

These inattentive individuals tend to be as academically impaired as those of the Hyperactive-Impulsive Type, but they do not tend to bring as much attention to themselves because of their more passive and socially withdrawn behavior. Consequently, they frequently get missed diagnostically and fall through the cracks. This group is usually diagnosed later, around middle-school age, when the demands for organization, homework, responsible behavior and independent functioning increase, and they can no longer keep on top of it. More girls than boys appear to fall within this diagnostic group, perhaps contributing to the so-called lower incidence of ADHD in girls than boys. The ADHD, Predominantly Inattentive Type group is that group which was formerly identified as ADD without Hyperactivity and then Undifferentiated Attention-deficit Disorder (UADD). There is still debate among researchers whether this group is part of ADHD or is a separate disorder.

It Takes More Than Symptoms

This list of symptoms associated with ADHD is provided as a general guide for diagnosis. However, simply meeting at least six of the symptoms in the inattention and/or hyperactivity-impulsivity groups listed above does not confirm a diagnosis of ADHD. Much more information is required, including a detailed developmental history; observations of the child's behavior and functioning across home and school settings; perhaps psycho-educational testing (including intelligence and achievement testing) to rule in or rule out a learning disability or problems in processing language; and/or a psychological evaluation to determine the existence of possible emotional difficulties such as anxiety or depression.

Many parents look at this list of symptoms associated with ADHD and remark that at one time or another most children display some or all of these behaviors. This is true. The point to remember, however, is that ***ADHD is not a disorder of abnormality, but of excess.*** That is, children with ADHD display these behaviors persistently and to an excessive degree compared to what is typical for their developmental age. So, although most children are sometimes inattentive, impulsive, restless, careless or forgetful, children with ADHD display these problems more often, more severely and more chronically.

Parents of children with ADHD often complain that their child seems immature compared to other children his age. This is because ADHD interferes with his ability to do such things as regulate his behavior and emotions, follow through with daily tasks, stay organized, manage time, follow social and behavioral rules, and function independently and responsibly. For children with ADHD, these problematic behaviors are almost the rule rather than the exception.

To be diagnosed ADHD, an individual must show some of the ADHD-related symptoms before age seven, even though he may not have been diagnosed until a later age. Also, the symptoms must be present for at least six months to help rule out the possibility that the symptoms are a reaction to a recent stress event such as divorce, illness or a family move.

Since ADHD is a developmental disorder that pervasively affects the individual's functioning, the individual must demonstrate this constellation of behaviors in at least two settings, such as home, school or the workplace. If the symptoms are noticeable in only one setting, the explanation may be more related to a "poor fit" between the individual and the setting, rather than ADHD. Very importantly, to be given the diagnosis of ADHD, the ADHD-related behaviors must clearly interfere with the individual's functioning socially, academically or at work. If the behaviors are very mild and are not found to impact an individual's functioning, the need to give the diagnosis at all is questioned. Finally, if an individual has been diagnosed with a more serious disorder, such as Pervasive Developmental Disorder, Schizophrenia, or other psychotic disorders, a diagnosis of ADHD is not given.

SUMMARY

- ADHD affects 3 to 5 percent of the school-age population. It appears to be manifested more often in boys than girls, but girls may be underdiagnosed.

- There are three classifications of ADHD:
  ADHD, Predominantly Inattentive Type
  ADHD, Predominantly Hyperactive-Impulsive Type
  ADHD, Combined Type

- Many researchers now view ADHD as primarily a disorder of impulse control (dis-inhibition) rather than a disorder of attention or hyperactivity.

- ADHD is not a disorder of abnormality but of excess. Although most children are sometimes inattentive, impulsive and restless, children with ADHD display these problems more often, more severely and more chronically.

ADHD Through The Lifespan

As we look at the developmental history of individuals with ADHD, from infancy through adulthood, we see a wide array of behavioral characteristics and outcomes. Individuals who are diagnosed ADHD do not necessarily manifest all of the characteristics or turn out the same. Numerous factors determine the developmental course and eventual outcome of children with ADHD.

The usual onset of symptoms is between 3 to 4 years of age, although the range of onset is between infancy and 7 years of age.[1] Children who seem to manifest their symptoms after seven are identified later, usually because their ADHD symptoms did not interfere with their earlier academic or social functioning. As the demands in school became more complex and expectations for social responsibility increased, these children could no longer function successfully. This group of later-identified children tends to be those who are bright (and/or had exceptional support from parents or teachers) and thereby were able to more effectively compensate academically and socially until the demands at school and home exceeded their capacities.

INFANCY

Researchers have examined the early developmental history of children who were diagnosed with ADHD. They have uncovered some common developmental markers or signs.

Many children with ADHD were reported to have difficult temperaments as infants. They tended to cry more and could not be easily soothed. They often developed colic or were generally more irritable. Feeding problems were more common, including milk allergies and resistance to many foods. The transition from the bottle to regular foods was often difficult. They had irregular sleep patterns including repeatedly waking up, startling themselves and crying. They did not easily follow a schedule or reacted strongly to changes in their schedule. They were considered to have a high activity level and often had to be watched more closely so that they did not flip off the changing table or roll off the bed. These infants tended to be not as cuddly and often resisted being held. Infant vocalizations and babbling were sometimes delayed.[2]

PRESCHOOL (2-5 YEARS OLD)

Ginny sat in my office, very discouraged and almost in tears. Her 4-year-old son Andy had just been kicked out of his second preschool for hitting and pushing the other children. She knew that his teacher couldn't keep a child who was so disruptive, but now she was faced with taking time off from work to scramble and find another place for Andy—again. She worried that no setting would take him and that she would have to quit her job.

Andy had always been a challenge. He was very sensitive to the feel of his clothing and would go into a rage if his clothes didn't feel "just right." Getting him dressed and out the door in the morning was a huge battle. It seemed like any kind of transition was met with fierce resistance, whether it was getting ready for bed, coming in the house for lunch, going to church, or turning off the TV. Andy's frustration tolerance was very low, and if he couldn't get a toy to work, he threw it against the wall. Ginny lamented that his moods were as unpredictable as the weather, but she sure would appreciate a three-day forecast! Andy seemed unable to occupy himself and was always complaining that he was bored. If he did find something to play with, it didn't last long before he was underfoot. Ginny knew that she couldn't get much done around the house unless Andy was entertained. Sending him to a neighbor's house to play was no longer an option.

At four years of age, Andy already had a reputation in the neighborhood. Other children refused to play with him because he was too aggressive and too bossy. Mothers discouraged their children from playing with Andy because he was a "bad influence." Ginny witnessed how the other children ran away from Andy when they saw him coming, and it hurt to see her son rejected. She knew the rejection spilled over onto her, too, because she was never invited for coffee and was

not asked to join the neighborhood babysitting pool. She felt isolated in her own neighborhood.

Many children with ADHD can be identified as early as preschool. However, there is a reluctance to diagnose a child this early because of the wide range of what is considered "normal" behavior at this stage of development. It is often difficult to determine whether an overly rambunctious 3-year-old is more spirited or actually has an attention deficit.

Most children with ADHD show their symptoms as preschoolers. Parents who are concerned about their preschooler's behavior, however, are frequently told that their child will likely outgrow the symptoms. It's true that many youngsters go through a phase of "overactivity" and uncontrolled behavior but they outgrow it before they enter school. Early diagnosis could incorrectly label these normally exuberant children as ADHD. To avoid over-diagnosing ADHD at this early age, some researchers suggest that a preschooler should display his behavioral symptoms for at least a year, rather than the standard six months, before the diagnosis is given.[3]

Those children who tend to show more aggressive behavior, such as throwing things, kicking, hitting and biting, tend to be those who are more severely hyperactive and therefore more easily diagnosed. The critical feature in determining whether a child this young may have an attention deficit is whether or not the child's symptoms *significantly* impair his functioning behaviorally, socially or pre-academically.

The developmental history of those with ADHD reveals a wide range of behavioral symptoms during the preschool stage. These children continue to have sleep problems and are now characterized as restless or fitful sleepers. Parents may notice that their child's sheets are bunched up in a ball at the foot of the bed. Toilet training difficulties are common, and it often takes longer to train these preschoolers. Difficulties with gross- and especially fine-motor coordination are commonly found, and there is a higher incidence of enuresis (wetting) or encopresis (soiling).

Preschoolers with ADHD have a higher percentage of speech and language delays. Other behavior problems are often associated with prolonged language delays. There is speculation that these language delays adversely affect development of internal language, the conversations we have with ourselves to reason, plan ahead and direct our behavior. Perhaps the delay of this internal language contributes to the impulsive behaviors of children with ADHD.

Preschoolers with **ADHD** are also described as overly active, with boundless energy, and always "up and on the go." These children seem to constantly need to feel and touch everything around them. Parents state that they couldn't take their eyes off their preschooler for fear he'd get into something, dismantle a room or disappear while shopping. Their impulsive behavior frequently leads to more accidents, including more bumps, scrapes, bruises, and stitches. They must be watched carefully when playing outside to ensure that they don't wander off or dart into the street.

Preschoolers with **ADHD** tend to be disorganized even while playing. They may flit from one activity or toy to another, not spending much time with anything for very long. Toys don't last long before they are broken because of the child's rough play. These children don't easily share toys and may aggressively defend their territory with a hit or a kick. Aggressive behavior toward siblings and peers is frequently reported.

The problems with difficult temperament from infancy continue as well. The preschooler with **ADHD** may still have a hard time with change or transitions. He may refuse to wear a new pair of socks because they "feel funny" or because they are the wrong color. He may become very upset with any sudden changes in his schedule and will have a hard time adapting. He may frequently refuse to leave the playground or some other activity he is enjoying. He may protest longer and tantrum louder. He may be excessively demanding of parents' time and attention and seem to be always underfoot or always calling for help. He may become excessively frustrated if things don't go his way. Parents are often frustrated in their attempts to get their preschooler to cooperate, even with the simplest of requests. He may defy usual punishment methods and refuse to go to time-out.

In preschool, teachers may complain about the child's disruptive or loud behaviors and aggression toward peers. It may be hard to get him to join the group, and he may often wander around the classroom. He may intrude on the play of other children and act bossy toward them. The more aggressive youngsters may be asked to leave their preschool or daycare setting.

SCHOOL AGE (5-12 YEARS OLD)

Max's third-grade teacher suggested that he be evaluated for attention problems. Although she knew he was a bright boy, she was concerned that his behavior was interfering with his ability to get his work done. He never seemed to start his deskwork unless she stood right by him. Either he was talking to other students, or he was digging in his backpack for a pencil or eraser. He was forever moving around in his chair, getting up to sharpen his pencil, or asking to get a drink of water. When Max *did* work, he was usually heard humming, singing or making other distracting noises. "Max, get back to work" or "Max, stop bothering me" were common refrains in the classroom. Being patient was not Max's strong suit, so he often blurted out in class without raising his hand, rushed through his worksheets with poor handwriting and lots of mistakes, and pushed to be first in line. Although Max was extraverted and outgoing, he had only a few friends. He seemed unaware that the other kids were turned off by his behavior.

Max's parents complained that they couldn't get him to follow through with anything. The biggest battle was homework. Max often forgot his papers or books at school and usually couldn't remember if he had an assignment. If his parents tried to get him to sit down and do his work, he had a thousand excuses why he couldn't. Evenings were usually turned into crying and shouting matches, and Max's mother concluded that nothing was worth this much family disruption.

Max's brother and sister saw that he got out of doing most household chores and seemed to monopolize their parents' time with all of his problems at home and school. They were especially annoyed that Max was always going into their bedrooms and helping himself to their stuff, which he usually denied doing. Accusations, name-calling, teasing and put-downs were constant. The whole family was fed up with Max's behavior!

The majority of children with ADHD are referred for assessment during their first three years of school. By school age they bring more attention to themselves because their behavior now makes academic and social success difficult. Teachers are not as willing to tolerate such behaviors, especially when they have 29 other students in the classroom.

Expectations for children's behavior also increase. They are now expected to comply with requests from teachers and other adults, sit still for longer periods, pay attention to tasks without constant adult intervention, be self-directed, control impulses and frustrations, have more patience, and develop certain cognitive and motor skills. Lack of these skills results in academic and social failure. School underachievement becomes a hallmark feature of the disorder and creates much anxiety in the child, leading to feelings of inferiority, lack of motivation, and perhaps depression.

The child with **ADHD** often continues to have temper tantrums into middle childhood, while most children have outgrown these outbursts after the preschool years. Also, more sibling rivalry is found in families of children with **ADHD**. Siblings grow increasingly frustrated with the **ADHD** child's embarrassing and "obnoxious" behaviors and become resentful that their brother or sister with **ADHD** gets more attention, has fewer household chores, and seems to get preferential treatment from Mom and Dad.

Parents and other adults make more requests of the school-age child because by this time he is expected to handle more responsibilities at home, at school, and in the neighborhood. But parents of a child with **ADHD** find that they have to supervise their child for even the simplest of routines if they want the job to get done.

School-age children with this disorder begin to experience the pain of social rejection as peers no longer tolerate some of their intrusive, impulsive, controlling or immature behaviors. Parents may find that their child is not invited to many birthday parties or sleepovers, and he may be excluded by other neighborhood children. For a child who is athletic, sports can be his main social link and ticket to wider acceptance. But most children with **ADHD** find friendships with younger children, who are more willing to tolerate their less mature social behaviors.

Academic difficulties are the hallmark of the disorder at this stage of development. Nearly 20 to 25 percent of these children have reading problems, most of which are documented by the second grade.[4] Educational performance is erratic, and teachers report variable academic achievement, often differing from day to day. School assignments are often lost or uncompleted, and it's not unusual for students to falsely report to their parents that they have no homework in order to get out of doing it or to cover up the fact that they forgot their books or worksheets at school — again. These children usually resist doing homework, and this often turns into a nightly battle with parents, creating a tremendous amount of conflict that continues throughout the student's school career.

These students are generally disorganized at home and especially at school. Disorganization interferes with their ability to keep track of assignments and needed materials, as well as with their ability to start and hand in assignments. Teachers complain that these students continually turn in assignments late if at all, blurt out in class, get off track, bother other students, demand a lot of teacher attention, rush carelessly through their work, or disrupt the flow of the classroom. Given the increased level of negative feedback that these children receive by this age and the mounting school failures that they experience, signs of low self-esteem become apparent.

By later childhood, the pattern of academic difficulties, family conflict, and social rejection are well ingrained. About 30 to 50 percent of children *with severe cases of ADHD* may develop more serious conduct and social problems, including bullying, intimidating, physical aggression toward other people or animals, frequent lying or breaking promises, property damage, petty thievery, or truancy.[5]

By the end of sixth grade, 30-45 percent are receiving special education for academic and/or behavior problems. Many have experienced academic failure. Over 50 percent will have engaged in either individual or family therapy, and 60 to 80 percent will have been on stimulant medication to control ADHD symptoms.[6]

ADOLESCENCE

Tom was afraid to tell his parents that he failed another class, seriously messing up his chances of graduating on schedule this spring. His parents had told him he would lose the car for good if he failed one more class. He thought he had lost the car for sure with that last speeding ticket, but he convinced his parents that he would be more responsible and wouldn't disappoint them again. Once again, he blew it.

Tom knew that his poor grades would wipe out any chance he may have had to try out for the school play. People had always told him that with his "gift for gab" and his constant wanting to be the center of attention, he should be on stage. But he can hear his dad now, "You can't seem to find enough time to do your schoolwork, but you can find time to act in some silly play. Besides, you never finish anything you start. How about those trumpet lessons you wanted so badly, and then quit after four lessons? Or what about your great dream to be a baseball player that fell apart because you couldn't even get yourself to practices?"

The going has been pretty rough between Tom and his parents the last few years. It seems like they are "on his case" about everything. They constantly remind him to pick up his room, mow the grass, take out the trash, hand in his assignments, return his library books, pay his overdue fines, write his thank-you notes for his birthday gifts, sweep the garage, and get off the phone. Tom says his friends aren't micromanaged the way he is. When he tells his parents he's not a little kid anymore, they always have the same response, "Well, stop acting like one."

Tom's parents have become more concerned about their son recently. He has always been a moody kid, but now his mood swings are more dramatic and last longer. He spends too much time locked away in his room or out with his friends. He stays out later and later at night, continuously "forgetting" to call to let them know where he is going to be. A few times his parents thought they smelled smoke and alcohol on his breath. He seems to be lying more about what he's doing or where he's going. They worry that he's headed for trouble but don't know how to prevent it.

Adolescence is difficult enough for most kids and their parents. This is a time when hormones are raging, impulsive behaviors increase, and emotions erupt. Kids are normally trying to establish their own identity separate from their parents'. They are more apt to question authority, resist rules, and defy parents' attempts to "micromanage" them. Parents lose their influence over their adolescents as the power of peers takes over. For most (but not all), the typically challenging period of adolescence becomes even more challenging with the added factor of ADHD.

By the time a child with ADHD reaches adolescence, levels of hyperactivity diminish and attention span and impulse control may improve somewhat. However, children do not typically outgrow the disorder by this time. It has been estimated that as many as 70-80 percent of these children continue to display ADHD symptoms into adolescence.[7] The major concerns of parents and adolescents at this stage are not the primary ADHD symptoms of inattention, impulsivity and overactivity. The main reasons parents and their children seek help at this point include poor schoolwork, trouble with authority figures, peer difficulties, low self-esteem, depression, and family conflict.

Most adolescents without ADHD will more easily pass through this stage if they have achieved success in academics, social relationships, or extra-curricular activities. Unfortunately, the adolescent with ADHD often has difficulty succeeding in these same areas.

Even with average to above-average intelligence, the course of academic difficulty continues into adolescence, and 58 percent fail at least one grade by high school.[8] Adolescents with **ADHD** are chronic underachievers, and school performance may be several years below placement. Students at this stage typically complain that school is boring, and they develop a well-ingrained pattern of putting off homework or anything else that requires mental effort and sustained concentration. They have a hard time dealing with the different personalities and varying expectations of their many teachers. They may now have reached a point where they no longer care about their grades because they can't keep up with the increased homework demands and have had too many failure experiences in school. Their scores on standardized achievement tests are lower in the areas of math, reading and spelling because they don't "test well" and because they have now developed gaps in their academic skills. Teachers often comment that these students don't work up to their potential or that they are "lazy and unmotivated." Truancy continues to be more of a problem for teenagers with **ADHD**. A higher number of these students are suspended or expelled from school, and 35 percent quit school, a rate four times higher than the national drop-out rate.[9]

Adolescents with **ADHD** continue to have problems with their peer group. They are viewed as immature because they may engage in loud, reckless or dangerous behaviors in attempts to impress others or improve their popularity. They are not good self-observers, so they don't see that their actions alienate peers. They are not as likely to try out for sports. If they do, they tend to quit prematurely because they lose interest or can't get to practices on time. These teenagers are more apt to gravitate toward other peers who are impulsive and seek thrills. As many as 35 percent are also diagnosed as conduct disordered, with the most common antisocial acts being stealing, thefts outside the home, and fire setting. Adolescents who are both hyperactive and conduct disordered are two to five times more likely to use cigarettes, marijuana, and/or alcohol. The higher incidence of substance abuse is likely related to their poor impulse control and higher need for stimulation.[10,11]

Adolescents with **ADHD** have a slightly higher incidence of automobile accidents.[12] Parents may be faced with the dilemma of deciding whether or not to allow their impulsive and relatively immature adolescent to even get a driver's license. If they say "no," they worry about the angry reaction of their child and the social repercussions for him. If they say "yes," they worry about their child's safety and their insurance rates.

Adolescents with **ADHD** suffer from low self-esteem and are given to unstable moods. Their increased moodiness is due partly to the biology of **ADHD** but is also a reaction to their history of failure at home, at school and in their social world.

ADULTHOOD

Mary desperately wanted to know why life for her has been so hard. She doesn't see other people struggling to keep it all together the way she has to. Although she has a good job as an art director for a major advertising firm, no one understands all of the energy it takes behind the scenes to keep her head above water. Mary feels she has no ability to place limits on herself. She stays up late at night, getting "stuck" on video games for hours. Her office and home are cluttered with piles of papers, mail, and magazines strewn around. You'd think that by now she would have figured out a filing system, but her "system" is to pile it higher. She feels overwhelmed just thinking about cleaning and organizing her space, and she has no idea where to start.

Making decisions about most things, including ordering from a menu, causes her a lot of stress because she can't make a choice when faced with too many options; it's too confusing. She feels like she's walking a tightrope all the time, and the least bit of disruption or change makes her feel like she is in a free fall. She's always on edge and often snaps at her husband for minor things. He calls it her "terminal PMS." She wonders why he puts up with her.

Mary lives in constant fear that she will be fired from her job. She struggles with time management, which can be deadly in a career that is driven by deadlines. She's used to staying up all night to meet a deadline because she put off doing the work. She admits that she has now trained herself to operate in crisis mode, feeling charged by the adrenalin. She's often late for appointments and meetings with clients because she misplaced her appointment book, lost track of time, or didn't allow herself enough time to get there. She detests getting to appointments early because she gets bored waiting and thumbing through old magazines.

Mary has never been one to sit and relax because it's too boring. She dislikes going to movies because she has to sit too long. She seldom watches TV for the same reason. She can't sit and read a book because her mind wanders. She even gets bored walking from her car to her office and will either count her steps or walk and read a magazine at the same time in order to make the walk more stimulating. It's a wonder she hasn't walked right into traffic.

Most people do not outgrow ADHD. Approximately 50 to 65 percent of those diagnosed with ADHD in childhood will continue to manifest ADHD symptoms in adulthood.[13] It is estimated that over 10 million American adults have ADHD. The syndrome may look different in various ways in adulthood because of normal maturation, unique coping strategies, and the cumulative effect of life experiences.[14]

Perhaps the most common complaint lodged by adults with this disorder is the pervasive feeling of underachievement: not having lived up to one's potential, regardless of the person's individual successes. They often feel like they are living a sham, afraid that others will find out that they aren't as smart or as competent as they think they are.

Disorganization may be the thorn in their side as they misplace important papers, miss deadlines, forget appointments, and leave piles of clutter around their home and office with the promise that they'll get to it "some day." Just as disorganization was usually the culprit behind their chronic underachievement in school, it is now one of the biggest factors in work nonproductivity. Chronic procrastination often grows out of the disorganization, because starting tasks seems too overwhelming and too confusing. A common complaint is, "I don't know where to start."

Adults with this syndrome tend to be impatient, cannot tolerate boredom, and are easily frustrated. This leads to an almost insatiable search for stimulation as they jump from one thing to another (usually not completing any of them) and find it hard to sit and relax for any length of time. In fact, these adults often complain that relaxation makes them anxious because they feel they should be doing something. Their intolerance of boredom and high need for stimulation can cause them to go from job to job as they quickly lose interest or complain that they are no longer challenged.

Although most adults with ADHD are gainfully employed, their work history may not be as successful as their peers', and they tend to achieve lower socioeconomic status. They change jobs more frequently and have more part-time jobs outside their full-time jobs. Work performance reviews tend to be lower, with complaints of unfinished tasks, the need for more supervision, tardiness, and general disorganization. These adults tend not to do well with sedentary desk jobs or work that makes many demands for organization and detail. However, adults with ADHD tend to flourish in a work environment that does not emphasize their weaknesses, that stimulates them, and that allows for activity and variety.

The hyperactivity of youth is now restlessness that looks like nervous energy in adulthood. Adults with ADHD stand up and pace when they have to sit for long, drum their fingers on whatever is near, mindlessly hum, shift about in their chairs, tap their foot, or abruptly get up and leave the room. Others usually view this behavior as rude or annoying.

Their inattention makes it hard for these adults to listen to a conversation, read a page in a book or magazine without drifting, or tune into details. On the other hand, they may hyperfocus on something and not be aware of anything else going on around them. Some adults report that this hyperfocusing is actually their attempt to harness their concentration and control distractions. If they allow themselves to stop what they're doing, they're afraid they'll get off track and never get back to it. They may interrupt or monopolize a conversation, not because they are inconsiderate, but because they feel that if they don't say it all now, they'll lose their train of thought.

The impulsivity of adult ADHD can be seen in the tendency to say what comes to mind without thinking about its appropriateness, or in their penchant for spending, drinking or gambling too much. These adults often jump into projects without considering all that is involved or start something and then stop impetuously, concluding that it's too hard, takes too long, or is too boring.

Mood swings and problems with anger control are hallmark characteristics of the adult with ADHD. Their bad moods can seem to come out of nowhere, and they may overreact to little things. Family members or co-workers report that they have to walk on eggshells around this person because they never know when he's going to blow.

Increased anxiety, self-doubt and feelings of insecurity are also common. Approximately 79 percent of adults with ADHD complain of symptoms such as anxiety and sadness, or they have physical complaints.[15] These adults have grown sensitive to the fears of failure and have learned to doubt their competency. They may overcompensate through perfectionistic and compulsive behaviors or engage in excessive and exaggerated worry.

Many adults with ADHD are intelligent, creative, and unconventional. They have learned to channel their need for stimulation, driving them to boundless heights in their professional and personal lives as they tackle and conquer one challenge after another. They are often found in "right-brained" professions such as advertising, art, music or acting.

Relationship and marriage problems are more prevalent in the lives of those with ADHD. Spouses often complain that they can't rely on the individual; that he/she is "hot tempered" and tends to overreact; that he/she is self-centered, moody or stubborn; and that they can't get him/her to follow through or finish household chores.

As many as 20 to 45 percent of adults with ADHD continue to manifest anti-social behaviors and 25 percent may be diagnosed with Anti-social Personality Disorder. Approximately 18 percent will have contact with the police or the court system, although most of these contacts will involve only traffic violations. Alcohol and marijuana use is slightly higher in early adulthood, but this lessens with time.[16]

Early academic difficulties may take a toll in adulthood, as barely 5 percent of adults with ADHD graduate from college, compared to 25 percent for the general population. Overall, these adults have lower educational attainment than their non-ADHD counterparts. Many adults with ADHD do much better once they are out of school, because the school environment was too restrictive and emphasized their weaknesses. Once they are in a setting that allows them more freedom, spontaneity, and options, they tend to do much better and realize their untapped potential.

IF WE COULD PREDICT THE FUTURE

Understandably, as a parent you would like to know how well your child will do in the future. Will he be happy and well-adjusted? Will he make it through school? Will he be able to make and keep friends? Will he get into trouble dealing with authority or the law? Will he go to college? Will he get a job? Will you have to support him when he's an adult?

Unfortunately, it's not possible to guarantee with certainty how well your child will do in the future. There is not one single factor that can predict his eventual outcome. What we do know, however, is that your child's future well-being depends upon much more than his individual characteristics. Equally if not more important are his social and school environments and the childrearing practices in his family.

We also know that children who have received a combination of interventions have better adjustment than children who received no intervention or children who received only one form of intervention. The most effective treatment is **multi-modal intervention**, which may include a combination of parent education in ADHD, behavior management strategies at home and in school, medication, academic support and/or special education, social skills training, family counseling, and individual therapy for the child. This multi-modal treatment is most effective if it is ongoing from early childhood through adolescent years.

Research has shown that there are at least eight specific factors that are most powerful in predicting future outcomes of children with ADHD:[17,18,19]

1. **Intelligence**

   Children with higher intelligence have been found to do better academically and to attain higher levels of education and employment. They tend to adjust better to life and to be emotionally more stable.

2. **Family socioeconomic status (SES)**

   Children with ADHD are found in all socioeconomic groups. However, children from families of lower socioeconomic status tend to have more significant degrees of ADHD. Further, those from higher SES tend to have a more positive outcome. They tend to have higher academic achievement, go farther in school, and do better in employment.

   There may be several reasons for the differences in outcome. One reason may be that women in lower socioeconomic groups tend to have less access to good prenatal health care. They may also have poorer nutrition. This increases the probability of pregnancy and birth complications and may have an effect on their babies' developing nervous systems, thus increasing the risk for significant ADHD. Also, there is a higher incidence of family conflict, divorce, and parental emotional difficulties in families of lower SES, all of which can increase the severity of ADHD symptoms and undermine the effectiveness of parenting. An additional factor is limited financial resources for having their children evaluated and treated. Families from higher SES are more likely to seek and follow through with treatment.

3. **Quality of peer relationships**

   The single most powerful predictor of adult emotional adjustment is the quality of social contacts and friendships in childhood. Those children with ADHD who have a history of generally positive social relationships tend to generate more social support and acceptance from others and, consequently, adapt better to their ADHD and to the frustrations of home and school. Those individuals who experience peer relationship difficulties in childhood, however, tend to have more interpersonal problems in adulthood.

4. **Degree of aggressiveness and conduct problems in childhood**

   A history of aggressive behavior in younger childhood is one of the best single predictors of antisocial behavior and poor emotional adjustment in adolescence. It is very difficult to extinguish aggressive behavior in children with ADHD once it gains a foothold, and it usually continues as a progressive pattern into adolescence. Higher aggression levels are found in children from lower SES and in those whose parents use aggression as a form of discipline, whose parents have more psychological problems, and where there is marital discord. Treatments for those with high aggression should focus specifically on the aggression problems as well as the parental emotional and marriage problems.

   Aggressiveness and conduct problems in childhood predict a poorer outcome in educational adjustment, achievement and social relationships. The more aggressive group of children with ADHD have lower academic attainment, more school suspensions and expulsions, greater substance use and abuse, more frequent and recurring conduct and social problems, and poorer occupational attainment and emotional adjustment into adulthood.

5. **Degree of parental problems**

   Parents of children with ADHD are more likely to have ADHD themselves. There is also a higher incidence of marital problems, antisocial behaviors, alcoholism, depression or anxiety, and learning disabilities in parents of children with ADHD. Parents who struggle with these various problems experience more stress in their parenting and tend to use less effective, more aggressive, and inconsistent parenting strategies. They tend to have more difficulty following through with treatment recommendations and to drop out of therapy prematurely. Children with ADHD who grow up in families with such difficulties are more prone to develop these difficulties themselves. Therefore, a higher degree of psychopathology in parents is related to an increased risk of emotional difficulties in the adolescent and adult with ADHD.

6. **Degree of parent-child conflict**

   Parenting a child with ADHD is a challenge for even the most patient and competent parents. In response to a child's difficult ADHD-related behaviors, parents become frustrated, angry, anxious and irritable. These parental responses, however, have a negative impact on the relationship that the parent and child develop together. This in turn affects the child's future development. How conflict is handled within a family becomes the model that the child uses to handle conflict in his own world, apart from his family. The more conflicted the interactions between the child with ADHD and his/her parent(s), the more likely these conflicts and generally aggressive behavior will persist into adolescence and adulthood.

7. **Severity of ADHD**

    Those with more severe ADHD tend to not do as well academically, be more prone to fail or drop out of school, and be more likely to have a higher incidence of run-ins with the law.

    The degree of hyperactivity is considered to be one indicator of the severity of ADHD. Children who are more hyperactive tend to have greater achievement problems in later school years. The degree of impulsivity is another indicator of severity of ADHD. Those children who are better at delaying gratification tend to obtain higher scores on intelligence tests, have higher educational achievement, develop more competent social skills, and are more successful at resisting temptations that lead to problems in adolescence.

8. **Age of diagnosis and treatment**

    Generally, those children who are diagnosed earlier, and consequently begin treatment earlier, tend to have a more positive outcome. Although treatment cannot erase ADHD, the earlier treatment begins, the more likely that problems can be lessened. Since ADHD affects a child's functioning in so many areas, providing only a specific treatment for a specific problem has limited effectiveness. Children with ADHD have been found to do better in adolescence and adulthood when they have received multi-modal treatment.

SUMMARY

- Although symptoms of ADHD generally appear between infancy and seven years of age, some individuals may not be *diagnosed* until adulthood.

- ADHD manifests itself in different ways at different stages of a person's life.

- Many professionals are reluctant to diagnose preschoolers as having ADHD, because their rambunctiousness may still be within the wide range of normal behavior typical at this stage of development.

- The majority of children are diagnosed during the first three years of school because their behavior now makes academic and social success difficult.

- School underachievement is a hallmark of ADHD.

- Approximately 50 to 65 percent of those diagnosed with ADHD in childhood continue to manifest ADHD symptoms in adulthood.

- The most effective treatment for ADHD is multi-modal, including parent education, behavior management, medication, academic support and/or special education, social skills training, family counseling, and/or individual therapy for the child.

CHAPTER

3 Causes: Fiction and Fact

MYTHS

There is an abundance of misinformation about the possible causes of ADHD. Despite the fact that little or no scientific information supports many of the believed "causes" of this disorder, these notions are still popular among many people. Some of the more persistent myths are:

Poor Parenting

Many believe that poor parenting causes ADHD. You may have heard this suggestion (or perhaps more accurately, this indictment) from relatives, strangers, school principals or teachers, and even from some mental health professionals. Strangers may conclude that you are too lenient when they see your child running down the aisles of the grocery store, and you just "let it happen." Your mother may complain that her grandchild is just fine when he's at *her* house. Your child's teacher may suggest that you should be more involved in your child's homework. A psychologist may have told you that your child is "acting out" the strain in your marriage.

It is true that parents of a child with ADHD tend to interact with their child differently than parents with a "normal" child. Dr. Russell Barkley, an eminent researcher of ADHD, conducted well-designed research studies to investigate these parent-child interactions.[1] He found that mothers of hyperactive children are more commanding, controlling and negative. At the same time, they are also less attentive, less responsive and less positive toward their hyperactive children than mothers with normal children. Likewise, he found that hyperactive children are less compliant, more negative, more off task, and less able to follow through on requests than children without ADHD.

However, Dr. Barkley also found that when medication produced positive changes in children with ADHD, the mothers of these children changed as well. They became less controlling and less negative, and more responsive and more approving. These studies indicate that the negative interactions of the parent are often the *result* of the child's behavior, not the cause of it. The relationship between parent and child is not just a one-way street. Parents influence their children, and children influence their parents. When the behavior of the child with ADHD improves, the responses of the parent improve.

Parents don't "teach" their children with ADHD to behave the way they do. Parents, however, *do* react to the behavior of their children. As children with ADHD become noncompliant and negative, parents often become more commanding and controlling as a means to manage their child's behavior. As parents increase negativity and control, children with ADHD increase noncompliance and negativity. And so the vicious cycle begins.

The two-way street also runs to your child's friends, teachers and others. It has been found that teachers are considerably more negative and controlling with students with ADHD than they are with students without ADHD. Also, peers tend to react more negatively to children with ADHD than to normal children. No one would conclude, however, that either teachers or peers caused the child's ADHD. More accurately, they are reacting to the ADHD behavior, just as parents do.

Although we know now that parenting does not cause ADHD, we also know that ineffective or reactive parenting practices can make matters worse. We also know that the emotional difficulties of parents can negatively impact the situation.

Brain Damage

In the early 1900s, hyperactive behavior was hypothesized to be the result of brain damage. This notion gained prominence following the 1918 encephalitis epidemic in the U.S. Many children who recovered from this disease were found to be exceptionally hyperactive, impulsive and distractible. Years later it was found, however, that many children who were hyperactive did not show evidence of brain injury.[2] Consequently, it was theorized that although brain damage could not be found, these individuals likely had minimal degrees of brain dysfunction. Even though there was no hard evidence that could prove brain dysfunction, it was reasoned that this difference in brain function could be inferred from how children acted.[3]

Physicians began to look for neurological "soft" signs during an exam as part of the process in making the diagnosis. Soft signs are suggestive of immature neuromaturational development and may include gross- and fine-motor incoordination, poor eye tracking, clumsy finger sequencing, difficulty with rapid alternating hand movements, clumsy hopping on one foot, or slight hand tremors. Subsequent research that investigated this practice of uncovering soft signs found that these neurologic signs were also found in children with conduct disorders, major psychiatric disorders, and children with learning disabilities. Many hyperactive children displayed no neurologic soft signs on examination. In other words, we could not rely on the presence of soft signs to confirm a diagnosis of hyperactivity.[4]

Food Additives

The belief that hyperactivity was caused by an allergic reaction to food additives, particularly food dyes, preservatives, and salicylates, gained prominence through Dr. Ben Feingold in the 1970s.[5] He claimed that over half the cases of hyperactivity in the country were the result of adverse reactions to these substances. He believed that if these children were placed on a controlled diet, the majority would show dramatic improvement within a couple of weeks. Feingold Associations sprang up all over the country to provide support to parents of hyperactive children. Dr. Feingold's information was largely anecdotal, however, and did not stand up under the scrutiny of controlled research.

Sugar

There are many claims that sugar makes children hyperactive and hard to control. Sugar has even been linked to aggressive behavior and violent crimes. Many physicians and mental health professionals will recommend to parents that they place their children on sugar-restricted diets if their behavior is exceptionally hyperactive or uncontrollable. Various researchers have speculated that sugar acts on the brain in different ways to produce these adverse effects, but there is no consensus about what is actually happening in the brain.[6]

Those well-designed studies that have rigorously looked at a possible connection between sugar ingestion and ADHD have found only small, if any, effects of sugar on behavior. Dr. Keith Conners, most noted for his research on diet and ADHD, states, *"None of the findings in sugar studies justify eliminating sugar from the diet of children."* [7] It would appear from the research that if there is a more vulnerable group, it is children of preschool age. However, even the connection between sugar and behavior at this age is very small.

KNOWN CAUSES OF ADHD

Researchers agree that there is probably not one single cause of ADHD, but likely multiple causes.

Prenatal Factors

There are various prenatal factors which have been associated with ADHD. It is not known for certain, however, whether these factors cause ADHD or just occur more frequently in the history of those with ADHD.[8,9]

It is known that smoking during pregnancy is positively correlated with ADHD. Also, fathers of children with ADHD have been found to smoke more than fathers of children without ADHD. Continued research on the effects of second-hand smoke may uncover some answers.

Another connection has been found between maternal alcohol consumption during pregnancy and ADHD. Furthermore, research has shown that the amount of alcohol consumption has been proportionally related to the degree of inattention in the child at four years of age.

Other prenatal factors that have been positively correlated with ADHD include maternal caffeine ingestion, maternal convulsions, poor maternal health, fetal distress, and low birth weight.

Heredity

There is much evidence to suggest that genetics play a part in causing ADHD. This disorder does tend to run in families, and it has been found that children with ADHD are four times more likely to have another member of the family with ADHD. It is estimated that 15 to 20 percent of mothers and 20 to 30 percent of fathers also have ADHD. Overall, studies of genetics and ADHD suggest that the degree to which genetics contribute to the symptoms of ADHD is about 50 to 65 percent. Often fathers of children with ADHD comment that their child reminds them of themselves when they were young. It is estimated that the risk of a child with ADHD having a female sibling who also has ADHD is approximately 13 to 17 percent, and the risk of having a male sibling with ADHD is 27 to 30 percent.[10]

Neurochemical Imbalance and Brain Structures

We now know that ADHD has something to do with the brain. The parts of the brain implicated in ADHD are the frontal region just behind the forehead (prefrontal lobes), an area in the midbrain situated on top of the brain stem (limbic system), and the pathway connecting these two parts of the brain (striatum).[11]

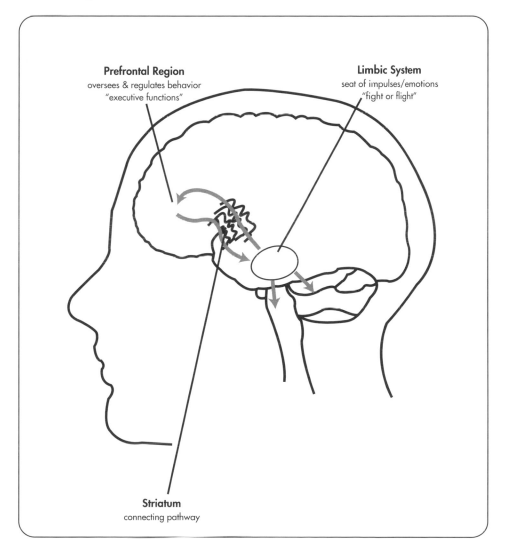

Prefrontal Region
oversees & regulates behavior
"executive functions"

Limbic System
seat of impulses/emotions
"fight or flight"

Striatum
connecting pathway

   The **prefrontal region** of the human brain is the center of self-control and self-regulation. It helps us **inhibit** our **impulses** and **urges** and thus allows us to control our emotions, thoughts and actions. It helps us plan and organize our behavior so we can make goals for the near or distant future. By controlling our impulses, the prefrontal region allows us to consider the consequences of our behavior before we engage in that behavior, and it allows us to monitor our behavior so we can make changes if it is appropriate to do so. It allows us to sustain attention, ignore distractions, and persist in our efforts so we can reach our goals. It allows us to consider lessons from past experience so we can more thoughtfully direct our behavior. Together, all of these responsibilities of the prefrontal lobes are called **executive functions:** the function of overseeing and regulating behavior to meet goals. Dysfunction of the prefrontal lobes can lead to poorly controlled and poorly regulated behavior, also known as **dis-inhibition.**

The **limbic system** is the seat of **emotions** and is also responsible for **motivation** and **memory.** The limbic system receives information from the senses (sight, hearing, touch, smell). It then compares the new sensory information with information stored in memory to form an emotional response. If this integrated information suggests that the individual is in "danger," it will quickly activate the "fight or flight" response in lower brain structures. The limbic system also sends this integrated information upward to the prefrontal region of the brain, where it is sorted and analyzed against previously learned information and past experiences in order to make rational sense out of it. In this process, the prefrontal region acts as a damper switch by putting the brakes on the more impulsive limbic system until it can formulate an appropriate and reasonable response. It then sends this controlled message back to the limbic system for action.

The **striatum** is part of a complex system of nerve bundles that **connects the limbic system with the prefrontal regions** of the brain. It is this pathway that allows the limbic system to send messages to the prefrontal lobes and allows the prefrontal lobes to send messages back to the limbic system. From there, appropriate responses radiate out through the brain and the rest of the body.

Current research now suggests that areas of the prefrontal lobes, limbic system and striatum may be variably understimulated in some individuals with ADHD. When a part of the brain is understimulated, it can't perform its functions effectively or consistently.

A number of studies have investigated the brain function of people with ADHD. Some studies have measured brain activity in children with and without ADHD using EEGs while these children performed tasks requiring mental effort. The results showed that children with ADHD had reduced brain activity in the frontal area of the brain compared to children without ADHD.[12]

Other studies comparing children with and without ADHD found that children with ADHD had reduced blood flow to the frontal area, limbic system in the midbrain, and the striatum connecting these two parts of the brain. Blood flow relates to brain activity, so reduced blood flow in the brain of those with ADHD means reduced brain activity.[13]

Landmark studies conducted by Dr. Alan Zametkin and his colleagues at the National Institute of Mental Health found that adults with ADHD metabolize glucose, the fuel of brain nerve cells, at a slower rate when compared to non-ADHD adults while performing an auditory attention task. Slower glucose metabolism in the brain relates to brain underactivity. The area of reduced glucose metabolism was concentrated in the frontal section of the brain.[14]

Although we don't know why those with ADHD have brain underactivity, some studies suggest that it may be related to lower levels of certain brain chemicals or neurotransmitters.[15] Those regions of the brain implicated in ADHD are known to be typically rich in two neurotransmitters, dopamine (DE) and norepinephrine (NE). Neurotransmitters are responsible for relaying messages throughout the brain system, and dopamine and norepinephrine are specifically associated with inhibiting behavior, i.e., putting the brakes on behavior. Various studies have found that these two neurochemicals are deficient in some individuals with ADHD. In a sense, it would seem that neurologically speaking, the "brake fluid" is low in these individuals, leading to uninhibited and poorly controlled behavior.

ADHD: A DISORDER OF INHIBITION

ADHD is now believed by various prominent researchers to be a neurologically-based disorder of self-regulation, or what is more technically termed **dis-inhibition.**

The dis-inhibition model of ADHD essentially states that the frontal region of the brain is underactive and therefore cannot do its job effectively or consistently. A critical "job" of the prefrontal lobes of the brain is to inhibit impulses and urges so that one can control and regulate behavior. This is called **inhibition**. An underactive frontal region of the brain interferes with an individual's ability to control emotions, thoughts and actions. It interferes with the ability to put the brakes on the limbic system (and the emotions which it generates) long enough for a more rational response to be considered. This is called **dis-inhibition.** This neurobiologically-based disorder of inhibition explains the far-reaching and varied symptoms associated with ADHD, perhaps primarily ADHD Hyperactive-Impulsive and Combined Types.

A WORKING MODEL OF THE NEUROBIOLOGY OF ADHD

To better understand the brain process related to ADHD and how it affects behavior, let's look at what ADHD would look like if you could draw it. Keep in mind that a very complex (and not completely understood) neurobiological process is extremely simplified here for illustration purposes.

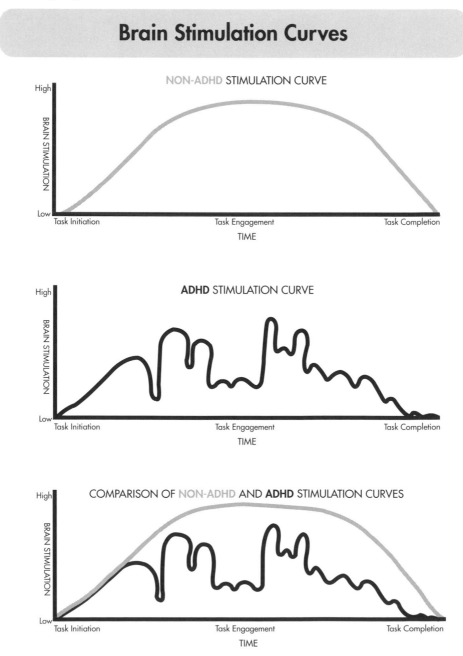

This first illustration depicts what ADHD does *not* look like. This curve represents activity level in the prefrontal lobes of the brain and corresponding behavioral functioning. At the left end of the curve, there is little activity, representing an individual's resting state. As the individual begins to engage in a task, brain stimulation increases at a rate and to a level that fits the requirements of the task. The curve levels off at the top, indicating that the individual has reached an optimal plateau of brain stimulation at which he is effectively paying attention, controlling impulses and frustrations, regulating his behavior, persisting, and ignoring distractions. After a period of time, the level of brain stimulation decreases to match the demands of the task or because the task has been completed.

Now look at the second stimulation curve. This represents the functioning of an individual with ADHD. The many peaks and valleys represent neurological stimulation and corresponding functioning that fluctuate and vary over time. This is a picture of variability and inconsistency. Does this remind you of anyone?

Finally, look at the bottom stimulation curve which contrasts the functioning of an individual *without* ADHD and an individual *with* ADHD. Although the task at hand requires a level of brain stimulation represented by the smooth, inverted U curve, the brain activity level of the individual with ADHD fluctuates, never consistently meeting the level of stimulation required to effectively perform or complete the task. Looking at this diagram, the "valleys" represent brain *understimulation*. They correspond to dopamine (and maybe norepinephrine) depletion. Behaviorally, these valleys represent reduced behavioral inhibition or impulse control resulting in fluctuating attention, ineffective regulation of activity level, poor persistence, lack of effective response to consequences, and poor emotional control. **This is a picture of poor self-regulation.**

Variability and Impersistence

Now that you see the dramatic peaks and valleys in the brain stimulation of those with ADHD, you can understand why we say that **ADHD is a disorder of variability and inconsistency.** That is, individuals with ADHD do not show symptoms all the time, in every place, with every task, and with every person. The symptoms related to ADHD vary considerably depending upon such factors as the nature of the task, the setting and the time of day. For example, an individual with ADHD will have greater difficulty with tasks that make great demands for executive functioning (i.e., frontal lobe functioning). These are tasks that require the individual to sit still, pay attention, control impulses and emotions, get organized, and persist even if the task is long or boring. This pretty much describes homework for most kids. Although many children do not enjoy homework, it is torture for kids with ADHD. As these kids attempt to do homework (assuming they haven't reached the point of complete resistance), their attention comes and goes, their frustration tolerance fluctuates, they work carefully for a minute or two and then impulsively race through the task to get it done. On the other hand, if the task is not too complex, does not take too long, is inherently interesting and stimulating to the individual, and does not make great demands on sustained attention, organization, and impulse control, the individual with ADHD can probably do as well as most people.

This pattern of variability and inconsistency can be seen as you observe a child with ADHD in the classroom. One minute he may be paying attention, the next minute he may be spacing out, the next minute he may be working on a few math problems, and the next minute after that he may be losing his cool. His behavior, his productivity, his emotions, and his academic achievement may fluctuate from task to task, minute to minute, hour to hour, or day to day.

The failure to understand the variability and inconsistency that is so characteristic of ADHD is what often leads parents and teachers to say, *"I know he could pay attention and do this work if he tried. He seems to have no trouble playing Nintendo or watching TV for an hour. He's just lazy and doesn't care."* In this case, the difference between the child's ability to play Nintendo for hours and his inability to sit and do his homework for twenty minutes is due to the difference in the nature and demands of the two tasks. Simply put, Nintendo is neurologically more stimulating; homework puts his brain to sleep. Exciting activities like Nintendo provide their own stimulation. In contrast, your child must fight the losing battle of manufacturing stimulation to get his homework done. **Don't assume that because your child with ADHD is willing and able to do something fun or easy but refuses to do something that is more difficult and challenging, he is just being stubborn. And don't assume that because your child does well in school one day and not the next, that he's just being lazy. His variability and inconsistency may very well be the result of how his brain is wired.**

This working model of variable stimulation also illustrates why we say that **ADHD is a disorder of poor persistence and motivation.** An individual is going to have a hard time sticking with something to its completion if his attention is waxing and waning, his impulse control is weak, his frustrations are hair-trigger sensitive, he is easily bored, and he is easily distracted or drawn off task. More than likely, he will give up, find something that is more stimulating, or just avoid the task altogether. **What looks like low motivation in the child with ADHD is not necessarily a *choice* , but a *result* of his neurologically-based ADHD.**

Raising the Valleys

Understanding how brain activity works provides a basis for more intuitively understanding how to manage the symptoms of ADHD. Essentially, one must "raise the valleys" of understimulation to more effective levels. This will "even out" your child so that he can function more optimally. "Raising the valleys" requires that you modify the environment, the tasks, and the overall style of how you interact with your child. In this way, you compensate for his neurological differences and provide a stability that he cannot produce on his own.

As a result of current studies, researchers now theorize that stimulant medication is one means of directly "raising the valleys" to even out behavior. Dr. Zametkin and his research team have found that the low level of brain activity in adults with ADHD was temporarily corrected when the adults took stimulant medications commonly used for treating ADHD.[16] Likewise, studies which have used EEGs to measure brain activity in children with ADHD have found that brain activity increased with stimulants. Also, studies that compared brain blood flow in children with and without ADHD have found that blood flow increased to near normal levels in children with ADHD when they were given stimulant medication. More information on medications used for ADHD is found in Part Five, " Medication Management."

Another way to "raise the valleys" and even out behavior is to modify the environment or task in such a way that you indirectly provide an effective level of stimulation for your child. These have their greatest effect on his executive functioning abilities. They involve such strategies as increasing structure, shortening the length of tasks, providing more hands-on involvement for tasks, and decreasing monotony and repetition. Specific strategies for modifying the environment and tasks are detailed in Part Four, "Behavior Management Strategies and Methods."

A third essential way to "raise the valleys" is to modify the way that you interact with your child to minimize his emotional reactiveness (limbic surges), direct his behavior, and increase compliance. It is best to avoid trying to reason your child into compliance. Instead, you want to enforce clear and quick limits, give shorter commands, provide immediate and consistent reinforcement, and give more positive attention and feedback. These methods are also discussed in Part Four.

As we learn more about the neurobiological basis of ADHD, we gain better understanding of the effects of ADHD on behavior. We can now more easily move from focusing on flawed character to an emphasis on inability. Our expanding knowledge of ADHD has legitimately placed it in the ranks of a bona fide disorder and away from indictments of poor parenting, laziness, stupidity or moral defect.

Understanding that ADHD is a biologically-based disorder that affects an individual's ability to inhibit impulses and regulate behavior leads many people, including parents, teachers and relatives, to say, "Aha, now I get it!" They can now finally understand why the child seems to have difficulty mustering up the motivation for many tasks and why he gives up so easily in the face of frustration. They can more easily understand why he often doesn't follow rules and why he doesn't consider consequences before he acts. They also gain insight into why they get stuck in an exasperating cycle of repeated reasoning and arguing, trying to get the child to do what he was asked to do.

SUMMARY

- ADHD is not caused by poor parenting, brain damage, food additives, or sugar.

- There is likely not a single cause of ADHD. Rather, there are multiple causes, including prenatal factors, heredity, a neurochemical imbalance (resulting in brain underactivity) and differences in brain structures in the prefrontal lobes and midbrain (limbic system).

- The dis-inhibition model of ADHD states that difficulty with self-control (i.e., controlling emotions, thoughts, and actions) comes from underactivity in those parts of the brain that oversee and regulate behavior.

- ADHD-related variability and inconsistency of behavior and the lack of persistence with difficult or boring tasks are related to fluctuating understimulation in the brain.

- There are various ways to compensate for understimulation in the brain: medication, modifying the environment and modifying the style of interaction.

ADHD Affects Motivation

Behavioral theory tells us that behavior is determined by its consequences. If we do something that is followed by reward or reinforcement, we will likely do it again. Conversely, if we do something that is *not* followed by reward or reinforcement (or is followed by punishment), we are less inclined to do it again. The reward or reinforcement can come from external sources, such as getting a paycheck for doing a job, or it can also come from internal sources, such as feeling proud and competent for getting the job done. For most of us, it takes an "average" amount of reinforcement to motivate us. The same does not hold true for those with ADHD.

Motivational difficulties are a fundamental aspect of ADHD. Children with ADHD perform or behave significantly better when they receive immediate reinforcement or consequences at a high rate. They also do much better when they are engaged in highly rewarding activities such as computer games or various hobby or play activities that they really enjoy. They tend to persist and work better if tasks are broken down into smaller chunks so they can see an endpoint before their frustration builds up and their motivation gives out. Under these circumstances, they persist in their efforts and perform almost as well as non-ADHD children.

However, when individuals with ADHD are in situations where there is not a high rate of immediate reinforcement; where there is little inherent stimulation; and where it just takes too long, is too complex, or involves many steps, they give up, and their behavior deteriorates dramatically. This is evident, for example, when we observe children with ADHD trying to perform in the classroom, do their homework or sit through a church service. These are all environments or situations where reinforcements may be few and far between, stimulation is low, demands for sustained attention and impulse control are high, and it just lasts too long.

These behavioral difficulties are linked to the underlying neurology of ADHD. Neurobiological understimulation makes it hard for your child to sustain attention, control impulses, avoid distractions, temper frustration, organize steps to a task, and persist. As much as he might want to successfully complete tasks, he will not have much motivation to perform tasks which make these kinds of demands. Therefore, those tasks that are especially challenging for him are ones that require a lot of concentration and/or self-control, involve a lot of organization or multiple steps, are not very stimulating or reinforcing, and take a relatively long time.

These descriptors pertain to many tasks which your child faces every day, including getting ready for school in the morning, doing household chores, doing homework, going to church, and running errands, to name just a few. So-called normal levels of reinforcement (internal or external) will likely not motivate your child to perform these tasks because, from a *neurobiological standpoint,* they are difficult for him. It takes more reinforcement, reward and stimulation to keep your child motivated and engaged. This is what we mean when we say ADHD is a disorder of motivation.

Motivation for your child does not come easily from within unless the activity or task in which he is engaged is highly rewarding to him. If the activity or task is not intrinsically rewarding, he will lose attention, give up prematurely, or perhaps even refuse to begin the task. Typical nonrewarding activities include homework and daily chores. This requires that the task or situation has to be restructured, reinforcement has to be external, and this reinforcement has to be more powerful than for children without ADHD. In other words, others have to create the motivation externally because it doesn't come easily internally for your child. This is why restructuring the environment, restructuring tasks, and using behavior modification strategies are essential for managing ADHD. They are all ways to increase motivation. We discuss these strategies in Parts Three, Four and Six.

SUMMARY

- Children with ADHD are motivated differently than other children. Long-term consequences are not as motivating as immediate reinforcements and the intrinsic value of events (i.e., how much a child wants to do an activity).

- Motivation often has to be externally provided because it is not internally generated by the child with ADHD.

CHAPTER

5 ADHD Affects the Ability to Follow Rules

If you are a parent of a child with ADHD, you are all too familiar with the fact that your child continually breaks rules. He probably breaks the same rules over and over again, no matter how many times they are stated. Consider this scenario.

> Your 8-year-old child with ADHD has a penchant for going into his big brother's room and taking his belongings, such as candy, toys, tapes, and books. You tell him that the rule is, "Stay out of your brother's room and don't take his stuff." At least twice a week, however, you hear the two of them yelling and arguing because, once again, "Sticky Fingers" has pilfered some of his brother's prized possessions. You ask him why he continues to take his brother's stuff even though he knows he's not supposed to. He replies, "I don't know."

Or consider this example:

> Your daughter loves to be with her friends after school, but you need to know where she is. You tell her the rule is that she must call and check in with you to get permission to go to a friend's house. Despite this rule, your daughter continues to come home from school one to two hours late most nights. You're often making lots of phone calls, trying to track her down. When you finally find her, she says something like, "Oh, I meant to call, but I forgot."

In both of these cases each child knew the rule but repeatedly broke it. Instead of doing what they were supposed to do, they did what felt good to them at the moment. It's not that they didn't know the rule; they didn't follow the rule.

Children with ADHD do not easily follow rules; they do not easily internalize rules that control behavior. When a "normal" child hears a rule a few times, he is able to follow that rule for the most part. It guides his behavior accordingly, not only at the point of hearing the rule, but also on an ongoing basis and into the future. He does not have to hear the rule repeatedly in order to "behave." Also, the "normal" child is able to generate his own rules or guidelines for behavior. He is able to delay his impulses long enough to "talk" to himself and regulate his behavior. He can use internal speech to guide behavior and consider consequences to his behavior. He can say to himself *before* the fact, "I'm supposed to check in with Mom before I go anywhere. Even though I'm in a hurry, I'll really make Mom angry if I don't take the time to call."

However, because of his neurologically-based dis-inhibition, **the child with ADHD is managed by the moment and directed by impulses rather than managed by rules and directed by consequences.** In essence, *his impulses overrule the rules.* He literally can't wait long enough to use internal speech to guide his behavior. As a result, these children frequently break rules. It's not that they don't know the rules; they just can't consistently follow them. They can't easily control their impulses long enough to use the rules. In the examples, the impulse to eat a piece of candy or play with his brother's toy overruled the rule to keep hands off his stuff, and the impulse to have fun with friends overruled the rule to call home and check in. The impulse at the moment was too powerful compared to the consequence in the future.

It is important to understand that breaking rules may not be completely within the control of your child. He may intend to follow a rule, but his neurologically-based inability to control impulses pushes him past the rule. When you talk to him about breaking a rule, he might even be able to tell you which rule he broke. Barkley says, "It's not that he doesn't know what to do; he doesn't do what he knows." He is managed by the moment, not by rules.[1]

A child with ADHD has a defective internal control system. Because he does not *internalize* rules to govern his behavior, you must *externalize* rules for him. That is, you must act as your child's external control system. Rules must be externally visible and have a high profile. This can be done by posting rules on the wall or in your child's bedroom, sticking Post-It ® notes in strategic places as reminders, making job charts that state the rules for completion of a job, repeating rules frequently, anticipating and discussing potential problems before your child enters certain situations, and discussing ahead of time what specific consequences will follow if rules are broken.

You must also adjust your expectations for how well your child will follow rules. It is probably unrealistic for you to expect that you can state a rule once or even a few times in order for it to govern your child's behavior. *Don't* expect your child to do what he's supposed to do no matter how often you talk about it. More than likely, you will need to give your child reminders to do things for which you feel he shouldn't need them. For example, even though your child knows he is supposed to make his bed every day, you may have to remind him.

You may need to restate certain rules on an ongoing basis throughout an activity or until your child has completed what he was told to do. For example, it is unrealistic to expect that your young child with ADHD will stay by your side in a store after hearing the rule only once. More realistically, you will have to repeat the rule throughout the shopping trip, acting as your child's external control system. Likewise for older children, you may have to continually repeat rules such as, "Pick up your clothes," "Take a shower," "Take out the trash," or "Mow the lawn." **It will help you if you face the reality that you must follow the mantra, "Repetition without emotion";[2] that is, know that you will have to repeat rules and give reminders like a broken record, but do it calmly, without anger, criticism or shame.**

ADHD is a *performance* deficit, not a *skill* deficit. When your child has broken a rule or has done something wrong, you may have asked him, "Why did you do such a dumb thing?" Then you probably launched into a long-winded lecture explaining why it is so important to follow these rules, hoping that this lecture will finally convince your child to follow the rules from now on.

This attempt to reason your child into compliance might be marginally helpful for the non-ADHD child who may have not yet learned the rules. We can assume that his failure to follow the rules was a result of a *skill* deficit, i.e., he hadn't learned the rule yet. Once he learns and understands the rule, he will probably follow it most of the time. This is not the case with ADHD. Your child may understand the rules, and he may even know how to execute the rules, but knowing and doing are two different things. His poor impulse control interferes with his ability to *perform* or follow the rules.

SUMMARY

- The child with ADHD is managed by the moment and directed by impulses, rather than managed by rules and directed by consequences.

- Parents must act as their child's external control system by establishing explicit rules, repeating them frequently, and keeping them simple; by anticipating and discussing potential problems ahead of time; and by specifying in advance the consequences for breaking rules.

- "Repetition without emotion": reinforce and repeat without shame, impatience or anger.

Part Two

What ADHD Looks Like in Real Life

Children with ADHD do not necessarily act alike. Some may be revved up as though their motors are in overdrive. Some may not be so hyper, but they're spacey and disorganized. Others may be fidgety, impulsive, and talk incessantly, while still others may be moody, overly sensitive and very oppositional. This is one reason why ADHD is so perplexing — its symptoms are so varied. So even though researchers have provided a list of clinical symptoms to help determine if a child has ADHD, parents often look at these symptoms and remark, "I can't tell if this describes my child."

If we look at all the various and individual behaviors associated with ADHD, we find some common behavioral *patterns*. These are the real-life patterns of behavior that you may see and struggle with every day. Your child may show all or some of these behavioral patterns, and the intensity of these patterns may vary for each child.

Pattern 1: **Inattention**
Pattern 2: **Impulsivity**
Pattern 3: **Hyperactivity**
Pattern 4: **Poor response to consequences**
Pattern 5: **Noncompliance**
Pattern 6: **Inconsistency**
Pattern 7: **Difficulty delaying gratification**
Pattern 8: **Emotional overarousal**
Pattern 9: **Poor persistence**
Pattern 10: **Difficulty with change and transitions**
Pattern 11: **Disorganization**
Pattern 12: **Social Problems**

6 Twelve Common Behavioral Patterns

1. INATTENTION

"He never finishes what he starts."

"She is so easily distracted."

"She's our little space cadet."

"He forgot his homework — again"

"He never seems to listen."

"She is a daydreamer."

Sound familiar? Your child with ADHD will have difficulties with attention, especially if tasks are relatively long, monotonous, or boring. Although all children have difficulty paying attention from time to time, those with ADHD have noticeably more difficulty than others their age.

Some people erroneously believe that if a child can pay attention to some things, he cannot have ADHD. How many times have you seen your child spend hours watching TV but struggle to pay attention in the classroom? Or have you seen him plaster his nose in a science fiction book, yet become drowsy and bored when reading his history book? **Most of us can pay attention better and longer when we are doing something we enjoy. And most of us have a hard time paying attention to something that is long and boring. But most of us can *force* ourselves to pay attention to those things in which we are not all that interested when we know it is important to do so. Those with ADHD, however, cannot easily "force" themselves to pay attention, even when they know it is important to do so. It's not that they can't pay attention at all; they lack the ability to activate and *sustain* their attention at will.**

Types of Attention Problems

Attention is not a simple, all-or-nothing thing. There are many types of attention, including focused, selective, divided, sustained, vigilance, and distractibility.

If your child has problems with **focused attention,** he may often look like he is daydreaming or preoccupied with other thoughts. He often does not start his work in school or tasks at home immediately upon being asked. You may have to repeat yourself many times, say his name out loud, or get eye contact with him before he pays attention and starts to move.

If **selective attention** is the problem, he may focus upon the wrong thing. Instead of listening to what you are telling him to do, he is paying attention to how your nostrils flare when you are angry. Or instead of getting the main gist of a story, he is more interested in the pictures. Problems with focused and selective attention appear to be the main attention problems associated with ADHD, Predominantly Inattentive Type.

A problem with **divided attention** is apparent when your child has difficulty completing two simultaneous tasks. For example, he may have difficulty listening to his teacher and taking notes at the same time.

A problem with **sustained attention** may be seen if your child does not stick with a task for very long and/or flits from one activity to another. He may start many tasks but never finish any of them. In the classroom, he may start a worksheet but soon gets up to sharpen his pencil or bug the student next to him. Research suggests that sustained attention is the main type of attention problem underlying ADHD, Hyperactive-Impulsive and Combined Types.

A problem with **vigilance** means that your child has difficulty getting ready to respond. For example, during a spelling test, he is unable to listen for the next spelling word from the teacher. Out on the baseball field, he may be thinking about that last high fly ball as the next one goes whizzing by him.

Children easily drawn off task may have a problem with **distractibility.** These kids are like heat-seeking missiles; if there is something more interesting going on, they'll find it, no matter what they were *supposed* to be doing. Underlying this problem is difficulty in controlling the urge or impulse to seek stimulation, to seek something more interesting or fun. This means that if your child is engaged in a task that is boring to him, he will shift "off task" toward something around him that is more interesting. In the classroom, for example, he may find socializing with another student more fun than doing 30 math problems, or he may feel that what is happening outside the classroom window is more interesting than listening to his teacher talk about square roots. At home, you may find him playing when you sent him upstairs to brush his teeth. In all of these situations, your child has difficulty suppressing the urge to engage in something more fun or stimulating. On the other hand, your child can glue himself in front of the television and never hear you calling him to answer the phone. In this case, his television program was so stimulating that it grabbed his attention, and he couldn't easily let go.

The apparent source of distractibility does not always have to be external. Your child may often find his own thoughts and imagination more interesting than what is going on around him. Consequently, his teacher may tell you that he daydreams excessively in class or seems to be "in his own world." Often, his own world is more interesting than the outside world.

Situations in Which Your Child May Not Show Attention Problems

Further confusing the attention picture is the fact that there are situations in which your child will not show any signs of an attention problem. There are at least four factors in the environment which determine this. If your child is in a situation which is **novel, interesting, intimidating, or one-to-one,** he may not appear to have an attention deficit at all. This may be why **in about 80 percent of the cases, these children do not show their ADHD behaviors in the doctor's office.**[1] The doctor's office is often new or novel and, therefore, more stimulating. The child may be watching closely to see what the doctor is going to do to him next, so it is interesting. Doctors are authority figures to most children, so they are intimidating. And it is often just the child and the doctor (and sometimes the parent) in the office together, so it is one-to-one.

Similarly, children with ADHD often do not show their symptoms during one-to-one testing. A psychologist or clinician evaluating a child for ADHD usually administers tests to the child by himself, creating an "ideal environment," which minimizes the effects of ADHD. It is very different from the conditions in the classroom, home setting or the real world. In addition, the one-to-one testing situation is very structured and thus organizes the child's behavior for him. Although testing may last a few hours at a time and continue over a few days, there is a clear beginning and end. The psychologist often sets the pace of testing according to the child's mood, motivation and attentional capacity. The clinician allows breaks if it is apparent that the child is tired or losing motivation, and frequently gives some form of overt or subtle feedback to keep the child on track. External distractions are minimized in the one-to-one setting, so the child is not as easily drawn off task. These testing conditions are dramatically different from those in the typical classroom where there is less structure, more distractions, less immediate feedback, fewer work breaks, more expectations for independent functioning, and greater demands on organization and follow-through. This situation continues day after day.

It is no wonder that physicians or psychologists often erroneously conclude that a child is not ADHD. After all, he didn't act like he had ADHD in their office. These conclusions often leave parents discouraged and feeling unheard. If this has happened to you, you probably wondered if you had been overreacting all this time to your child's behavior and questioned whether *you* were actually the one with the problems.

Attention and Memory Problems

Another problem associated with inattention is poor memory or forgetfulness. How many times have you reminded your child to bring home his homework only to repeatedly find that he forgot it at school, or that he doesn't even remember if he has any? Have you complained that your child can remember something you told him when he was 4 years old, but he can't remember what you asked him to do 5 minutes ago? How often have you found yourself scrambling at the last minute to find your child's backpack or lunch or shoes because he can't remember where he put them?

Memory is a very complex process, and there are many types of memory. A person can have good memory for some things and terrible memory for other things. Attention and memory go hand-in-hand so it is common to find some types of memory problems in children with ADHD. After all, one must pay attention to information before that information can be stored in memory.

Daydreamers or children who are highly distractible may not acquire as much information as their classmates because they don't "take in" or pay attention to the incoming information. Some children with ADHD don't pay attention long enough to really process the information so that they can remember and understand it. This affects the **depth of processing.** For example, if your child studies for a test, but gives it only superficial attention, he may not learn the information well enough to do well on the test. He will likely have gaps in his learning and not completely understand the concepts that he was trying to learn.

Sometimes children with ADHD have great memories, but for the wrong things. They pay attention to and remember the unimportant information or the nonessential detail, but don't pay attention to what they need to remember. For example, your child may study for a test only to find when he takes it that he memorized information not on the test. Or you may be thrilled that your child remembered he has a homework assignment, only to find that he forgot his backpack at school. Or he remembered to tell you he took a telephone message for you, but he forgot to write down the caller's name and phone number.

Commonly, children with ADHD have problems with **prospective memory**, or remembering to remember. This type of memory problem usually shows itself when your child forgets *to do* something that he was told to do or that he was going to do. He forgets to bring home his homework, forgets he was going to run an errand for you, or forgets he was going to call you if he was going to be late. Prospective memory relies on the child's ability to cue himself to remember what he was supposed to do. He has to remember to remember. Children with ADHD who struggle with the constant flow of external and internal distractions have difficulty remembering to self-cue.

This difficulty with prospective memory often creates problems for children with ADHD when it comes time to remember to take their medication or to get their daily homework sheet signed by their teacher before they leave class. School personnel will often comment that the child has to learn responsibility and they cannot keep reminding him to take his medicine or get his papers signed. Teachers or parents often comment, "He's old enough to remember, I shouldn't have to remind him." But prospective memory is not simply a function of age or being "old enough" or being responsible. Many adults with ADHD struggle with prospective memory problems as well. Prospective memory problems are a function of the ADHD and its impact on memory.

Finally, many children with ADHD have difficulty remembering what they are supposed to do while they are doing it, or they have difficulty keeping information in their memory long enough to manipulate and use that information. Called **active working memory**, research indicates that it is function of the frontal lobes of the brain.

Dr. Mel Levine, in his book, *Keeping A Head In School*,[2] compares active working memory to having a television screen in your mind. While you're listening and watching the information on the television, parts of the screen keep going out and the information gets lost. Your child may experience attention-related problems in active working memory when he reads. He may read a paragraph, but by the time he gets to the end of the paragraph he may forget what the beginning of the paragraph was all about. He may also have problems working a math problem such as division because while he's dividing the smaller number into the larger number, he may forget what to do next. He may struggle with active working memory problems when doing written language tasks because he may have difficulty keeping his thoughts in his mind while also trying to spell, punctuate, sequence the words and get them down on paper.

2. IMPULSIVITY

Impulsivity is the more common term for dis-inhibition. As we discussed in Chapter Three, recent research suggests that this is the fundamental problem underlying ADHD[3] (particularly for those who are ADHD, Predominantly Hyperactive-Impulsive Type and Combined Type). That is, individuals with ADHD have a significant problem with stopping and thinking before they act. They often act first and think later. They learn by trial and error rather than by past experiences. This is why they are often "repeat offenders." Even when they have gotten into trouble in the past for doing a particular thing, they continue to do that same thing over and over again, despite the consequences. It's not that they don't *know* what to do. They can, in fact, often state the rules to you. It is more a problem of not *doing* what they know. **The problem is not in knowing the skill, but in controlling impulses long enough so that they can apply the skill.**

Dis-inhibition also interferes with a child's ability to put the brakes on his emotions. His knee-jerk reactions to situations make it difficult or impossible to step back and separate his feelings from the facts. Reason goes out the window, and emotions take over. At these times, not only is it useless to try to reason with your child, it often makes matters worse. It is this emotional dis-inhibition that often makes these kids seem so immature.

Dis-inhibition also shows itself in the difficulty that school-age children and adolescents have in planning ahead, forming long-term goals or managing time. Planning ahead involves putting the brakes on impulses long enough to consider the future. Because those with ADHD are typically responding to the here and now, to the moment, they often don't take the time to consider what is coming in the future. Eventually the future becomes now, and they haven't prepared what they intended to prepare or do what they intended to do. They mismanage time, move at their own pace, and are often late because of their difficulty in considering the future and strategizing how to get there.

As you observe your child's behavior, you will see endless examples of his problem with dis-inhibition. You see it when he blurts out in class or has a difficult time waiting his turn in line. He may rush through his work to get it finished, or take a quick look at a chore and decide it's too big or overwhelming to do. He may intrusively join in with other children when they are in the middle of a game or constantly interrupt when someone else is talking. He may impulsively dash out into the street without looking or carelessly throw a baseball inside the house. He may explode in anger over seemingly minor incidents or lash out and bop his sister on the head before you realize what happened. In a split second he darts away from you in the grocery store even though you just reminded him to stay by your side.

The remaining nine categories of behavioral patterns that follow can all be related in one way or another to dis-inhibition. As you read the descriptions, you will gather a full appreciation of the far-reaching and troubling effects of dis-inhibition.

3. HYPERACTIVITY

Contrary to common belief, **not all children with ADHD are overactive or "bouncing off the walls."** Hyperactivity is seen in degrees from subtle to obvious. The most obviously hyperactive individuals seem to be full of energy and are observed to continually be "on the go." Their "motor" won't turn off. They can't settle down. In contrast, those who are more mildly hyperactive are often characterized as restless, fidgety, unable to relax or impatient.

In actuality, hyperactivity for the child who has ADHD does not mean that he displays an excess *amount* of activity, but that he has difficulty *regulating* his activity level to fit the situation or the task at hand. His apparent energy level may be too much and too disruptive for the situation, such as when he is crawling under his seat in the movie theater. Or his movements may seem irrelevant, purposeless or annoying given the situation, such as when he keeps fiddling with his Nerf® ball while you're trying to have a serious conversation with him. In both situations, his apparent energy level does not fit the situation.

Some researchers believe that these seemingly over-charged, purposeless or off-task movements may actually be related to the child's neurologically-based understimulation. Dr. Sidney Zentall from Purdue

University suggests that the overactive, restless, or extraneous movements of the child with **ADHD** are his attempts to stimulate himself when faced with a relatively understimulating task or environment. In this sense, these apparent purposeless behaviors take on a real purpose.[4]

Other researchers suggest that hyperactivity and impulsivity are both expressions of a child's difficulty inhibiting his behavior. The overactive behaviors, as well as the more subtle restless and fidgety behaviors, arise from the individual's difficulty in controlling the urge to move around, to get up and look at something or do something more interesting. In some situations, therefore, your child has difficulty controlling and regulating his excitement and impulses as he goes from an energized situation such as the playground to the more calm and sedate classroom. Consequently, he continues to be loud, rambunctious and rowdy while his classmates have already settled down.

4. POOR RESPONSE TO CONSEQUENCES

"Nothing seems to work with my kid!"

Parents will comment that they just can't find any consequence or form of punishment that seems to control the behavior of their child with **ADHD**. Whereas normal children seem to change their behavior if they are grounded or sent to time-out, these methods are usually less effective for the child with **ADHD**.

Children who are not **ADHD** usually work for rewards fairly easily. Unfortunately, for the child with **ADHD** it's hard to find something that provides enough motivation to change his behavior. Although parents may finally find the "right reward," it typically works for only a short time. As a result, parents conclude that their child is just being stubborn, is not really trying or, once again, they have failed in their parenting.

Consequences That Work

Recent research offers explanations for why consequences often don't work. Some researchers hypothesize that the child's difficulty in responding to consequences and reinforcement is related to brain function. They suggest that reinforcements and consequences may be less effective in controlling the behavior of children with **ADHD** because the centers in the brain which respond to reward/punishment are less sensitive or understimulated. As a result, **ADHD**-related behavior is not as easily inhibited or regulated by the threat of punishment or the enticement of reward. Other researchers suggest that the reduced power of rewards and consequences is a result of the difficulty or inability to stop and think about the consequences or rewards of a behavior before engaging in that behavior.

Whatever the underlying reason for why rewards and consequences are less effective with children with ADHD, we do know that **rewards or punishments need to be more powerful to have an effect.** Essentially, the rewards or punishments have to be stimulating enough to motivate your child to overcome his neurobiologically-based poor impulse control so that he can comply.

There are four basic things you can do to make consequences more powerful:

- **Immediate**

  More powerful consequences do not necessarily mean more expensive rewards or harsher punishments. Consequences (positive or negative) are more powerful for the child with ADHD if they are delivered **immediately** after the behavior occurs.

  Failure to apply consequences immediately is often the main reason why consequences for these children are ineffective. For example, you may try to encourage your child to get better grades in school by offering him a big reward at the end of the quarter if he brings his grades up. He may be enthused about this idea for the first week but then quickly falls into the old pattern of not getting the work done and achieving poor grades. When this happens, you get even more discouraged and conclude that the situation is hopeless and your kid is lazy.

  The problem, however, is not with a lazy kid but, among other things, a reward that was not immediate. Weeks or months go by between getting an assignment in and getting a report card at the end of the quarter. For a child who is managed by the moment, this is an eternity! The promise of a big reward at the end of the quarter is definitely not an immediate consequence when your child is receiving low grades at the beginning of the quarter. This delayed consequence will not be powerful enough to motivate your child past the here and now for very long.

- **Consistent and Frequent**

  Consequences also have to be delivered **consistently**, that is, every time the behavior occurs. In fact, your child's behavior may deteriorate or become considerably worse if he was expecting a positive consequence and does not receive it. Popular video games satisfy the criteria of immediate, consistent and high rate of reward, which may explain why children with ADHD can effectively pay attention for so long to these games.

- **Interesting**

  A more powerful reward is also one that is more **interesting**. You might often decide for your child what his rewards should be. Unfortunately, what may be considered a good reward by you may be considered a boring reward by your child. A child who struggles with low motivation is not going to get fired up for a boring reward. Be sure to get your child's input into the rewards or consequences that would be the most motivating for him.

- **Varied**

  Finally, a more powerful reward has to have **variety.** Remember, there is an underlying neurochemical explanation for the fact that children with ADHD soon become bored with rewards. To compensate for this deficit, rewards have to be changed frequently so that they maintain their interest and stimulation value. So perhaps for your child, working for a rented video may work for a few weeks, and then changing to working for a Friday night sleepover may be more motivating for a while.

5. EXCESSIVE NONCOMPLIANCE

All too often you meet a brick wall when you ask your child to do something. More than other children, he seems to whine, argue, complain, talk back, or ignore you when you ask him to follow through on something, even something as simple as hanging up his coat or brushing his teeth. Children with ADHD are excessively noncompliant. In fact, it is estimated that as many as 65 percent of children with ADHD are oppositional or defiant.[5,6] The main triggers for noncompliance are commands or requests from parents and teachers. It is no wonder these children are often described as "hard to parent" or "hard to teach."

Noncompliance of children with ADHD needs special explanation — it escalates. What may start out as difficulty with complying eventually turns into outright resistance. At least two dynamics are going on here. First, the ADHD-related inattention, impulsivity and poor regulation of activity interfere with these children's *ability* to follow through with what parents or other adults ask them to do. Second, their inability to do the task correctly or completely frustrates adults, leading to nagging, anger and increased control. After enough negative interactions with adults, children with ADHD eventually develop a secondary layer of active defiance or more passive resistance, such as refusing, arguing, ignoring or "forgetting" so that they can avoid the whole thing. In a short time, this noncompliance is generalized to the majority of requests made by adults. More about the "cycle of non-compliance" is discussed in Chapter 18.

Children with ADHD are not totally noncompliant. They are more likely to comply if the request involves something that they like, involves just a little amount of effort, or if there is the promise of an immediate reward or pay-off. For example, your youngster is more likely to comply with your command, "Get in the car" if he knows he is going out to rent a video rather than going with you to the dry cleaners. Your adolescent is more likely to comply with doing his homework if he knows that he can't get together with his friends until his assignments are finished.

Children who are hyperactive-impulsive tend to be more actively noncompliant and defiant than those who are predominantly inattentive. The reduced self-control and greater impulsivity of the hyperactive-impulsive children lead to more overt acting out and active verbal and physical refusals. In contrast, the more inattentive children may be more passive in their resistance. More often, they may tend to "forget" or to be "too tired" to do something.

6. INCONSISTENCY

We have now come to understand that variability and inconsistency are hallmarks of ADHD. Unfortunately, many people look at the inconsistency and variability of the child with ADHD and conclude that he can't possibly have an attention deficit because he can pay attention to some things, and he isn't always "hyper." Parents often assume that if their child can sit and watch TV for an hour, he should be able to sit and do his homework for 45 minutes. When he doesn't, they assume he is "just lazy" or he is doing this "just to make me angry." Teachers may erroneously conclude that because a student was on task last period, he should be able to continue paying attention for the next period. If he doesn't, it's because "he just isn't trying."

Conditions which Contribute to the Inconsistency of ADHD Symptoms

A child may exhibit his ADHD-related symptoms depending upon:
the environment;

the nature of the task with which the child is engaged;

the individual with whom the child is interacting;

the time of day; and/or

the immediacy of reinforcement or punishment.

* **Environment**

    Environmental factors are significant in determining the manifestation of ADHD-related behaviors. Children with ADHD often do not exhibit problematic behaviors in situations or settings that place little demand on them to control their behavior. Consequently, many times your child cannot be distinguished from non-ADHD children on the playground. However, in settings which demand that he sit still, pay attention for long periods of time, stay motivated, follow complex directions, control impulses, stay organized, and follow rules, he has considerable difficulty. These are the typical demands in the classroom, which explains why most of these children are first diagnosed when they enter school.

    Conversely, your child will exhibit fewer ADHD-related behaviors in environments that are well-structured but flexible, stimulating but not over-stimulating, allow some amount of movement (which helps keep them aroused), provide much ongoing feedback and positive reinforcement, and do not make excessive demands for sustained attention and effort.

* **Nature of the task**

    The nature of the task in which your child is engaged also affects his behavior. Children with ADHD will have more difficulty and display more ADHD-related behaviors doing those tasks which are relatively long, boring, or complicated, and which demand planning, organization and regulation of behavior. This describes many school-related tasks (including homework), as well as routine chores around the house (such as taking out the garbage, making the bed, brushing teeth and hair, and getting ready for school). Your child will be more successful at tasks that are stimulating and inherently interesting to him, are relatively short and fit his attentional capacity, are broken down into segments, and provide opportunities for hands-on involvement.

- **Individual with whom the child is interacting**

  Children with ADHD also respond differently depending upon the person with whom they are engaged. They generally tend to be more cooperative with their fathers than with their mothers. This does not mean that mothers are less effective parents, but mothers tend to spend more time with their children than do fathers, even if the mothers are working outside of the home. Consequently, there are more opportunities for children to display their negative behaviors with their mothers. Also, mothers tend to monitor and enforce more of the drudge and maintenance tasks within the household, such as brushing teeth, picking up clothes, and doing homework. Children with ADHD have difficulty complying with these typically monotonous, unstimulating chores.

  Also, mothers and fathers tend to respond to their children differently. Mothers are more likely to use reasoning and to talk more with their children when they are trying to convince them to comply and are less likely to use punishment or force. Fathers, however, usually talk less, don't employ reasoning as much, and discipline more quickly when the child is noncompliant. Fathers also tend to be more intimidating given their typically larger size and deeper voice.

- **Time of day**

  The time of day also affects the behavior of children with ADHD. Your child likely does better in the morning hours. As the day wears on, his attention and impulse control decrease, and his hyperactivity or restlessness increase. Consequently, school behavior and academic performance are considerably worse in the afternoon. Given this, it is important to schedule more demanding academic tasks or household chores in the morning and leave the recreational, less demanding activities for the afternoon. Waning attention and motivation in the afternoon also create potential problems if your child is typically expected to do his homework during this time of the day.

- **Immediacy of reinforcement or stimulation**

  Finally, children with ADHD will manifest fewer of their symptoms if they are in a situation that provides immediate reinforcement or punishment for behavior. If your child is engaged in activities that are highly rewarding or provide reinforcement immediately, such as with Nintendo or other video games, he may perform like any other child. Likewise, if your child is given *immediate* reinforcement for positive behavior, his behavior will improve more dramatically. One reason that behavior management programs at home or at school sometimes fail is that the rewards or punishments are given too long after the specific behavior(s) occurs. Consequently, parents and teachers should work to "tighten it up" when giving the child reinforcements, feedback or consequences for his behavior.

7. DIFFICULTY DELAYING GRATIFICATION

Children with ADHD are extremely *impatient*. When they want something, they want it NOW, and they won't stop badgering you until they get it. They seem unable to accept the word "No." They will ask for something and simply will not let the issue drop until they have worn you down and you have given in.

You see your child's difficulty with delaying gratification when he does not stop to do simple, routine things when there is something else he would rather be doing. When he comes home from school, he throws his coat on the floor and heads straight for his after-school snack. Or if his friends are waiting outside to play and he hasn't picked up his room yet, you may find his toys and dirty clothes stuffed underneath his bed while he's outside playing ball. Waiting in line is torture, so he pushes to be first in line. Money usually doesn't last long; it just takes too long to save it. If you give your child an allowance, it's probably gone by the end of the day. Although most kids badger their parents on car trips with the unending question, "Are we there yet?" your kid just doesn't let up as he repeats the question every ten miles. There are probably many times you'd like to put him up on the luggage rack!

Difficulty delaying gratification also shows its effects in school. It's hard to raise his hand and wait for the teacher to call his name, so your child might blurt out his answers, monopolizing or disrupting class discussions. He will rush through his work because it takes too long, sacrificing quality in the process. His worksheet may be done, but it's sloppy, incomplete and incorrect. He may skip to the end of a book to see how it ends before he's even read the first chapter.

When teachers devise incentive programs, they may forget about these students' difficulty delaying gratification. They may motivate these children to complete their work, but inadvertently reinforce impulsivity and inaccuracy. In one classroom, the teacher told the student with ADHD that if she finished her work, she could play checkers with another student as a reward. This student loved to play checkers, so she was motivated by the idea. She soon started getting all of her classwork done very quickly. Unfortunately, it was usually wrong and sloppy. In this example, the teacher focused on motivating the child to *complete* her work, but *accuracy* was compromised in the process. The student should have been rewarded for completion *and* accuracy.

8. EMOTIONAL OVERAROUSAL

It is usually the child with ADHD who tends to overreact to situations. You are frequently left scratching your head wondering how your child could get so upset over such a little thing. He feels his emotions very intensely, and he lets you know it. He may laugh too loud, scream or cry often bringing much attention to himself. He is more prone to temper tantrums, and they are usually fairly dramatic. Living with the child with ADHD often feels like riding an emotional roller coaster as you experience his mood shifts with their exaggerated highs and lows.

Children with ADHD seem to be very reactive to their environments. Their behavioral dis-inhibition prevents them from "putting on the brakes." Therefore, they easily get caught up in the emotions of others around them. You might say that your child is the barometer for family stress. His behavior mirrors, and perhaps exaggerates, the emotional climate, tension or stress around him. If Dad comes home from work upset, it will not be too long before your child is upset. Or if Mom is short-tempered today, more than likely your child will be also.

Relatedly, children with ADHD do not effectively cope with frustration. Your child may become easily upset if faced with a difficult or challenging task and will likely give up in frustration rather than persist. His modus operandi is to go around a challenge rather than face it. This style becomes especially problematic once your child is school-age because learning in the classroom, completing worksheets, and doing homework all involve challenges and a certain degree of frustration. Students with ADHD are the ones who tend to give up sooner and frequently ask their teacher for help before they have applied much effort themselves.

Your child may be a poor loser in games, and he may become overly upset in competitive activities if the situation is not going his way. A younger child may bang a toy or throw it if it is not working the way he wants it to.

Anger is a common problem with children with ADHD because of their poorly controlled emotional impulses. Your child may frequently get into fights on the playground with the slightest or no provocation. An accidental bump in line from another student may be countered by a forceful push and foul language. Neighborhood children may stop playing with your child because he always gets angry and bosses them around.

Your child's anger at home can affect the whole family, causing you and his siblings to walk on eggshells. You may dread waking your child up in the morning to go to school because you know he'll bite your head off. Giving him a simple request such as, "Start your homework" may be met with angry defiance. Although he persistently goes into his sister's room and takes her stuff, he lambastes her hard if he catches her in his room. Family outings can be ruined by your child's bad mood as he sulks in the car, taunts his siblings, and stubbornly refuses to change his attitude.

9. POOR PERSISTENCE

"He's lazy and doesn't care."

"He never finishes what he starts."

A common complaint by teachers is likely that your child doesn't finish his work. He gives up more easily, gets frustrated sooner, and leaves half the worksheet incomplete. Consequently, he has more homework than other kids. At home you deal with his unfinished homework and household chores. You wonder how much homework your child is going to get done before you find him goofing off or throwing a fit. You send him out to mow the lawn, but he only does the front yard because he's exhausted or bored. He may tackle a new project with initial enthusiasm only to soon complain that it's too boring and "dumb." He may convincingly talk you into allowing him to take trumpet lessons and then constantly complain when he has to practice.

You have probably observed that the longer your child is doing something, the more you see him become physically restless, yawn frequently, become distracted, rush through and make careless mistakes or put in minimal effort, complain that "this darn thing takes too long," or just get up and leave in the middle of it. He may resist doing the job or project altogether.

Perhaps more than any other symptom, children with **ADHD** are maligned because of their difficulty with persistence. They are characterized as lazy and not caring. The common admonition from adults is, "You just need to try harder." There are probably no words of "encouragement" that kids with **ADHD** detest more. The "You just need to try harder" is usually met with defiance, resentment, and eventual apathy. **Telling a child with ADHD to "try harder" is like telling a carpenter without a hammer to pound harder.** It's difficult to finish a job if you don't have the right tools. The "tools" the child with **ADHD** lacks are the neurological wiring to sustain motivation, control impulses and frustrations, maintain attention and ignore distractions through long, complex, boring or nonrewarding tasks. **This lack of persistence is the result of neurobiological dis-inhibition. It is not a character flaw.**

ADHD is a disorder of poor persistence. If an individual is motivated by immediate reward and high stimulation; if his attention is waxing and waning; if his impulses are poorly controlled; if his frustration tolerance is minimal; if he's drawn off-task by the sights and sounds around him; and if he's prone to seek stimulation through his own daydreaming because he's easily bored — the simple reality is that he's going to have a problem with persistence.

10. DIFFICULTY WITH CHANGE AND TRANSITIONS

Children with ADHD often become disorganized with change and transition. Sometimes small transitions, such as stopping play to come to the dinner table or getting ready for bed, become major battles. More significant changes such as overnight guests, vacations or a parent on a business trip can throw your child into a tailspin which lasts for days.

The school-age child with ADHD may have a number of transitions throughout the day which he finds difficult to handle, including going from the morning routine at home to the structure of school, taking an often chaotic bus ride, going from the structured classroom to unstructured recess, or going from the unstructured lunchroom setting back to the structure of the classroom. Younger children with ADHD may have difficulty at school transitioning from snack time to reading time or going from work station to work station. They may dawdle or even refuse to join the group. For older students with ADHD, going from class to class every period may be a series of difficult transitions. They may often be late for class, forget their books in their lockers, or rush so much that they fail to write down their assignments. The behavior of these students may be more disruptive than their peers during transitions, and it usually takes them longer to settle in following transitions.

Generally, children with ADHD tend to do better when going from a structured to unstructured, focused to unfocused, or formal to informal setting. For example, if your morning routine at home before school is fairly chaotic and unstructured, and then your child rides a noisy, overstimulating school bus, he will have more difficulty settling into the more structured classroom setting. His dis-inhibition hampers his ability to put the brakes on his "revved up" emotions and behavior. You can help by creating a calm, structured routine at home before school. It may also be necessary for your child to sit at the front of the school bus and away from the usual chaos that goes on toward the back of the bus.

If your child is on medication, he may have two additional types of transitions in his day. As his morning dose of stimulant medication begins to wear off (usually just before lunch), he may become more restless, off task, and prone to blurt out more. It is important for teachers to be aware of this possibility and not inappropriately penalize him for behavior which may be more difficult for him to control due to medication effects. Also, at the end of the school day when his second dose of medication wears off, he *may* go through what is called "rebound": a brief escalation of ADHD symptoms. Unfortunately, this is usually the time when you see your child most! If you are not aware of rebound, you may erroneously conclude that your child is getting worse or the medication doesn't work. Medication rebound is discussed in more detail in Chapter 20.

11. DISORGANIZATION

When you go into a classroom, you can usually tell which desk belongs to the child with ADHD. It's the one with the lid that doesn't completely close because of all the papers that have been stuffed into it. It's the one where the assignment due three weeks ago is crumpled up and pushed to the back of the desk under that overdue library book.

Organization requires pre-planning and reflective thinking, which are difficult for the child with ADHD. As a result, he may be very disorganized, sloppy, and forgetful. He has a hard time finding things like books, assignments, his backpack, or his jacket, usually as the school bus is coming down the road or you're waiting for him in the car because you should have been to work fifteen minutes ago. As you can see, poor organization also affects time management.

The condition of your child's bedroom often becomes a battleground for arguments. Dirty clothes are left on the floor, along with old food, papers, books and trash. You might be afraid to look under the bed for fear of what you might find.

Perhaps the environment most affected by your child's disorganization is school. Throughout the school day there are many demands placed on his organizational skills. At a minimum, he must get himself to class on time, keep his books, pencils, folders and worksheets together, write down his assignments, and remember what is due on what day. Once he enters middle school or junior high, demands for organization increase because he must deal with a greater number of teachers, move from class to class, and keep up with the increased homework load. At the end of the school day, he must be sure he has all the books, notes, and assignments he will need for that night, and he must make time in his day to organize and complete his homework. Without a lot of outside structure and direction, the student with ADHD often fails to keep this all together.

A primary problem with organization is often at the root of the underachievement so characteristic of students with ADHD. Teachers may misinterpret your child's failure to write down an assignment or hand in homework as laziness or a lack of caring. Furthermore, teachers may insist that your child is now "old enough to be responsible" and should not need to be supervised to do these things. Your child may therefore be penalized or marked down in grades. In reality, your child probably cannot organize all the steps required to write down assignments or get papers to and from school. Likewise, his resistance or refusal to do homework may be related to his difficulty organizing all the steps involved in approaching a complicated homework task. He may not even know how to get started and may give up before he tries.

12. SOCIAL PROBLEMS

Most children with ADHD have social problems to some degree. Your child's high activity level, loudness, impulsiveness, and poor self-control often alienate playmates. Other parents are reluctant to invite your child over to play because of his wild behavior, the work it takes to monitor him while he's at their home, and possibly the fear that he may negatively influence their own children. Peers may avoid playing games with him because he may try to change the rules during the game, grab game pieces, or play out of turn. If he loses, he may accuse the other children of cheating and burst into tears.

In school, your child may be the class clown or the child who bears the brunt of the teacher's reprimands. He may blurt out in class, bug the student sitting next to him, push to be first in line, and get into trouble on the playground. He may eventually develop a reputation among other students as the kid you should stay away from.

Chances are your child does not read social cues that are important but often subtle. Therefore, he does not pick up on the facial expressions, tone of voice or body language of other people that may send a signal to him that he should change his behavior or that he is acting inappropriately.

He has a poor sense of social "cause and effect," and therefore does not see how his behavior affects others. In fact, he is more likely to project the blame for his own behavior onto someone else, such as his parents, siblings, friends or teachers.

He also does not easily put himself in someone else's shoes. As a result, others may see him as selfish and self-centered. He gets stuck in his point of view and stubbornly defends his way of seeing things, trying to "save face." In fact, you can turn blue in the face if you persist in trying to convince your child to change his perspective or to see it your way.

Your child may have a tendency to overinterpret the actions of others toward him as being hostile. Therefore, he is more likely to respond with aggressive counter-attacks over minimal, if any, provocation. Often, you may be left wondering why he reacted so fiercely to something so innocent.

Given all of these social problems, your child may have a hard time making and keeping friends. He is probably regarded as socially immature. Children his own age are less tolerant of his ADHD-related behaviors and, consequently, he may often find friendships with younger children.

Of all the problems associated with ADHD, problems in social behavior are often the most enduring.

SUMMARY

- The symptoms and behavioral patterns of ADHD are numerous and complex; a child may not show all of the symptoms, and the intensity of the symptoms vary for each child.

- If an individual with ADHD is in a situation which is novel, interesting, intimidating, or one-to-one, he may not appear to have an attention problem.

- Impulsivity, also called disinhibition, is believed to be the fundamental problem underlying ADHD.

- Not all children with ADHD are hyperactive.

- Being hyperactive does not mean the child has an excess *amount* of energy; he has difficulty *regulating* his activity level to fit the situation or task at hand.

- Rewards and punishments need to be immediate, consistent, interesting and varied to have an effect.

- As many of 65 percent of children with ADHD are excessively noncompliant, but they are more likely to comply if the request involves something they like, involves just a little amount of effort, or has the promise of an immediate reward.

- The symptoms of ADHD are inconsistent. They vary depending upon the environment, nature of the task, individual with whom the child is interacting, and time of day.

- Children with ADHD usually feel their feelings more strongly. They are more sensitive to any tension and stress in the family, and this is often reflected in their behavior.

- The child's neurologically-based difficulty with persistence causes others to erroneously conclude that he is lazy or does not care.

- Disorganization is often the underlying cause of the underachievement characteristic of ADHD.

- Most children with ADHD struggle with social problems.

Part Three

Parenting Principles

ADHD is a disorder that can be managed but not cured. If you set out to change the nature of your child or to make him "normal," you will be disappointed. The goal for any child with ADHD should be to minimize the effects of his disorder, teach him compensatory skills, and structure the environment so he can succeed.

It is important to remember that regression is part of ADHD. It is easy to get lulled into believing that your child no longer has ADHD when things seem to be going well. Conversely, when your child has a bad day or a bad week, it is equally easy to conclude that none of these management strategies works. As a result, parents prematurely abandon appropriate strategies or bounce from one strategy to another, only making matters worse. As with many things in life, it is important to take each day as it comes and realize that the road ahead is bumpy, but you're moving forward.

It is also important to buffer your child from the misinformed reactions of other adults. Many parents are uncertain whether or not they should tell teachers, neighbors, or relatives that their child has an attention deficit. They fear that their child may be targeted as the "bad kid," or that others will treat him differently or discriminate against him. On a personal level, parents often feel embarrassed that others may think it is their fault their child has this disorder.

Unfortunately, reluctance to inform adults who have a relationship with your child allows misunderstandings to develop. Adults may incorrectly assume your child is "spoiled" or a "bad character" and react in ways that make matters worse.

It is important for other adults to know that your child has a disability that interferes with his ability to pay attention, control impulses and regulate his activity level because his brain works a bit differently, not that he is undisciplined or uncaring.

So, how do you avoid falling into the ill-fated trap of trying to re-construct your child and make him "normal"? How do you begin to parent him more realistically and effectively?

Successfully parenting a child with ADHD requires a solid founda-tion of management principles that come from our understanding of the disorder and its effect on behavior. Once you understand these principles, you will more intuitively understand how to manage your child's behavior. The following six parenting principles provide the foundation to more effectively respond to the ever-changing needs of your child:

1. Form Realistic Expectations
2. Distinguish Between ADHD-Related Behavior and Willful Noncompliance
3. Consider How Your Temperament "Fits" With Your Child
4. Parent Proactively
5. Avoid Over-Punishing
6. Give Positive Redirection and Specific Feedback

CHAPTER

7 Principle 1: Form Realistic Expectations

How often do you get angry with your child? If you're like most parents of a child with ADHD, you probably feel angry a lot of the time. You may be angry because your child forgot to bring his schoolwork home again. You might be angry because your child is arguing with you again. You might be angry because your 10-year-old child is acting like a 6-year-old again.

It is normal for parents to feel angry with their children sometimes, and it is normal for parents of a child with ADHD to feel angry more often than most parents. But the *intensity* of your anger is determined by your expectations. For example, you might be a little annoyed if your child comes home from school 10 minutes late, but it's okay because his behavior is still generally within your expectations. You might be fairly angry if he comes home from school 30 minutes late because now his behavior is getting outside of your expectations. But you might be rip-roaring mad if he comes home from school two hours late because his behavior is totally outside of your expectations. Your anger increased in direct relationship to the expectations you have for your child's behavior.

Parents usually form unrealistic expectations for their child with ADHD. The intensity of parents' frustration and anger is usually directly related to their expectations for that child, expectations that are often times unrealistic. If your expectations are out of whack, your anger will be out of whack! Those parents who are truly most effective in parenting their child with ADHD are those parents who have formed realistic expectations based upon a solid understanding and *acceptance* of the disorder.

ADHD has one important feature that makes it unlike many other disorders: it is invisible. There are no physically distinguishing characteristics to separate the child with ADHD from any other child. Unfortunately, if we can't see a disorder, we tend to deny that it is really there. If a child was in a wheelchair, no one would expect him to walk, and he certainly would not be punished for his inability to do so. Because we can "see" that the child can't move his legs, and because his inability to move his legs does not change from day to day, we *believe* that he can't move his legs. In contrast, you can't *see* ADHD, (like you can "see" the paralysis of a child in a wheelchair), even though you certainly *experience* the behavioral ramifications of this disorder. The inability to see ADHD may cause you to unconsciously reject the disorder.

In addition, it does not help that the symptoms of ADHD vary and fluctuate from day to day and even moment to moment. If a child with ADHD can pay attention to one thing and not the next, can control his temper in one situation and not the next, can remember his homework one day and not the next, we fall into the trap of believing that the child is doing this on purpose. We reject the fact that there is an underlying disorder that contributes to these annoying behaviors. More importantly, we tend to form unrealistic expectations.

Another common problem is that after a while parents stop using the strategies necessary to manage their child's behavior, almost as if they have "forgotten" their child has ADHD. That is, they erroneously *expect* that after a while their child will outgrow his annoying behaviors or that he will eventually catch up to his siblings and friends and act like other kids. They become increasingly frustrated and annoyed with their child because he is not meeting their expectations. He is still forgetting his homework, still arguing, still making messes and not cleaning them up, still not using good judgment. In other words, he still has ADHD.

Children do not outgrow ADHD simply because we want them to. Given that they have so many difficulties in so many areas, these children are immature compared to their agemates. Some have said, in fact, that **because ADHD so greatly affects behavioral functioning, we should subtract approximately 30 percent from their age level when we form our expectations for how these children should behave.** For example, if your child with ADHD is 10 years old, you should more realistically look at him like a 7-year-old and base your expectations on that age level.

Although children with ADHD certainly do improve with age and maturation, there will likely always be that lag behind normal peers and siblings, particularly in the area of simple, day-to-day functioning. This includes following through with tasks (including the seemingly simple ones such as getting dressed and making the bed in the morning), being organized, staying focused, following schedules, managing time, controlling emotions and impulses, and following rules and guidelines. Not being able to perform these tasks is directly or indirectly the result of your child's underlying neurobiological disorder. **The desire or expectation that he will outgrow these problems does not change his underlying neurologic status.**

In contrast to the pattern of over-expectations, sometimes parents fall into the trap of under-expectations. They inadvertently hinder their child's maturation and independence by over-doing, guided by the belief that their child's ADHD renders him incompetent in most areas.

Parents overdo for their child with ADHD in a variety of ways. They overdo when they do their child's homework rather than supervise it; when they make their child's bed or pick up his messes rather than require their child to do it; or when they excuse their child's aggression because he has ADHD rather than insist that he apologize.

Remember, ADHD is a performance deficit, not a skill deficit. Your child can do what other children can do, but he needs more structure, supervision, reinforcement, consistent limits and immediate consequences.

It is hard to strike a balance between over-expecting and under-expecting. To help you more realistically adjust your expectations, at least in the area of household responsibilities, consider the "Household Jobs Participation Chart" on the next page. This chart was taken from Elizabeth Crary's book, *Pick Up Your Socks*.[1] The chart is not scientific, but it generally indicates which tasks children typically do around the house and the level of parental support involved for each task. At first, a child needs parental help to do a task. As he gets older, only reminders or some supervision is needed until finally, the child can complete the task alone.

Household Jobs Participation Chart

The chart lists common household tasks, the percentage of children involved with the task, and the average age of children at different levels of involvement.

Symbols:
H means the child will need help with the task,
R means the child needs reminding or supervision, and
A means the child does a task as needed without reminding or supervision.

Task	Percent children involved	Ages and involvement

Task	Percent children involved	Ages and involvement (2 3 4 5 6 7 8 9 10 11 12 13)
Dress self	99%	H-----------R--------------------------------A
Brush teeth	99%	H--------------------------------R--------------A
Bathe self	99%	H----------------------------R-------------------A
Pick up belongings	99%	H----------------------------R--------------------A
put dirty clothes away	99%	H--------------------R------------------A
Hang up clean clothes	97%	H------------------------------------R-------------A
Make bed	93%	H---------------------------------R-----A
Tidy room	98%	H---------------------------------------R----------A
Wipe spills	93%	H------------------------------------R-----A
Vacuum floors	79%	H------------------------------------A-----R*
Clean sink	75%	H-----------------------------A-----R*
Take out trash	72%	H-----------------------------A-----R*
Care for pet	72%	H----------------------------R-----------A
Do laundry	54%	H------------------ R-/A 14yr, 4mo
Set table	93%	H---------------------------------R-----A
Wash dishes	75%	H----------------------------R-------------A
Fix snack	89%	H---------------R----------------------------A
Cook meal	71%	H-----------R--------------------A

Data from a study of Washington state families by Elizabeth Crary, 1989
*Children require supervision again after becoming independent

The chart illustrates that the process of developing responsibility for household tasks for normal children is slow. For example, there are more than six years between the average age children help clean the sink (6 years old) and the average age they do it without supervision or reminding (12 years old).

As one would expect, the ability to perform chores increases with age. The average 4-year-old's involvement is to help others with household jobs, while the average 10-year-old can do many tasks alone. Interestingly, the chart shows that as children get older, they need to be reminded about some tasks they previously did independently.

Now look at this chart again, but with your child with **ADHD** in mind, reducing 30 percent from his age. So if your child is 10 years old, for example, look at the level of responsibility for a 7-year-old. The level of responsibility typically demonstrated by a 7-year-old may more closely reflect the level of responsibility which your 10-year-old with **ADHD** can handle.

It is important to form realistic expectations in areas other than just household chores. This means you need to learn as much as you can about **ADHD** and become an expert on the subject. You can become an expert by reading books, going to workshops, renting videos on **ADHD**, joining professional groups such as CH.A.D.D. (Children and Adults with Attention Deficit Disorders), and joining parent support groups. Information about professional and support groups, books and videos is included in Appendix A in the back of the book. Once you understand **ADHD**, you can better help your child and yourself.

When you truly understand and accept **ADHD**, you will know that your child's fundamental deficit in inhibition affects his behavior, and you will adjust your expectations accordingly. You will understand that his neurologically-based deficit in self-control interferes with his ability to separate his emotions from his reason, so he is more emotional and quick to anger. This renders him very reactive to his environment, and his behavior varies widely depending upon what's happening around him. You will understand that he has difficulty thinking before he acts, so he repeatedly engages in the same inappropriate or self-defeating behaviors despite his past experiences and the consequences.

When you truly understand and accept **ADHD**, you will understand that your child is managed by the moment rather than by rules, so he repeatedly breaks the rules. You will understand that his defective self-control impairs foresight, so he has difficulty working for long-term goals, anticipating problems ahead of time, and managing his time. You will find he has difficulty delaying gratification, so he is impatient and finds it hard to avoid temptations and distractions, finish things, and accept "No." Generally, if you truly understand and accept your child's ADHD, you can expect that he might:

- Be overly-emotional and quick to anger
- Be easily frustrated and impatient
- Apply the least amount of effort to difficult, boring tasks
- Not easily learn from past experiences
- Blurt out
- Talk excessively
- Start assignments without reading directions
- Take things that don't belong to him
- Refuse to share
- Take too many risks
- Not manage money well
- Not manage time well
- Not plan ahead
- Be disorganized
- Not stick with a task
- Repeatedly break rules
- Be unaffected by consequences
- Miss details
- Miss social cues
- Daydream
- Not sit still
- Make noises
- Work inconsistently
- Forget
- Resist homework
- Underachieve
- Engage repeatedly in the same annoying behaviors
- Have good days and bad days

This list of expectations can be daunting, and you may not want to accept it. Unfortunately, when we don't want our child to be a certain way, we resist the fact that he *is* this way. Consequently, we fail to adjust our expectations and continue down the road of unrealistic expectations and demands, ineffective parenting, and anger. You don't have to *like* that your child with ADHD is this way, but you do have to *accept* that he is this way. Only then can you be an effective parent.

Once you accept your child's ADHD-related behaviors, you are free to appreciate his strengths. You can cherish his individualism and accept that he is who he is. You can stop trying to remake or reconstruct him into something he is not. You can help him capitalize on his strengths and be his fiercest advocate in the process. You can appreciate the fact that even though many of his behaviors may frustrate you now, they may serve him well in the future.

If shaped and managed, your child's energy can allow him to accomplish more than most; his verbal abilities can open doors that would be closed to others; his spontaneity can make his life rich and full; his creativity can propel him to imagine and realize what others wish they would have conceived; his willingness to take risks can lead him to adventures that many dream of but are too afraid to try; his unconventionality can make him shine above the crowd; his stubbornness can force him to accomplish what others would have given up on long before; and his competitiveness can drive him to the top of those endeavors which truly ignite him.

SUMMARY

- Parents often form unrealistic expectations for their child with ADHD, leading to excessive anger and overreactions.

- Children with ADHD tend to be less mature. Therefore, we should subtract 30 percent from their age level when we form our expectations for how these children should behave.

- Parents who adopt realistic expectations for their child with ADHD are more likely to bolster his self-esteem and nurture his full potential.

Principle 2: Distinguish Between ADHD-Related Behavior and Willful Noncompliance

Some of your child's noncompliance arises from his ADHD, interfering with his following rules and performing certain requests. At other times, however, your child's noncompliance is more willful, more oppositional or defiant. How do you tell the difference, and what do you do about it?

THREE TYPES OF NONCOMPLIANCE

There are basically three types of noncompliance:

1. Your child *does not start to do what he is told* within a reasonable amount of time. Reasonable is usually about 5 to 10 seconds. For example, you ask your child to pick up his jacket, and he responds that he can't now; he's watching TV. You repeat your request, perhaps a little more sternly, and your child starts to argue that he "always has to do everything around this house." He refuses to budge.

2. Your child *starts to comply, but he does not sustain compliance* until the task or request is completed. An example would be that your child started to get ready for school, but when you went to check on him 10 minutes later, he was playing in his bedroom.

3. Your child *fails to follow previously taught rules*. For example, despite the fact that you have told him many times to use a quiet voice in the house when the baby is sleeping, he starts to play very loudly.

Learning to distinguish between ADHD-related behavior and willful noncompliance is critical to the success of any behavior management program for ADHD. Each group of behaviors must be dealt with very differently. Noncompliance that is related to your child's ADHD results from his *inability* to comply effectively or consistently. Accordingly, it must be dealt with by making changes in the environment, changing the way you react to these behaviors, and teaching your child appropriate coping/compensatory skills (all of which are discussed in following chapters).

Behaviors that are the result of willful noncompliance, however, occur when your child *chooses* not to behave appropriately. This type of noncompliance must be dealt with through consistent consequences and proactively breaking the cycle of noncompliance.

Understanding this distinction and responding appropriately are vital for your child's eventual outcome and self-esteem. By the time those with ADHD are adolescents, many have had a long history of negative feedback from their environment and a string of failures in many areas. This eventually takes a toll on self- esteem. A history of negative interactions also plays a significant role in fostering oppositional behaviors in the child with ADHD. Over time, repeatedly hearing "Stop it," "Quit doing that," "Can't you sit still?" "How many times do I have to tell you?" and "Knock it off" teach your child that his world is very controlling, nonaccepting, and overly restrictive. In response, he protects himself with increasingly defensive, oppositional behaviors.

Look back again at the three types of noncompliance. Type #1 is an example of *willful noncompliance*. Assuming your child has your attention and you have made the request in a respectful manner, he has made a choice not to comply. This behavior is not primarily ADHD-related and therefore must have firm and immediate consequences.

Type #2 *is ADHD-related*. Your child has good intentions and starts to comply. In the process of performing the task, however, he gets off task, perhaps pulled by the more powerful enticement of toys in his room. In addition, getting ready for school is a multi-step, tedious, and nonrewarding task. It is difficult to complete because of his inability to sustain attention and his difficulty persisting with tasks that are boring or unrewarding.

Type #3 *is usually ADHD-related* and is likely an outgrowth of the child's difficulty following rules. Your child may quiet down immediately upon being told to do so and may even appear apologetic and promise that he will not do it again. Shortly thereafter, however, the rule to play quietly is overpowered by his impulses and by his difficulty monitoring himself on an ongoing basis. Not surprisingly, his volume escalates again. This breaking of the rule was not intentional but was a by-product of the fact that he could not retain the rule long enough to govern his behavior.

Parents frequently say that they have difficulty knowing whether their child's noncompliance is ADHD-related or willful noncompliance. It's not always easy to determine this, especially since noncompliance which may begin as ADHD-related can be masked by an exasperating layer of secondary behaviors that are more willful. For example, children with ADHD usually have difficulty complying with daily routines such as getting ready for school in the morning. Initially their difficulty following through with this routine may be related to their ADHD; that is, it is difficult to sustain attention and persist at tasks that are not intrinsically rewarding and that are boring. Their inability to follow-through with this seemingly easy routine is understandably annoying and frustrating for parents. Consequently, parents respond with repeated commands, increased control, and perhaps yelling or even punishment.

After a time, the child will develop an aversion to this routine, given his negative association with it. The secondary aversion includes resistance, ignoring, arguing, or outright refusal. Unfortunately, parents are thrown off by these more willful secondary behaviors and punish the child for willful noncompliance when the underlying problem is actually an inability to comply successfully given his ADHD. In these situations, the most effective strategies are to change the nature of the task or request, or to use behavior modification strategies that increase motivation so that the child can more easily comply. We have much more on these strategies in following chapters.

A simple way to determine whether your child's noncompliance is ADHD-related or willful noncompliance is to give him a command and see what happens next. If your child starts to comply but does not finish what was requested, it is likely ADHD-related. It is important to understand that your child is having difficulty completing the task because of his ADHD. The first thing to do is to ask your child to repeat your request to make sure he was paying attention. Poor attention often interferes with your child's ability to remember what was asked of him. Also, stay in the same room with your child when issuing the request to make sure he heard the request and that he starts to comply. Sometimes parents leave the room too soon or shout the request from a different room. When they go to check on their child and see that he has not complied, they don't know whether or not he even heard the request initially, whether he started to comply but got off task, or whether he refused to start in the first place.

Likewise, if your child does not follow a pre-stated rule, but then tries to comply (although perhaps unsuccessfully) when given a respectful reminder, it probably is ADHD-related. For example, although the rule is to make your bed in the morning, your child continues to forget. If you remind him respectfully, and he complies, view this as ADHD-related noncompliance.

However, if your child actively or passively refuses to comply after the initial request, it likely is willful. Before you come to this conclusion, however, take a look at the request and ask yourself if the task is difficult for your child given his ADHD. If this is the case, you may need to restructure the task or modify the request.

Behavior is much too complex to put into tidy categories. Therefore, these are not fail-safe distinctions. Nonetheless, you will increase your chances of responding more appropriately, and in ways that will help your child, if you follow these general guidelines. More specific strategies for dealing with ADHD-related and willful noncompliance are in Chapters 17 and 18.

SUMMARY

- Noncompliance that is related to ADHD results from an *inability* to comply effectively or consistently. In contrast, willful noncompliance occurs when a child *chooses* not to behave appropriately.

- ADHD-related noncompliance must be dealt with by making changes in the environment, changing the way you react, using behavior modification, and teaching your child coping/compensatory skills.

- Willful noncompliance must be dealt with through consistent consequences and by breaking the cycle of arguing and yelling.

Principle 3: Consider How Your Temperament "Fits" With Your Child

Many children with ADHD have what is called a difficult temperament. That is, they are *born* with a behavioral style that is often unquestionably hard to manage. Many parents will say that from day one their child had his own unique personality, his own temperament.

Three researchers, Drs. Stella Chess, Alexander Thomas, and Herbert Birch, conducted a landmark study following children from infancy to young adulthood.[1] They were trying to identify the unique temperament traits of 133 children and observe their temperament development through the years. These researchers identified three different groups of children: easy children, slow-to-warm-up children, and difficult children. A large group of children with ADHD, particularly those who are Hyperactive-Impulsive and Combined Type, tend to manifest some characteristics of a difficult temperament.

DIFFICULT TEMPERAMENT

Children with difficult temperaments display some combination of the following nine temperament traits:[2]

1. **High Activity Level**. Very active; always into things; makes you tired; "ran before he walked"; gets wild or revved up; loses control; hates to be confined.

2. **Inattention**. Has difficulty paying attention and concentrating, especially if not interested; doesn't listen.

3. **Impersistence**. Does not stick with things and tends to give up.

4. **Poor Adaptability.** Has difficulty with change and transitions; continues to whine and pester if he wants something; stubborn; gets "locked in" and does not easily change to something else; long and hard tantrums.

5. **Initial Withdrawal.** Does not like new situations, places, people, food, clothes; clings, protests or tantrums if faced with something/someone new.

6. **High Intensity.** Is generally loud; overly intense; exaggerated emotions.

7. **Irregular.** Does not follow regular patterns for sleeping, eating, bowel habits; unpredictable, rapid mood changes.

8. **Low Sensory Threshold.** Is very sensitive to stimulation around him, such as noise, lights, touch, tastes, texture, temperature; fussy about clothes because they don't "feel right"; overreacts to bumps or bruises; picky eater.

9. **Negative Mood.** Basically grumpy, whiny, complaining, irritable, unhappy.

From *The Difficult Child* by Stanley Turecki, M.D. and Leslie Tonner, Copyright © 1989 by Stanley Turecki, M.D. and Leslie Tonner. Used by permission of Bantam Books, a division of Bantam, Doubleday Dell Publishing Group, Inc.

Understandably, a child with these difficult temperament traits can be a challenge to parent. These children can push the limits of even the most patient and skilled of parents. Although it has already been established that parenting does not cause ADHD, we do know that parenting can influence and shape a child's behavior.

A key factor in the effectiveness of parenting your child with ADHD is the "goodness of fit" between you and your child. Each of the nine temperament traits has a continuum from low to high intensity. Any given individual can be near either end of the continuum or fall somewhere between these extremes.

As you think about your temperament vis a vis your child's, you may already have a sense about how important the match-up is between your temperaments. You can analyze the goodness of fit between you and your child by doing the following exercise. Take a look at the continuum of temperament traits. For each trait, plot your child on the continuum to indicate where he tends to fall. Next, plot yourself on the continuum to indicate where you tend to fall for each trait. Compare where you fall in relationship to your child for each trait.

Continuum of Temperament Traits

HIGH ACTIVITY	LOW ACTIVITY

POOR ATTENTION	GOOD ATTENTION

LOW PERSISTENCE	HIGH PERSISTENCE

POOR ADAPTABILITY	HIGH ADAPTABILITY

HIGH INTENSITY	LOW INTENSITY

INITIAL WITHDRAWAL	OUTGOING

IRREGULAR	REGULAR

LOW SENSORY THRESHOLD	HIGH SENSORY THRESHOLD

NEGATIVE MOOD	POSITIVE MOOD

Too Close for Comfort

A child who manifests an extreme degree of some or all of the above-mentioned difficult temperament traits will likely not "fit" well with a parent who also manifests a high degree of some or all of these same traits. For example, if you tend to overreact or respond very impulsively, and your child does too, you will likely become embroiled in many power struggles that quickly escalate. Neither you nor your child is applying the necessary controls to keep the situation manageable, to keep it in equilibrium.

This unstable dynamic describes the relationship between Ann and her son Paul:

> Paul, a second-grader, had been diagnosed with ADHD. His mother Ann had a very difficult time controlling Paul's behavior, especially when it came to doing what he was told to do. Ann complained that Paul was easily excitable, overreactive, and extremely belligerent. The two of them seemed to have power struggles over even the simplest of requests, such as, "Get ready for bed," "It's time to get up for school," or "Come eat dinner." Paul's usual reaction was to ignore, whine, complain and then yell. Paul seemed to quickly spiral out of control, often to the point that he was hitting, throwing and screaming. He blamed his mother for causing him all of his troubles and often shouted that things were never going to change!
>
> Ann complained that Paul's behavior "drove her nuts." She was distraught over his belligerence and worried that he was turning into a delinquent. She found herself always yelling at Paul and arguing with her husband. She began to have panic attacks. Ann frequently called her doctor when she and Paul would have one of their "episodes." Although these conversations would calm her down and she would once again resolve to try her doctor's suggestions, she quickly became agitated and started arguing with Paul all over again when he did not comply. She would usually conclude that the situation was hopeless and that things were never going to get better.

The relationship between Ann and her son was out of balance. Paul was at the extreme end of the continuum of temperament traits for poor adaptability and negative mood. Ann also was at the same end. As a result, they did not balance each other, and instead both quickly spiraled out of control in their interactions.

Too Close for Comfort

Never the Twain Shall Meet

Another situation that can create a bad "fit" between you and your child with ADHD is if you are on the opposite extreme from your child on any given temperament continuum. In this case, the extreme difference or distance between the two styles can create conflict. You become exceptionally intolerant of your child's style because it is so different from your own. For example, if you are very conscientious, perfectionistic, and have very good follow-through, you may have a hard time understanding a child who cannot finish what he starts, seems careless, and rushes through his work. As a result, you may be overly demanding of him. Consider the case of Kyle and his father:

> Kyle was a very bright fourth-grade boy who had been diagnosed with ADHD, characterized predominantly by poor impulse control, restlessness and fidgetiness. Kyle's parents described their son as extremely careless, forgetful, and irresponsible. He inconsistently followed through on what he was told to do. He would often start to do what he was told, but then get off track, failing to complete tasks on his own. His schoolwork was often incomplete, and when it was complete, it was done hastily and carelessly. His grades were suffering.
>
> Kyle's father, Lowell, was also very bright and had done well in school and in his career, working very conscientiously and persistently to obtain his goals. He was now head engineer at a major design firm. His belief was that to be successful, one had to buckle down, pay attention to detail, and always keep working until the job was finished. He was thoroughly exasperated with Kyle's irresponsibility and could not understand why Kyle failed to change his ways when he "knew" how important it was for his future.
>
> Lowell found himself constantly lecturing Kyle on the importance of follow-through and responsibility. During these "conversations," Kyle was always fidgeting with something in his hands or looking around the room. His father interpreted this behavior as signs that Kyle was not listening and was being very disrespectful, fueling his exasperation. These conversations usually spiraled to heated arguments that ended with Kyle being grounded for not listening and not improving his behavior.

In this example it is clear that Kyle and his father were on the opposite extremes of the continuum for several traits. Kyle had high activity, poor attention, low persistence, and high irregularity. These traits were very much in contrast to his father, who had well-controlled impulses; excellent sustained attention and persistence; and successful task completion. He also was very predictable in his follow-through. Lowell's expectations for his son were high and were an outgrowth of his own self-expectations. He had difficulty understanding Kyle's temperament and how it inter-related with his ADHD, because his son was so different from him. This contrast in temperaments hindered Lowell's ability to view Kyle's difficulties from a different perspective, causing him to be very frustrated and relatively intolerant. For several traits, father and son were too far apart to allow any tempering, learning or helping to take place.

Never the Twain Shall Meet

The Laid Back Parent

Another potentially "poor fit" is a hyperactive child and a parent who is too tolerant, laid back, and believes in "live and let live." Strangers in the grocery store watch these parents and mutter, "Why don't they control that kid?" Some of these parents are just worn down from the constant battle of parenting a challenging child. Others, however, are temperamentally passive and ultimately ineffective. They fail to provide the structure and limits that their children need out of the belief (or hope) that everything will work out in the end if they just leave things alone. The household is usually fairly unstructured and without routines. Homework gets done when it gets done. Bedtimes vary from night to night. Curfews go unchecked. The child is not expected to perform household chores. Behavior problems are often dealt with by looking the other way or concluding that "boys will be boys." This lack of external controls, structure and accountability is harmful for a child who does not have the ability to exert his own self-controls and regulate his own behavior.

Mark's teachers were calling his parents again. For the third time in one week, Mark had disrupted the class, this time by trying to stuff his head in his desk. The time before he brought a "whoopee" cushion to class and proceeded to make rude noises behind the teacher's back. Before that, he was firing spitballs at a girl's head. Mark's classmates got a kick out of some of his antics but also were frustrated that he didn't seem to know when to stop.

Mark's behavior was just as uncontrolled at home where he seemed to have free reign. He seldom came home right after school but roamed from one neighbor's house to the next to "bum a snack and say hi." He rarely made it home in time for dinner; he was too busy socializing. Once he finally made it home, the rest of his evening was spent parked in front of the television or talking on the phone with friends while his homework sat untouched in his backpack. Bedtime was any time but usually not before 11:00. On weekends Mark often slept in until noon, but what do you expect when you've been on the phone until the wee hours of the morning? Once Mark did rise from bed, he usually set off on his bike, not to be seen again until early evening.

Mark's parents knew that their son had a lot of energy, but, after all, don't most 13-year-old boys? Sure, Mark may go too far sometimes and perturb his teachers or other kids, but those people just need to "lighten up." Where is their sense of humor? They felt that Mark's teacher should worry about those things that are really important such as kids on drugs or kids who can't read. As for the kids at school who complain about Mark, well, they should toughen up and learn to live in this world. It's true that Mark doesn't have much structure at home, but you can't cage in a 13-year-old boy! Besides, Mark's parents retorted, it's too late to start setting limits now.

It is important for you to understand your own temperament in relationship to your child with ADHD. If you see that you don't help your child because you share some or many of the same difficult traits, it is imperative that you work at establishing balance by tempering your own difficult tendencies. Also, if you see that you are on opposite ends of a continuum in relationship to your child, it is important that you work at approaching a more tolerant middle ground. Finally, if your style is too laid back, it's time to become proactive and to be more involved. We discuss how to do this in the next chapter, "Principle 4: Parent Proactively."

SUMMARY

- Parents should examine how their own temperament fits with their child's. A parent and child who manifest some of the same extreme temperament traits are more prone to overreactions and poorly-controlled behavior when they interact.

- Parents whose temperament is extremely opposite or distant from their child's may tend to be too demanding, less tolerant and not empathic.

- Parents who are too laid back will not provide the needed external controls and structure for their child.

 Principle 4: Parent Proactively

A successful parent is *proactive* rather than *reactive*. This is not an easy principle. As parents, our days are filled with events that make us angry, frustrated, happy, sad, etc. Our tendency is to react to those feelings and to sometimes let them control what we think and what we do. However, there is another alternative.

The following four steps will guide you in being a proactive parent for your child with ADHD.

STEP 1: CHOOSE YOUR RESPONSE

Would you say that you are the product of your circumstances?

Would you say that you are the product of your feelings?

What effect does having a child with ADHD have on you?

What feelings do you have as a result?

We have come to understand through behavioral psychology that with every stimulus there is a response.

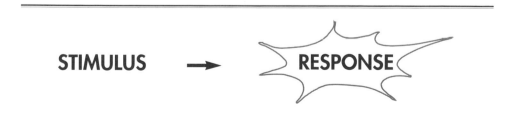

STIMULUS → **RESPONSE**

When an individual responds in a predictable way to a particular stimulus or event, we say the person has been conditioned to respond in that way. Remember Pavlov's dog. After the ringing of a bell was paired enough times with a piece of meat, the dog learned to salivate to the ringing of a bell. He became conditioned in that his response (i.e., salivating) was determined by the ringing of a bell.

Over time, many of us come to believe that our responses are *determined* by what is going on around us, by what is happening *to* us. Essentially, we tell ourselves in one way or another that "we can't help our reactions, we can't help ourselves." We may even define ourselves by our reactions: "I'm a sensitive person," "I'm impulsive," "I'm moody," I'm depressed." The problem is that these views become self-fulfilling prophecies. That is, when we believe that our response is determined by what is happening around us or to us, we give up our innate freedom to *choose our response.*

In reality, with every event, there are a variety of potential responses. We have the freedom to choose our response.

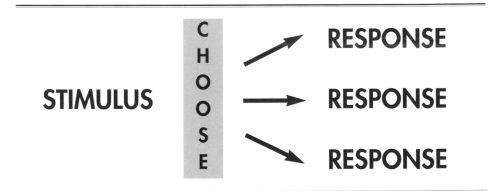

Understanding that we have the freedom to choose our responses is the essence of proactive parenting. In proactive parenting, parents take the initiative and the responsibility to choose their responses. They are change agents and actively make things happen rather than simply react to what happens to them.

Dr. Stephen Covey, in his book *The Seven Habits of Highly Effective People*,[1] emphasizes the proactive use of the word **"response-ability"** — the ability to choose your response. Proactive parents accept this response-ability; they choose their responses to their child's behaviors. They do not blame their reactions on their child's forgetfulness, obstinance, overactivity, impulsivity, recklessness or emotionality. They know that their own reactions are the product of their choices.

When parents allow their child's behaviors to determine their responses, they engage in **reactive parenting**. They are adversely affected by their child's behavior and blame their child for their feelings of ineptness, frustration, anger or depression.

"He makes me so mad."

"He makes me feel like I'm the worst parent in the world."

Unwittingly, parents choose to feel or react this way to their child's behavior. Those feelings of ineptness, frustration, anger or depression are their choice. As Eleanor Roosevelt once said, *"No one can hurt you without your permission."*

A common reaction to this principle is, *"Sure, that's easy for you to say, but just try living with a child who has ADHD and you'd feel this way, too. Don't tell me I choose to feel this way."*

Admittedly, this is a difficult concept to accept and practice. However, by accepting and actively embracing the concept that you can choose your responses to your child's behavior, you *empower* yourself. It is just the opposite of what parents of children with ADHD typically feel; what they tell themselves in their frustration and exasperation.

"He does this just to make me mad."

"She is so manipulative."

"He'll never change."

"My life would be so much easier if only he would mind."

The truth of the matter is you can think *whatever you choose* about your child with ADHD. Thinking is a function, an ability. It is not something that happens *to you*; it is an activity *in which you engage*. You actively select your own thoughts (even though you may feel that they just happen).

Thinking is an activity you use to create your own reality. Your thoughts are generated from within you, not from outside you. Therefore, in a very real sense, your *reality* is created from within you, not from what happens outside you. You can choose to think anything, and your feelings are a direct result of what you choose to think. Therefore, any feelings of ineptness, frustration, anger, or depression result from choosing thoughts that produce these feelings and then believing that these thoughts are reality, rather than the results of your thinking.

Whenever you put the focus or blame for your feelings outside of yourself, you give away the power to find the solutions. And you absolve yourself of response-ability. You put the control for change onto that person or thing that you are blaming. *"If only he would start minding, then I wouldn't get so upset."* When you adopt this way of thinking, you take on a *reactive* approach to parenting. You give up your choice to find proactive solutions and consequently lose your effectiveness to make changes.

Consider the thoughts of reactive parenting and the reality which they create:

"He makes me so mad!'" (I'm not responsible. My emotional life is governed by something outside my control).

"I don't have time to do all of this behavior modification with my son." (Something outside of me, i.e., limited time, is controlling me.)

"If only he would start minding me, then I wouldn't get so upset." (Someone else's behavior is making me less effective.)

This language of reactive parenting comes from a belief system that one's response is determined by another's behavior, that there is no choice involved. The reality that results from this language is: *I am helpless. There is no way that things can change.*

Reframe your thoughts

If you feel frustrated, exasperated or depressed, it will impact your effectiveness in dealing with your child. Parents' thoughts about their child and about themselves affect the parent-child relationship. If your thoughts are creating a negative reality and adversely affecting your relationship with your child, then your challenge is to examine those thoughts and proactively change or reframe them.

It is not easy to change your counter-productive thoughts. They seem to happen so automatically. But it can be done! Changing these thoughts takes practice. Like any new skill, the more you practice it, the more automatic it becomes. Here are some examples to help you practice changing or reframing your negative thoughts about your child:

Reactive Language	**Proactive Language**
There's nothing I can do.	I'll look at some other solutions.
He'll never change.	I can teach him some skills.
He refuses to sit still.	He needs to move around to stimulate his attention.
He's doing this just to manipulate me.	His ADHD makes it hard for him to follow the rules.

I have really messed him up.	It doesn't help to think this way; I'll look at how I need to change.
He makes me so mad.	I control my own feelings.
There's no controlling this child. Nothing works.	This is self-defeating. I have not tried everything.
I am so embarrassed by his behavior	It doesn't matter what others think. Helping my child is my goal.

STEP 2: KNOW WHAT YOU CAN CONTROL

Parenting a child with ADHD is not easy, and it can wear you down. To develop a more proactive parenting style, it is helpful to consider where you tend to focus your worries and energy.

There are many things about your child with ADHD that worry you: how your child does in school, what relatives think about his behavior and about your parenting, how your child feels about himself, or how to make your child do what he is told, etc., etc. The list probably goes on and on.

There is a powerful exercise you can do to put your worries in a productive perspective. Take that long list of worries that you have about your child and picture them in what you might call the "Worry Zone."

Worry Zone

These are all the things you worry about — some more than others, some more frequently, some with more intensity. But to whatever degree, these are the things with which you are preoccupied, that hit your hot button, that sap your energy, and that keep you awake at night.

The next step is to look at all those worries in the Worry Zone and think carefully about each one. Ask yourself a simple but hard question: Is there anything I can do about that worry? For example, can I make it go away, can I fix it, can I have some influence on it, is it under my control? Select those items to which you said "yes" and move them into a box inside the Worry Zone called the "Control Zone." Also, look at each worry to see if there is some related action that you could take that would positively impact that worry. Add those to the Control Zone list. For example, you might worry about how knowledgeable your child's teacher is about ADHD. You can't control what the teacher has learned in the past. But you *can* take the initiative, for example, to collect information about ADHD and present that to him/her in a respectful way. That action is in the Control Zone. The message is simple: don't worry and fret and get angry. Do something that makes you part of the solution, not part of the problem.

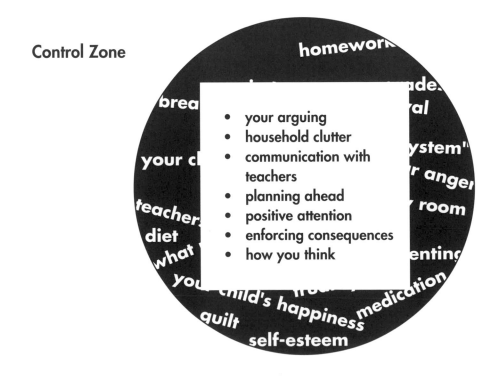

Control Zone

- your arguing
- household clutter
- communication with teachers
- planning ahead
- positive attention
- enforcing consequences
- how you think

As you look at the two zones, you quickly see that you are wasting valuable energy and time when you focus on the Worry Zone. In contrast, your power and effectiveness increase dramatically when you do those things in the Control Zone.

By determining in which of these two zones you direct most of your time and energy, you quickly see to what degree you engage in proactive parenting. Proactive parents focus their time and energy in the Control Zone. They focus on those things that they can change, things over which they have control.

Parents who focus their time and energy in the Worry Zone engage in reactive parenting. They spend their time preoccupied with those things over which they have no control: blaming their child or blaming the system; feeling victimized or inept; and engaging in reactive, self-defeating language. They dwell on what they must be doing wrong, on how they're failing as parents. When parents engage in blame toward self or others, they drain themselves of energy that could be more productively used to make changes. Rather than working to improve the situation and prevent future problems, they react in a conditioned, predictable way to their child and to circumstances. They neglect their area of control and thereby make the situation even worse. The Control Zone shrinks as emphasis and energy are directed outward toward the Worry Zone, thereby decreasing the parent's effectiveness and sense of control and increasing his/her sense of helplessness and anxiety.

In contrast, proactive parents who focus on the Control Zone find that it grows in size, pushing out on the Worry Zone and making it less powerful.

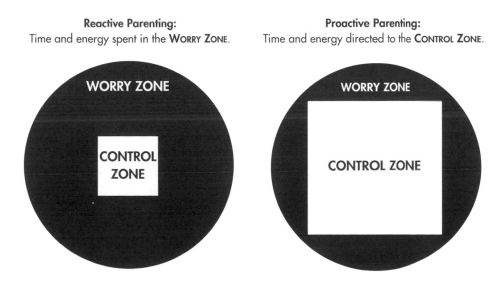

Reactive Parenting:
Time and energy spent in the **WORRY ZONE**.

Proactive Parenting:
Time and energy directed to the **CONTROL ZONE**.

WORRY ZONE

CONTROL ZONE

WORRY ZONE

CONTROL ZONE

As parents spend their energy on the Worry Zone they empower those worries to control them, even though they have little or no control over those worries. They drain energy from their Control Zone. By giving their time and attention to their Worry Zone, they simply increase their own feelings of inadequacy as parents, their feelings of victimization, and their sense of helplessness in being able to make changes. In the process, they are not helping their child and are probably hindering him.

To paraphrase Dr. Covey, it is not what your child is not doing or should be doing that's the issue. The issue is your own chosen response to the situation and what *you* should be doing. If you start to think the problem is 'out there,' stop yourself. That *thought* is the problem.

STEP 3: CHANGE YOUR ROLE

If you analyze the role you play in the problem, you may see the consequences of your own behavior. What you do with your child may be contributing to the problem and creating predictable outcomes. Once you understand how you may be part of the problem, you can work to be part of the solution. Make appropriate changes in what you do so that the problem is avoided or at least tempered in the future. When you consistently anticipate problems and make appropriate changes in what you do, you set up your child for success.

Parents who adopt a *reactive* parenting style overlook their role in creating the problem. They often operate on "automatic pilot," failing to pay attention to the way they interact with their child. They react to problems "after the fact," leading to over-reactions and harsh punishments. Without meaning to, reactive parents set up their child for failure.

What Parents Do To Set Up Their Child For Failure

Reactive parents engage in two primary processes that perpetuate problems, ultimately setting up their child for failure:

1. **More of the same**

The battle cry of the reactive parent is:

> *"No matter how many times I keep telling him to stop doing that, he keeps on doing it."*

One could ask this parent,

> *"Why do you keep on asking him to stop when it obviously doesn't work?"*

This is an example of a parent engaging in the vicious cycle of "more of the same" — repeatedly doing what doesn't work. Instead of analyzing the situation and making appropriate changes, the parent continues with more of the same, over and over again. The question is "why?"

If continually telling a child to behave in a store leads to more disruptive behavior; if repeatedly asking a child to sit still and pay attention does not change his restlessness; or if constantly demanding that a child do his homework results in the child avoiding his homework time and time again, why do parents persist in doing what doesn't work? In part, because it is human nature to focus more on how someone else's behavior is affecting us rather than considering the role that we play in the problem.

Dr. Harriet Lerner,[2] a noted psychologist specializing in relationships put it aptly:

> *Human nature is such that when we are angry, we tend to become so emotionally reactive to what the **other** person is doing to us that we lose our ability to observe our own part in the interaction. Self-observation is not at all the same as self-blame...self observation is the process of seeing the interaction of ourselves and others, and recognizing that the ways other people behave with us have something to do with the way we behave with them. We cannot **make** another person be different, but when we do something different ourselves, the old dance can no longer continue as usual.* (Lerner, 1985, p. 45.)

2. **Setting fires**

A reactive parenting style is analogous to setting fires and then punishing the child for not putting out the fire which you set! Reactive parents often unintentionally "set fires" for their child with ADHD throughout the day. For example, parents "set a fire" every time they allow their child to watch violent movies or play violent video games and then punish the child for being aggressive. It's not surprising that a child with poorly-controlled impulses would act aggressively when he is exposed to aggression.

The examples of fire setting are endless:

Example 1: A child with ADHD who is on medication is allowed to have junk food 30 minutes before dinner and then is sent to his room for not eating his dinner.

Example 2: A father engages in roughhousing with his hyperactive son just before bedtime and then gets angry when his son won't settle down and go to bed.

Example 3: Parents bring their 4-year-old child with **ADHD** to a fancy restaurant and then punish him out of their own embarrassment because he is running around and won't sit in his chair.

Example 4: A mother tells her child with **ADHD** that they are going to run *three* errands and then spanks her child because he has a tantrum while she is running her *fifth* errand.

Example 5: A parent gives his child with **ADHD** a multi-step direction and then punishes him because he did not follow through on what he was supposed to do.

Example 6: Parents leave piles of bills and paperwork around a cluttered house and then punish their child because he can't keep track of his homework;

Example 7:   Parents allow their preschooler to stay up way past his bedtime and then put him in time-out throughout the next day because he is irritable.

All of these are fairly typical situations that parents have experienced with their children with **ADHD** and which have left them feeling exasperated and angry. In each situation, however, the parent plays a role in creating the problem. A proactive solution is for the parents to analyze their role in the problem and make appropriate changes to avoid, or at least temper it the next time.

STEP 4: CHANGE THE ENVIRONMENT

Being a proactive parent also means analyzing situations and the environment to determine what factors or conditions create problems for your child, *given his disorder*. Proactive parents do this analysis ahead of time and on an ongoing basis. They come to know what causes problems for their child, what *situations* are difficult for their child, and what *factors in that situation* make it difficult for him. They ask themselves important questions based upon their knowledge of **ADHD** to determine the factors that create problems. Once they know the answers to these important questions, they can make effective changes in the environment.

Some of the following are common problem situations and a few of the important questions that need to be asked. Appropriate solutions follow each problem.

Problem 1: Poor Eating

Your child usually says he is not hungry and won't eat his meal at dinner time. You get angry and frustrated because you put a lot of work into fixing meals.

Questions: *Is your child on medication?* Stimulants often suppress appetite, so perhaps your child's poor appetite is a side effect of his medication.

Does your child typically follow erratic biological schedules? It is not unusual that children with ADHD follow their own time clock for eating, sleeping, etc. Just because it's dinner time for you does not mean he is hungry.

Is your child more prone to eat small snacks throughout the day? Often children on stimulant medication who are experiencing appetite suppression need small, healthy snacks throughout the day instead of three big meals.

Is there a lot of easily accessible junk food in the house? Children with ADHD are notorious for indiscriminantly snacking on junk food throughout the day because they "just can't wait" until dinnertime. Some even hide food in their rooms. Many power struggles with these impulsive children can be avoided if the "temptations" are removed. Rather than argue over junk food, keep it out of the house.

Proactive Solutions: It usually works best to let your child eat before he takes his medication to counteract appetite suppression (and to avoid medication-related stomachaches). If your child is not hungry at mealtime, don't insist he eat large portions. It is never good to create power struggles over food. Perhaps putting only a small amount of food on his plate will fit his reduced appetite and satisfy your desire to have him eat something. Another option is to allow your child to eat smaller "meals" throughout the day. Crackers with peanut butter, a few carrot sticks, and a glass of milk can satisfy his erratic hunger without a lot of fuss. Finally, get rid of the junk food and replace it with healthy snacks. Once your child learns that healthy snacks are the only option, he may even develop a taste for the stuff.

Problem 2: Poor Follow-Through

Whenever your child is told to do something, he rarely completes it. Before long, you're shouting in frustration.

Questions: *How many steps do your directions usually involve?* Children with ADHD have difficulty following multi-step directions or chain commands.

What is the nature of what you asked your child to do? Children with ADHD have difficulty doing "busy work."

What is the tone of voice that you usually use with your child? Granted, you are probably frustrated with your child before you even give the directions because you have come to know he will not likely follow through. Nonetheless, your child will be less inclined to comply when directions are given in anger.

Where were you when you gave the directions? If you shouted the directions from another room, you have no way of knowing for sure whether your child was effectively paying attention in the first place. Maybe he was watching TV at the time and could not split his attention between you and the TV.

Proactive Solutions: Limit the directions you give to your child to one or two steps. Ask him to repeat the commands aloud so that you know he actually heard you and was paying attention. Like it or not, you will have to check on him to make sure he has not gotten sidetracked. Remember, children with ADHD are stimulus seekers; if something more stimulating catches their attention, they will go for it like a heat-seeking missile and forget to do what you asked them to do. If your child has gotten sidetracked, gently remind him what he is supposed to do and don't berate him for failing to follow through. After he has completed the first few steps, praise him and give him a few more steps.

Also, consider what you asked your child to do. His failure to follow through could be because the task is too monotonous and boring. You may have to build in an incentive to motivate your child, or tell him, "When you do the dishes, then you can play outside."

When you ask your child to do something, use a respectful tone of voice and remember the golden rule. Ask yourself if you would be inclined to comply if someone was barking orders at you. Keep in mind that children with ADHD are very defensive and extremely reactive to their environment. If you tell them to do something in an angry or disgusted tone of voice, they will likely become immediately defensive and react to your tone of voice rather than to your request Once they start in their reactive "save face" mode, it's difficult for them to put the brakes on their emotions because of their emotional impulsivity.

Finally, always be in the same room with your child when you give him a command. Often parents shout directions or commands from a different room and never know if their child was paying attention or heard them calling. Children with ADHD have a difficult time splitting their attention between you and the television or their video game. Just because your child responds to you and says, "Okay, I'll be right there" doesn't mean he heard you. Also, if you are not in the same room with your child when you give a command, you won't know if he started to comply but got sidetracked or whether he just didn't start to comply at all. It is important to stay in the same room long enough to make sure he heard you and that he started to comply. Always give your child positive feedback when he does obey: "I appreciate that you did what I asked right away."

Problem 3: Homework Refusal

Your third-grade boy either refuses to do his homework or puts off doing it every day. Every night you demand that he go to his room and not come out until he has finished his work. He cries and calls you names.

Questions: *How long is each assignment, and what is your child's attention capacity?* If your child's attentional capacity (i.e., how long he can effectively pay attention) is only 10 minutes, and the assignment takes at least 30 minutes to complete, he can't pay attention long enough to do the assignment.

When are you expecting your child to do his homework? It is important to consider whether your child's medication is wearing off, if he is worn out from a long day at school, etc.

What else is going on when he is expected to do his homework? Maybe your child's favorite TV program is on, or his friends are outside playing, interfering with his motivation to do his schoolwork.

What room is your child in when he is trying to do his homework? Some children go to their bedroom to do their homework, which is an unstructured, unsupervised situation. Others try to do their work in the busiest room in the house with the TV blaring, the phone ringing, and people talking.

Does your child have all of the materials he needs to do his homework? Often adults interpret the failure of the child with ADHD to start tasks as primary resistance or lack of motivation when it actually may be related to underlying disorganization. These children often cannot organize their materials and their actions or the steps involved in getting started with a complicated task. Consequently, they avoid doing the task. Also, disorganized children with ADHD often forget if they have homework, or they may have a vague memory that they do have homework, but don't remember what it was. They also often forget their books, worksheets or assignment sheets at school.

Proactive Solutions: Homework is usually a very difficult task for all children with ADHD. It's a struggle for them to sustain the attention and motivation for the length of the task, to organize the steps and materials needed to perform the task, to avoid more stimulating and gratifying distractions, and to control the impulse to rush through the work to get it over with. Because of these neurologically-based difficulties, children with ADHD need structure and supervision to complete homework. Therefore, it is important to monitor such things as the time of day, the room he is in, the room you are in, the level of distraction, the length of the homework assignment(s), and the materials needed to perform the work.

It is best to schedule homework at the same time each night. It should be at a time when you can be close at hand and supervise. For many children with ADHD, doing homework right after school may not be the best time. It is a major transition time, and they may need to unwind after a hard day at school. Also, after-school time is often when they are experiencing an increase in their ADHD-related symptoms because of medication rebound. If your child is on medication and in rebound, late afternoons may be a difficult time for him to sit still and concentrate. It may be necessary to wait until he has settled down. Or you may find it helpful to administer a third, half-dose of his medication after school (if he's taking a stimulant) to help him get through this commonly difficult time of day. Consult with your physician about this possibility.

You may need to experiment with finding the best time for homework. Some children can do their homework after they have had an after-school snack and watched one TV program. Others may work best right after dinner. If your child is involved in after-school activities, make it clear to him that continuing in these activities is contingent upon getting homework done. If the schedule permits, it's best to break up the schoolwork, perhaps completing some of it before the extra-curricular activity and the rest when he gets home. Whatever you discover works best, it's important that homework is done the same time each day so that it becomes part of the daily structure.

Often parents expect their child to go to his room and complete his homework without supervision. This may be a realistic expectation for a child *without* ADHD who can pay attention, control impulses, persist in the face of boredom and ignore distractions. This is an unrealistic expectation, however, for a child *with* ADHD. It is also probably unrealistic to expect your child to have finished his homework, unsupervised, by the time you get home from work. More than likely, he will not do it; or if he starts, he will be off task more than on task, get very little done, get it done but done wrong, or rush through it just to get it done. Try to be in the same room or at least close by when your child does his homework. Do not send him off to his bedroom. Not only will your presence signal to your child that he must stay on track, but you can monitor the quality of his work and make sure he is not rushing through it. Older children may insist that they do their homework in their bedroom. Don't battle over this point. Allow your child to do his homework in his room with the stipulation that you will check in with him every 20 minutes.

Some children with ADHD try to do their homework in a room full of distractions with the TV on, music blaring, and siblings playing. In this type of environment, it's almost impossible for these children to screen out distractions, stay on task, and maintain a complete train of thought. Make sure that there are no visual or auditory distractions while your child is doing his homework. This means turn off the TV, radio, video games, and maybe even the phone. There is a small minority of children who claim that they work best with a low level of background noise such as music. For these children *perhaps* the background noise acts as a neural stimulator which essentially increases their arousal so that they can do the work. There are also some children who need to get up and move to a different place a few times when they are doing their homework. Again, this movement and change of scenery may effectively stimulate the child so that he can continue working.

It is also important to make sure that homework is not competing with something more stimulating or rewarding, such as a child's favorite television program or an after-school activity. Granted, homework takes precedence over television, but you can make television your ally rather than your foe. Why not videotape your child's favorite program and reward him with viewing it after he completes his homework?

It is also critical that tasks be broken down into smaller, more manageable chunks to fit your child's attention and motivational capacity. If you know that your child's ability to stick with a homework assignment is only 15 minutes, and he has an assignment that takes 30 minutes, show him how to break it down into two 15-minute chunks. Allow him a short break between each chunk, but be specific about how long the break is. You may need to set a timer that signals him when it's time to get back to work.

If your child has a longer assignment that is due in a few weeks, help him break it into segments that he completes over the time period. Ask him to record each segment of work on his homework calendar to help ensure that he works on each segment on the designated day. Don't allow him to put off doing these long-term assignments, which he is likely inclined to do. This only reinforces procrastination and the impulsive tendency to throw something together at the last minute.

Children with ADHD need to be taught how to organize their homework and how to get their homework to and from school. An effective way to accomplish this is to devise a home-school work contract that involves your child, your child's teacher(s) and you. With this system, your child is responsible for writing his assignments for each class in a daily assignment book or homework sheet (if your child has poor fine-motor control or writes slowly, his teacher should write down the assignment). His teacher then checks his assignment book to see if he has included all the necessary information for the assignment, such as page numbers, date due, etc. His teacher also checks to see if your child handed in the assignment due for that day. Finally, his teacher should initial the book in ink if everything was done or write a comment and explanation if assignments were missing.

It will be important to also request that your child's homeroom teacher or school counselor meet briefly with your child at the end of the day to review his assignment book and make sure that he has all of the books and materials he needs to complete his homework. Your responsibility is to check your child's assignment book to see if he handed in his homework for that day and to help him organize his materials for his homework that night. If your child complied with the terms of this contract, he can receive a previously agreed-upon reward such as special dessert, extra TV, a later bedtime, or spending money. If your child fails to bring home his assignment book or did not turn in a previous assignment, he is given a predetermined consequence, such as loss of TV, early bedtime, or reduction in allowance.

Once you make a functional analysis of the situation and the environment, you can make appropriate modifications, working to *prevent problems* before they happen or before they recur.

If you have appropriately structured the homework situation, but you are regularly spending an inordinate amount of time with your child to help him complete his homework, ask your child's teacher(s) to modify the homework, reduce the amount of homework assigned, or allow a time extension. Also, be aware that your child's off-task behavior or slow working style in the classroom may prevent him from completing his classwork. Consequently, it becomes homework. If this is a recurring problem, talk to your child's teacher about ways to improve his classroom productivity or to allow him more time within the school day to get the work done.

There are countless other ways that you can make modifications in the home environment to help your child succeed. Many specific examples are reviewed in Part Four, "Behavior Management Strategies and Methods."

Making modifications for your child to help him succeed can involve self-control strategies or various behavior modification strategies. A full explanation of self-control strategies is beyond the scope of this book. Books by Kendall and Braswell[3] and Braswell and Bloomquist[4] are good sources for more information about this intervention with ADHD.

SUMMARY

- Proactive parents *choose* their response to their child's behavior; they do not automatically react in a conditioned way.

- Proactive parents direct their time and energy in the "Control Zone:" on those things they can control or change. They spend as little energy as possible in the "Worry Zone:" on those things over which they have no control.

- Proactive parents avoid doing repeatedly what they have found through experience does not work. They anticipate problems ahead of time and make appropriate changes.

CHAPTER

11 Principle 5: Avoid Over-Punishing

It was a familiar picture. Fourteen-year-old Jimmy sat in my office, propped against the pillows on my couch, his hands fidgeting with the baseball cap in his lap, the way he'd done for the last six years. I knew Jimmy well and understood his mannerisms. Fidgeting with something calmed his nerves and helped him pay attention. But there was something different about Jimmy today. Something I had not seen in him before but had privately expected and feared for some time.

His shoulders were slumped, and he avoided eye contact as he stared down in his lap. There were no signs of his usual sharp wit and quick comebacks. I couldn't even get him to crack a smile. He sat silently, a sharp contrast to his usual lively chatter. I approached Jimmy carefully. It was clear to me there was something very wrong, and he was fragile at that moment. I told him I was concerned. He had never looked this down to me before. I told him I was willing to listen if he was wiling to share.

He sat silently for a few moments, moments that seemed like hours. His head hung low as tears started to fall. Then he began to talk. His voice was hardly audible, and I had to strain to hear. Jimmy whispered that he had come to realize that things were never going to be better between his dad and him.

He knotted his baseball cap tightly in his hands as he talked about how much he resented his dad. No matter how hard he tried, he couldn't be the kid his dad wanted him to be. He was tired of trying and failing, of constantly looking over his shoulder to see when the next angry explosion would come.

He had finally given up and didn't care about anything anymore.

He had fallen way behind in his homework and had no desire to catch up this time. Before, he was able to pull it out at the last minute, buckle down, and get the work done. He admitted that now he was lying to his parents, telling them he was doing his assignments. He dreaded the usual harsh words from his dad, the "You'll never amount to anything" lecture. He knew it was only a matter of time before they would find out the truth, but he didn't care. So what if he failed?

So what if his dad blew up and yelled at him again, called him an idiot again, grounded him for a month again, demanded that he quit sports again, or barred him from his friends...again. It's nothing he hadn't heard a hundred times before. He resented his dad for the constant slap in the face instead of a helping hand, for the words of anger instead of the words of encouragement. Most of all, he resented his dad because apparently his dad was right — he was a failure.

I had diagnosed Jimmy with ADHD when he was in third grade. He was now in ninth grade. He was a "classic" ADHD, Inattentive Type. He was bright (an I.Q. of 145), creative, resourceful, but terribly forgetful and disorganized.

Jimmy's dad was the communications director for a large company. His job demanded lots of organization and attention to detail. Truth be told, he struggled with some of the same difficulties when it came to follow-through and keeping his eye on the ball. But Jimmy was like a thorn in his dad's side. Despite Jimmy's diagnosis, his dad demanded, "If he's so smart, he *should* be able to remember to bring his homework home. He *should* be able to get decent grades. I *shouldn't* have to remind him to do the simplest of things like make his bed, clean his room, and take out the trash. And I shouldn't have to remind him to take that darn hat off his head when he enters a room!"

Jimmy's dad found that reminding, cajoling, nagging and reasoning didn't work with Jimmy. Jimmy continued to fidget with something in his hands when he was supposed to be listening. He continued to shovel food in his mouth and make annoying chewing noises as he ate. He continued to forget his homework. He continued to forget to call if he was going to be late.

Granted, Jimmy was not an easy child to parent. He was often argumentative, and he didn't easily back down. What his dad did not understand or accept was that the more he yelled, the more defensive Jimmy became. He refused to realize that Jimmy had a hard time putting the brakes on his emotions. The louder his dad's tirades, the more he pushed Jimmy past the point of no return. His dad's tolerance for Jimmy had grown paper thin, and eventually every offense, whether it was forgetting to screw the cap on the toothpaste or staying out past curfew, was met with harsh criticism, yelling, and some severe sentence to be served. He was blinded by a misguided goal: "I'll get that kid to straighten up if it's the last thing I do."

Despite months of parent training and education about the nature of ADHD, despite extensive counseling about the benefits of positive parenting and the risks of overreaction, Jimmy's dad continued to over-punish his son. What he didn't realize was that each angry episode whittled away at Jimmy's self-esteem. His spunk and spontaneity gradually were replaced with apathy, self-loathing and anger.

Jimmy continued down a slippery slope of underachievement and eventual failure. He grew to fiercely resent his dad and finally convinced his mother to let him live with a relative. He rarely spoke with his dad after that and avoided all possible contact.

Punishing Jimmy may have allowed his dad to vent his frustration and anger, and he may have convinced himself that by exerting power over his son he was maintaining some sense of parental authority. He may have won some skirmishes, but he ultimately lost the war — he lost his son.

The last I heard about Jimmy, he had been suspended from school for trying to intimidate a teacher. The principal said Jimmy had no respect for authority. I wasn't surprised.

Sadly, Jimmy's story is not only true, it is also being repeated in many households. Undoubtedly, the behaviors of children with ADHD can totally exasperate their parents. When parents are worn out from the seemingly endless conflicts and hassles of dealing with their child, when nothing else seems to work, when parents are frazzled and at the end of their rope, they may turn to punishment to force their child to behave *right now*. Before long, punishment becomes the main form of "discipline" as parents convince themselves that nothing else works. It is clear that parents who over-punish are frustrated. But it is also true that parents who over-punish are reactive and, ultimately, ineffective.

PROBLEMS WITH OVER-PUNISHMENT

When parents over-punish, they are engaging in the dance of "more of the same." That is, they persist in doing what does not work. If you have used punishment as your main form of discipline, you too have probably come to realize that it does not work. Although it might coerce your child into complying at the moment, punishment likely does not deter him from doing the same thing the next time. Punishing may put out the fire at the moment, but it does not fix the smoldering problem for the future. Why? Because now you have a chronically angry kid on your hands! Through over-punishment you may have put out a brush fire, but you've created smoldering ashes that will erupt into a blazing forest. **Change that is forced by anger rarely lasts**.

What constitutes over-punishment? Over-punishment can be physical or verbal. It can include harsh physical actions such as hitting, spanking, pushing, pinching, or grabbing. It can include harsh restrictions such as locking a child in a closet or in his room for a long time, grounding a child for an excessive period, or enforcing an exaggerated loss of privileges or possessions. It can include more insidious verbal attacks such as yelling, name calling, threatening, belittling or shaming. Whatever form it takes, over-punishment is never appropriate.

There are many problems with using over-punishment to manage your child's behavior:

1. When punishment is used excessively with children with ADHD, they soon become immune to punishment. *"Go ahead, hit me. See what I care!"* This may be due, in part, to the fact that the underlying neurobiological deficit in ADHD causes consequences, whether positive or negative, to lose their effectiveness fairly quickly. Not fully realizing this, you may mistakenly increase punishment when your child continues to misbehave, only to find that his behavior worsens. Children in general can become immune to pain if they are the victims of excessive corporal punishment. In their attempts to protect themselves and save face, they may become hardened, developing a tough exterior as a defense mechanism.

2. Over-punishment is usually doled out in anger, and when you are angry you tend to overreact. *"You have lost your allowance for a year, young lady!"* Consequently, the punishment may be too harsh and not fit the "crime."

3. Overly harsh punishments are almost impossible to enforce. Therefore, you often back down from enforcing them or "forget" about the punishment after a period of time. Consequently, your child learns that you don't mean what you say. If you do enforce such harsh punishments, you are usually punished just as much as your child because of the protracted inconvenience it creates for you. This can make you resent your child.

4. Over-punishment creates sneaky kids. More than likely, if your child is punished excessively, he will become resentful. Consequently, instead of trying to change his behavior, he will figure out how to continue doing what he wants to do without getting caught. *"I'll wait until Mom goes to work. She'll never know."*

5. Over-punishment fosters revenge on the part of your child. Rather than focusing on how inappropriate his behavior may have been, he more than likely will spend his time plotting how to get back at you. *"He'll be sorry he punished me."*

6. Over-punishment usually tells your child what you *don't* want him to do but rarely teaches him what you *do* want him to do. He is often left to figure it out for himself, and children with **ADHD** are not too good at this. *"You said I had to turn off the TV; you didn't say anything about doing my homework."*

7. Excessive punishment can further damage the already tenuous self-esteem of your child with **ADHD**. *"I can' t do anything right."*

8. Excessive punishment can also hinder your child's development of an internal sense of judgment. He will become conditioned to relying on harsh *external* "police" to monitor his behavior, thereby diminishing the development of his own *internal* monitoring system. He learns that something is wrong only if he gets punished; if he doesn't, what's the big deal? *"The way I figure it, it's O.K. as long as I don't get caught."*

9. Aggression begets aggression. Aggressive forms of punishment run the risk of increasing aggressive reactions in children. When you use aggression to control the behavior of your child, you are modeling that aggression is an appropriate means to make people do what you want them to do. *"Give that back to me or I'll pound you!"*

10. The excessive use of punishment may also create a negative or aversive climate in the home. Anytime an individual is in an aversive situation, his tendency is to want to escape. Consequently, if you tend to use punishment excessively, you may find your child distancing from you or closing down all communication in his at-

tempts to escape a negative situation. *"I'd have to be nuts to ever ask my parents for help."*

AN ABUSE OF POWER

Parents have power over their children. That's the natural order. Young children respond to the power of a parent because the parent is physically bigger and stronger. A child may also respond to a parent's power because the parent is more wise, protective, experienced and competent. A child may respond to the power of a parent as long as that child feels dependent upon that parent for what he needs. A child's needs include not only his physical needs such as food, clothing, and shelter, but also his psychological needs such as love, acceptance, and forgiveness.

Parental power goes awry when parents attempt to use their power to *coerce* their children into compliance, resorting to harsh and excessive punishment to train their children to behave.

Over-punishment of a child is an abuse of power. The tendency for abuse of power is increased when you have a child with ADHD. Since these children lack effective internal control, they require more external control. But even though they may *require* more external control, that doesn't mean they *want* it or *accept* it. This is a great source of frustration for parents. As these children impulsively resist control, parents increase control, usually with mounting frustration, anger and emotion. Children with ADHD react to their parents' increased anger with stronger anger or emotions of their own. As their anger escalates, these children are quickly pushed past the point of no return and can easily spiral out of control, unable to "put the brakes" on their runaway emotions. Unfortunately, a parent may then react with more punishment, essentially adding fuel to the fire. The child may finally give in under the weight of the parent's intimidating and threatening power, but his emotions remain as strong as ever.

This escalating scenario may repeat itself enough to convince parents that harsh punishment is the only thing that works with their kid! Through harsh punishment, they "successfully" control their child's behavior *at the moment*. What they may not realize is that they have sacrificed their child's long-term outcome for this short-term goal. Children may succumb to power at the moment but with serious side effects for the future.

The power of over-punishment is time limited. As the child approaches adolescence, he becomes less dependent upon parents, and parents gradually and inevitably lose power over their children. The adolescent is now more capable and resourceful at getting his needs met, independent of his parents. Peers replace parents in order of importance. They become more critical to a child's self-esteem and more influential over his behavior. As adolescents realize that they can meet their needs separately from their parents, they no longer fear the power of their parents.

An adolescent who has been coerced by over-punishment will eventually rebel against the over-powering parent. Parents who have relied on power and over-punishing to control their child are in for a rude awakening. You can hear these parents complain, "I just can't control him anymore." "He acts like he has no respect for authority." "He does whatever he pleases." Over-punishing parents will one day realize that their power is gone, and they have little, if any, influence over their child.

REPLACING PUNISHMENT WITH SELF-CONTROL

Over-punishing is the epitome of loss of self-control. It is the result of frustration that eventually grows into uncontrolled anger and resentment. Parents who rely on over-punishment and coercion to control their children are demonstrating through their actions that *they*, the parents, have lost control.

How can a parent expect a child with ADHD to develop self-control if that child is a victim of his parents' own lack of control? Slapping your child for hitting his sister is like telling him, "Do as I say, not as I do." **It is essential that you model for your child what you want from your child.** If you want your child to control his anger, control *your* anger. If you want your child to respond reasonably, *you* must respond reasonably. If you want your child to be forgiving, *you* must be forgiving.

There are a number of things you can do to stay calm and regain your own self-control.

- **Count to 10**
- **Leave the room**
- **Take Calming Breaths**

    The calming breath exercise is one of the most efficient techniques for achieving relaxation and regaining control quickly. Inhale deeply through your nose, expanding your abdomen as you take in the air. Then exhale slowly. Do this ten times, counting backward slowly from 10 to 1.

- **Turn on the Radio**

  The radio can be a great distraction. Leave the room and turn on some soothing music.

- **Be Aware of Anger Contamination from Past Relationships**

  Sometimes our anger is distorted or exaggerated because we are unconsciously superimposing the pain of an old relationship on a current one. For example, your child's walking away when you talk to him may re-ignite old feelings of resentment you felt as a child when your parents walked away from you in the middle of a discussion. That unresolved pain fuels the anger in your current relationship. To tell whether or not your anger toward your child is being contaminated, pay attention to the following four cues: 1) your anger is instantaneous or habitually knee-jerk; 2) you consistently view your child in black or white or global terms; 3) your interaction with your child creates a familiar physical feeling such as a lump in the throat or pain in the chest; and 4) your anger is out of proportion to the situation.

- **Avoid Reasoning and Arguing Your Child into Compliance**

  Don't get caught in the trap of believing that if you explain it one more time or just right, your child is going to stop dead in his tracks, thank you for your insight, and comply with your request. Remember that children with ADHD are driven by their impulses, and their impulse is to avoid this unpleasant thing you want them to do. Impulses are stronger than reason. Arguing and reasoning with your child increases his impulsivity, pushing him toward an emotional hijacking where there is no way physiologically that he can put the brakes on his emotions and listen to you.

- **Call Time-Out on Yourself**

  This strategy is especially useful for controlling the escalation of anger. When you notice the warning signs that an interaction is headed toward anger, give the "T" sign for time-out and simply announce, "Time-out!" Then leave for a predetermined period of time, perhaps an hour. Do not use any "you" statements such as, "You're making me angry." These statements lead to defensiveness and an escalation of anger. During your time-out period, do something physical to release your tension, such as taking a walk. Use a relaxation response such as calming breathing. Try to replace your angry thoughts with a calming or relaxing image, such as resting in a velvety grass meadow or floating on a warm air mattress. Do

not waste your time building a case against your child or rehears-
ing a speech. This will only get you more upset than you were before the time-out. When the time-out is over, go back to your child
and see if he is ready to talk calmly about the issue. If he is not,
schedule a time to do so.

- **Put Things in Perspective**

    Parenting a child with ADHD can wear you down and throw your
    perspective out of whack. Often, however, your level of aggrava-
    tion or anger may not be a realistic measure of the seriousness of
    the problem.

    Put the problem at hand in proper perspective. Consider the wide
    range of situations/problems that could possibly happen to you in
    your life and rate them on a 1 to 100 scale with "1" being "not bad
    at all" and "100" being the "worst possible thing that could hap-
    pen." For example, breaking a fingernail probably ranks a "1,"
    breaking your writing arm is probably a "50," and losing a loved
    one is likely "100." Now, go back and plug the current problem
    into the same scale. Hopefully, you will find that the problem to
    which you are reacting so strongly is not as big a deal as you thought.
    It may be aggravating but not earthshaking.

- **Be Aware of Your Own Stress**

    Pay attention to those times when you are more susceptible to stress;
    your child is an easy target for your anger at these times. Common
    stress times for parents include when they are rushed, when they
    are just home from work, when they are tired or not feeling well,
    and when they are angry with someone else. Try to avoid conflict
    with your child at these times.

- **"Begin With the End in Mind"**

    Too often we get caught up in the moment, trying to soothe our
    immediate frustration without thinking of what we want to ac-
    complish in the long term. To force our child to stop doing some-
    thing we don't like in the present, we are willing to berate and
    criticize him and thus risk his self-esteem for the future. To put the
    present in perspective, imagine yourself at your 85th birthday cel-
    ebration listening to your child give tribute to you as a parent, as a
    model for his life. What would you like him to say? Fashion your
    interactions with your child based upon that vision of the future.
    Keep your moment-to-moment actions in line with your long-term
    goal for your child.

- **Avoid Statements that Attack and "Put Down"**

  Statements that attack intensify your anger. Angry attacks on children seriously hurt their self-esteem and cause them to react defensively, to dig in their heels and strengthen their noncompliance. This only fuels your anger and hurts your child.

- **Talk to the "Right People"**

  It is usually helpful to talk to someone about your frustrations, but avoid talking to someone who will only fan the flames of anger. It doesn't help to talk to someone who shares your trigger thoughts, "You're right, he's just a spoiled brat." Talk to someone who will listen to you without offering you advice, agreeing with your criticisms, blaming you, or arguing with you.

- **Exercise**

  Physical exercise is a great way to reduce stress because it releases endorphins that act as natural tranquilizers for your body. Aerobic exercising, walking or jogging, bicycle riding, swimming, or jumping rope can all help to reduce stress.

IS THERE SUCH A THING AS PERMISSIBLE PUNISHMENT?

The most effective approach with children with ADHD is to begin with positives. Focus on what you want your child to *start doing* rather than what you want your child to *stop doing*. For example, you may want your child to *start* making his bed, to *start* going to bed on time, to *start* doing what he is told after the first request. Begin by praising or rewarding your child when he does these desirable things. This will automatically focus your attention toward your child's positive behavior.

After at least two weeks of using an initial positive approach with some degree of success, a mild punishment procedure can be introduced in conjunction with a positive approach. Even when a mild punishment procedure is added, however, the positive attention should continue to outweigh the negative.

Some forms of mild punishment are permissible. Mild punishments come in many forms, such as time-out, removal of privileges, or grounding. Mild punishments can help your child see that certain actions result in unpleasant consequences. However, any form of mild punishment should be used with dignity and respect for your child. It should occur within the larger context of positive discipline and proactive parenting. If you use punishment with your child, it should be mild, initiated immediately after the infraction, and used only when your child commits particular offenses. It should not be used whenever your child does something "wrong."

The following are examples of permissible punishment that you can use to manage the behavior of your child.

Verbal Reprimands

The mildest form of punishment that may be effective is verbal reprimands. Verbal reprimands, however, will be most effective if they are short, firm, delivered immediately after the infraction occurs, and delivered with eye contact and close to your child. When delivering verbal reprimands, parents have a tendency to talk too much, turning the reprimand into a lecture. The child then develops "parent deafness," tuning the parent out. Avoid these "lecturing verbal reprimands," which are guaranteed to make matters worse!

Removal of Privileges

It is usually more effective to remove a privilege or something your child enjoys, rather than to do something aversive such as spanking. The removal of privileges should have a direct connection to your child's offense. This helps him see the connection between his behavior and the natural or logical consequences. For example, if your child comes home late for dinner, he should lose the privilege of a warm dinner. If he leaves his bike out in the rain, he should lose the privilege of using his bike for a period of time. If he and his sibling argue over a toy, they should lose the privilege of playing with the toy. If your adolescent misses his curfew, he should lose the privilege of going out the next time.

Some children respond to the opportunity to partially earn back a lost privilege. For example, one child lost the privilege of watching TV after school for five days because he continued to let TV infringe on his homework time. However, he was allowed to earn back one TV program a night if he finished his homework correctly before 6:00.

Response Cost

This procedure is an extension of a behavior modification system in which your child earns points or tokens each time he does something he was asked to do. With response cost, your child forfeits previously earned points or tokens when he does something he was not supposed to do. For example, if your child earns five points for getting ready for school on time, he loses two points for delaying.

Time-Out

Time-out involves removing your child from a problematic situation. For example, your child is sent to his room for 5 minutes for arguing with you.

Both of these latter procedures are discussed in detail in Part Four, "Behavior Management Strategies and Methods."

SUMMARY

- Using punishment as the main mode of discipline may coerce a child into complying at the moment, but it eventually causes him to angrily rebel against authority.

- There are many repercussions from over-punishment: It makes children immune to punishment; it fuels parental and child anger; it is hard to enforce; it creates sneaky or revengeful kids; it damages a child's self-esteem; it hinders the development of a child's own internal judgment; it often increases a child's aggression; and it cuts off communication.

- As children approach adolescence, parents gradually lose power over their children, and peers become more influential.

- Parents can do many things to maintain their self-control and avoid over-punishing, including: leaving the room before they "lose it"; taking calming breaths; avoiding reasoning and arguing; putting things in perspective; monitoring their own stress level; and "beginning with the end in mind."

- Permissible, milder forms of punishment include: verbal reprimands, removal of privileges, response cost, and time-out.

Principle 6: Give Positive Redirections and Specific Feedback

POSITIVE REDIRECTIONS

Most of us tend to pay more attention to what we *don't* like instead of what we *do* like. This is particularly true for parents of children with ADHD, given that these children demonstrate so many negative behaviors. Your tendency may be to redirect or manage your child's behavior by telling him to "stop doing this" or "stop doing that." Unfortunately, he often replaces one negative behavior with another, thereby creating more frustration for you.

Consider this example:

> A father needs to catch up on some paperwork, so he brings his son with ADHD to his office building one Saturday. The father knows that some of his business associates will also be in the office that day, so it is important that his son "behave himself." As they enter the building, the son starts to run down the hall, making a lot of noise as he goes. Immediately his father yells out, "Stop running." The child responds by skipping down the hall.

In this example, one negative behavior was replaced by another. Children with ADHD are not good monitors of their own behavior. They are often unaware of what they are doing even as they are doing it. Therefore, in the example above, the child may not have focused on the fact that running down the hall and making a lot of noise could have disturbed other people who were trying to work, thus angering and embarrassing his father. To consider all of this would have required reflective thinking, self-monitoring, and a consideration of the consequences of his behavior. This process obviously would be difficult for a child who is very impulsive and who is managed by the moment and whatever feels good at the time. Accordingly, without more specific re-direction, he would simply discontinue one behavior and replace it with another that also feels good at the moment.

When re-directing your child, it is important to help him focus on an *appropriate* alternative behavior. This is done by telling him specifically and succinctly what you *want him to do*. Avoid telling him what you don't want him to do. In our example, the father could have re-directed his son by saying, *"Please walk down the hall quietly."*

SPECIFIC FEEDBACK

Just as children with ADHD may not be aware of the negative behaviors they are doing as they are doing them, they also may not be tuned into the positive behaviors they are doing as they are doing them. Therefore, when you give your child positive feedback, it is important to be specific about what he is doing that is positive.

For example:

> A child is sitting at the kitchen table drawing a picture. He has been engaged in this task for 15 minutes, which is an uncharacteristically long time for him. The child's mother notices what her son is doing and says, "I like the way you've been sitting quietly for 15 minutes and drawing a picture."

This mother's specific feedback focused her child on his positive behavior and let him know what he was doing. On the other hand, if the child's mother had said something more vague, such as, "Good job," he may not have known exactly what behavior he should try again.

Some examples of specific feedback include:

"I see you're listening because you're looking at me and watching closely."
"You put your clothes away without my even telling you. Great!"
"You got started on your homework right at 4:30. Good going!"
"Even though you were angry with your sister for going into your room, you kept your cool and did not hit her. That's great self-control!"

SUMMARY

- Children with ADHD are not good self-observers.
- Redirect your child's behavior by telling him what you *want* him to do rather than what you *don't* want him to do.
- When giving your child feedback, tell him specifically what it was that he was doing, e.g., "You started your homework as soon as I asked you. Good job!"

Part Four

Behavior Management Strategies and Methods

Understanding the six important principles that underlie effective management of ADHD sets the groundwork for specific behavior management strategies. We have already discussed that children with ADHD:

- Have a neurologically-based deficit in inhibition that interferes with their ability to stop and think, preplan, or organize themselves;

- Are less sensitive to consequences;

- Can sustain interest and motivation only if tasks/chores are intrinsically motivating, stimulating, or highly rewarding;

- Do not internalize rules that guide behavior;

- Are more noncompliant;

- Receive significantly more negative feedback compared to other children; and

- Develop negative secondary behaviors that are an outgrowth of their primary ADHD.

These facts make children with ADHD unique from other children and a greater challenge to parent. In fact, many traditional parenting practices have to be set aside or modified. However, there *are* specific behavior management strategies and methods that are very effective even with the diverse characteristics and complex difficulties facing children with ADHD.

These strategies and methods are grouped into seven different areas:

1. Structuring the home
2. Structuring the child
3. Teaching your child to structure himself
4. "Catching him being good"
5. Devising behavior modification systems
6. Breaking the cycle of willful noncompliance
7. Using active listening

The first three intervention areas involve strategies that help you increase structure in one way or another. Given that ADHD is basically a disorder of self-regulation, **structure is probably the most powerful and critical component of intervention.**

The fourth intervention area of behavior management focuses on turning around the cycle of negative parent-child interactions and working toward a more positive household climate. The fifth area teaches you how to increase your child's motivation and shape his behavior. The sixth intervention area details a specific method to increase compliance and decrease arguing and emotional spiraling. Finally, we explore how to listen and talk to your child in such a way that you decrease his defensiveness and therefore increase his willingness to change.

CHAPTER

13 Structuring Your Home

We've discussed how children with ADHD have significant difficulty with self-regulation. They do not easily structure themselves; therefore, they need others to structure their environments for them to help them function more successfully. For parents, this means considerable effort must be put into structuring and organizing the home. A disorganized, unstructured home throws your child with ADHD out of kilter, making his problems worse.

Be Aware of What You're Modeling for Your Child

It is unrealistic for you to expect your child with ADHD to stay organized, put his things away, follow through on instructions, and remember where he last put something if he sees his own parents leave piles of their clutter around the house, sees them put off doing household chores, sees them forget to sign important school papers, or sees them frequently forget where they put their car keys. It is essential that you "clean up your act" before you can realistically expect your child to do the same. By operating in an organized fashion, you provide a calmer climate and model more appropriate behavior for your child with ADHD.

If you are a parent who also has ADHD, keeping your home clutter-free and staying organized will be especially challenging. You may need to enlist the services of a professional organizer or ask a trusted friend or relative to help you clean up the clutter and get organized.

Follow Regular Schedules

Children with ADHD function best in a structured, predictable household and become overly anxious and disorganized in a chaotic one. It is very important to establish regular schedules for daily or routinely occurring activities. Mealtimes, bedtimes and homework should be scheduled for the same time every day. Certain days should be designated for such self-care responsibilities as baths or showers, hair wash, etc. For example, every Wednesday and Saturday night can be "hair wash nights."

Create a Message Center

Hang a bulletin board or marker board in a central place in the house, probably in the kitchen, and call it the family message center. Designate a special section on the board for each family member and also specify a general information section. Be sure that all telephone messages, memos, reminders, or special notes are written here. Examples are, "Dad home late tonight," "Sue, RSVP for birthday party on Saturday," and "Mike, start laundry when you get home." Family members should look here throughout the day to see if there is anything for them.

Make an Activities Calendar

Hang a large calendar by the message center. Write in all regularly occurring school events or obligations for your child, such as due dates for media center books, piano lessons, sporting practices, religion classes, etc. Also write in specific upcoming events or notices from school, such as field trips, book report due dates, science project due dates, special vacations, etc. Encourage younger children to draw representative pictures on the calendar for special days/events (e.g., draw a book for media center day). Teach your child to check the calendar as part of his daily routine so that he can see what is going on for that day, what is due in the coming days, and what changes are scheduled. *Have him cross out each day as it occurs.*

Use Baskets for School Papers

Children come home from school with a load of different papers on a daily basis. It is exceptionally difficult for the child with ADHD to keep track of all of them. To help organize these different papers, place a few baskets or bins by the message center and label them *incoming* and *outgoing*. Teach your child that all papers that do not need to be returned to school, such as completed and graded homework, should go in the incoming basket. Parents should go through this basket on a certain day every week and then toss or file its contents.

All papers that require that a parent respond in some way should go in the outgoing basket. Check this basket every day and sign forms or write checks as indicated. Older children should check the outgoing basket each morning and put their papers in their backpacks themselves. For younger children, parents should put the appropriate outgoing papers in the child's backpack.

Do Nighttime Preparation for the Following Day

Children with ADHD often seem to operate on a different time schedule than the rest of the family. When everyone else is bustling around the house in the morning trying to get ready for the day and get out of the house, your child with ADHD is often plodding along, going at his own pace no matter how much you try to rush him.

To avoid this morning time crunch, do as much as you can the night before. Before your child goes to bed, have him choose his outfit for the next day. Make sure he puts his completed homework in his backpack and places his backpack by the door where he leaves the house in the morning. Review your activities calendar for the following day to see if there are any field trips planned for which your child needs extra money or special clothing. Are media center books due? Does he need his instrument for lessons or equipment for sports practices/games, etc.? Check the outgoing basket to see if there are any special school papers that require your signature and need returning by the next day. Have your child prepare his cold lunch the night before. If your child is younger, it may help to set out his jacket, boots and mittens by the door.

Prepare for the School Day

All efforts should be taken to help your child's morning go smoothly before school. Children with ADHD generally are emotionally overaroused and cannot easily calm themselves. If your child has an upsetting morning at home, he likely will go to school upset. His teacher and classmates may then have to pay the price for your child's difficult start of the day.

One of the most important things you can do is to get up and be ready for the day before your child gets up. He needs your help. Don't assume that because your child with ADHD "is old enough," he should be able to get himself up and ready for school without your having to tell him. This may be true if he is getting up to go someplace where he wants to be; in this case there is a built-in motivational factor. Getting up for school, however, is usually not very motivating for these children. You can help by your example and supervision.

Routines are also important. Set an alarm to be sure your child gets up on time and early enough so that he can complete the established morning routine. Make sure he gets up at the same time every morning. Set a regular morning routine that follows a predictable sequence, such as get up, eat breakfast, get dressed, wash face, brush teeth, and comb hair. If you allow the TV on in the morning, don't let your child turn it on until this sequence is completed.

Limit Choices

Children with ADHD become disorganized and overwhelmed when faced with too many choices, often leading to unnecessary power struggles. It is good, therefore, to limit choices whenever possible. One area where power struggles seem to erupt is over what to wear. When choosing an outfit for the next day, limit the choice between two alternatives. Children also seem to gravitate toward wearing blatantly inappropriate clothing such as a sleeveless shirt on a cold winter day. To avert a power struggle here, put all out-of-season clothes in a closet out of your child's room. Also, put away some of your child's toys on a rotating basis to limit his flitting from toy to toy and to reduce the clutter in his play area. Let him select from only two options when trying to decide what to do, where to go, with whom to play, etc.

Post Household Rules

Just as children with ADHD should have limited choices, they also should have a limited number of important household rules. Too many rules are difficult to enforce, create a negatively vigilant climate, and lead to many unnecessary power struggles. Also, remember that children with ADHD do not easily internalize rules and therefore need ongoing visible reminders about acceptable and unacceptable behaviors within the household. Choose those rules that are most vital and practical. Then be consistent and creative in enforcing them. Post them in an area of the house where family members can easily see them, such as the refrigerator and in your child's room. Be sure to state the rules specifically and in the positive, such as "Please pick up dirty clothes, dishes, and toys" instead of "Don't leave messes." Sometimes it is more practical and effective to place colorful Post-It notes in strategic places around the house to remind your child of certain rules or routines. For example, place a Post-It note that says, " BRUSH TEETH" on your child's bathroom mirror or a note that says, "FLUSH" on the toilet.

State Expectations/Consequences Before the Fact

Stating your expectations and consequences just prior to an activity/ event helps organize your child by establishing clear guidelines for behavior. It also helps to organize you because you can avoid the predicament of having to "think on your feet" in the heat of the moment. For example, if your child tends to watch TV too much and it interferes with his doing chores, say to him, *"You can watch TV until 8:00. If you don't turn it off then, you have to go to bed."* Before going into a store, state to your child the few rules for acceptable behavior and the consequence, *"There are three rules: 1. I expect you to stay by my side. 2. Do not ask to buy anything. 3. No fussing. If you break any of these rules, we will leave the store right away."*

Build in Transitions

As you know, children with ADHD are generally not very adaptable. They especially have trouble changing activities, such as going from TV to getting ready for bed or leaving playmates to come in the house for supper. It is helpful to build in a transition time so that your child can "start to get ready" for the change. The process is simple: just prior to the change, tell your child that the change is coming. For example, if he is playing and it's close to bedtime, tell him that in 5 minutes he will have to start to put his toys away so that he can get ready for bed. Be sure to check back in 5 minutes to help start the bedtime process.

Use Timer Management

A kitchen timer can be used to set clear time limits or help a child manage transitions. It can also remove you from potential power struggles in the process. For example, if you give your child a command, such as to put his toys away or get dressed, tell him that he has a certain number of minutes within which to complete it. Then set the timer for that number of minutes. When the timer goes off, see if he has completed what he was told to do. If he did not, administer a consequence. To help with transitions, tell your child that he will have to *start* getting ready in a certain number of minutes. Then set the timer. This built-in transition time allows him time to change his mindset for the next activity.

Avoid Spur-of-the-Moment Outings

Children with ADHD often become over-excited and disorganized with spur-of-the-moment outings and large-group activities. Try to plan ahead for outings and explain to your child what is going to happen, the sequence of events, and how long you will be there. Shield your child from overstimulation in large-group activities (such as trips to the zoo or the amusement park) by keeping him out of the center of activity and limiting the length of his stay. If necessary, schedule breaks from the action throughout the activity to allow your child to calm down and prevent behavioral/emotional spiraling.

Avoid Fatigue

Avoid fatigue with your child. When children with ADHD are exhausted, their self-control often breaks down, and their hyperactivity becomes worse. Learn to read your child's body cues that may signal to you that he is starting to get worn down and may lose control. Watch for such signs as increasing restlessness, yawning, increased distractibility, inattention or impatience, increasing voice volume, more interruptions, grabbing things, or whining.

Allow One Friend at a Time

Children with ADHD usually gravitate toward other children who are rambunctious. Consequently, their play often escalates into loud, uncontrolled, and sometimes aggressive behavior. Additionally, there's an unwritten law that states: If three children play together, there will always be an "odd man out." To better maintain a reasonable level of control and reduce the chances of arguing and competition, it is best to allow your child to have one friend over at a time, especially for sleepovers.

Prohibit Violent Videos, Movies, TV

Children with ADHD have difficulty controlling their impulses, and the more severe the ADHD, the more aggressive the child tends to be. Therefore, it is best not to allow your child to watch violent TV programs, movies, or videos, or to play violent video games.

Prohibit Aggressive Play

Monitor your child's play for aggressiveness. Any forms of physical or verbal aggression should be "nipped in the bud" immediately and not be allowed to escalate. Do not allow excessively rambunctious play or horseplay, especially in the house. Children with ADHD often are not able to monitor their play and put on the brakes if events start to get out of control.

Schedule Family Meetings

Family meetings are an effective way to settle conflicts, negotiate rules, share concerns, plan outings, distribute responsibilities among family members, and strengthen family communication. It is important to schedule these meetings for the same time each week. Guidelines for family meetings are outlined in the *S.T.E.P. (Systematic Training for Effective Parenting) Parents' Handbook[1]* available in most bookstores.

Schedule Regular Snack Times

Schedule snack times so that your child is not indiscriminately asking for snacks or interrupting you in the middle of doing something else. Tell him he can have a snack, for example, at 10:30 in the morning and 3:00 in the afternoon.

Enforce "Kitchen is Closed"

When mealtimes are over and snack times have passed, tell your child that the kitchen is closed. This means no more asking for snacks or helping oneself to food. This rule also helps to control the amount and frequency of messes in the kitchen.

Break Down Larger Tasks

It is important to break down larger tasks into more manageable units and set a time limit for completion. For example, instead of asking your child to clean his room, break it down into a series of smaller tasks. Tell your child to first pick up and put away everything on the floor. Give him an appropriate amount of time to do so, then set the timer. Be sure to check on him often throughout the task and give him specific positive feedback. Then ask him to do another sub task, such as clean off his desk, and follow the same guidelines. If a job is too big for your child's attentional/motivational capacity, you can even spread it out over a few days.

Give Effective Commands

A major factor in your child's noncompliance or poor follow-through may be the way that you give him commands.

- Only give a command if you mean it and intend to back it up. Know what the consequence will be, positive or negative, before you give the command.

- State the command simply and directly but not as a request: "It's time to come in now. Say good-bye to your friends." Although your tone of voice should be business-like, it should not be harsh or disrespectful.

- Do not give too many commands at once. If your command is complicated, break it down into steps. Use as few words as possible.

- Make sure you have your child's attention when you are giving the command. It's best to be in the same room as your child when you make the request and establish eye contact when you talk.

- Reduce all distractions before you give the command. Don't compete with the television, radio or video games when giving commands.

- If necessary, ask your child to repeat the command to ensure he was paying attention.

- Don't leave the room immediately after giving the command; stay in the room at least until your child starts to comply.

- Immediately praise your child for following through.

Use "When-Then" Contingencies

Children with ADHD are more likely to follow through with a request if the consequence that immediately follows is highly rewarding. Keep this in mind when asking your child to do something. For example, if your child has left his toys all over his room and it's just about time for his favorite afternoon snack, tell him that *when* he picks up his toys, *then* he can have his snack. This will motivate him to comply. Don't let him talk you into allowing him to pick up his toys *after* he eats his snack. If you do, you will have lost his motivator.

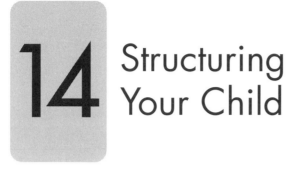

Structuring Your Child

As a parent of a child with ADHD, you know all too well the difficulty he has controlling his own behavior. Your child's neurologically-based dis-inhibition short-circuits his ability to regulate his own behavior. It is as though his *internal* control system is defective; it works sometimes, but not all the time, and not very well. To keep your child on track, you may have to act as your child's ***external* control system**. This means you have to put specific parameters and boundaries around your child's behavior and systematically direct and shape his actions. The following techniques can help provide needed structure for your child.

Give Positive Redirections

When redirecting the impulsive child, it is important to help him fo-cus on an *appropriate* alternative behavior. Otherwise, he may replace one unwanted behavior with a different one. This is done by telling him specifically and succinctly what you *want him to do* ("You need to walk down the hall quietly"). Avoid telling him what you don't want him to do ("Stop running!").

Give Specific Feedback

Just as impulsive children may not be aware of their negative behav-iors as they are doing them, they also may not be tuned into their *positive* behaviors. Therefore, it is important to immediately and spe-cifically tell your child what he is doing that is positive ("Thanks for unloading the dishwasher on your own. I really appreciate it!").

Increase What You Want

Think in terms of what you want your child to *start* doing rather than what you want him to *stop* doing. For example, you may often be frustrated because your child leaves his messes for you to clean up. Be on the lookout for those times when he does *pick up after himself.* Then give positive attention, praise, and/or tangible reinforcement.

To help you focus your attention on what you want your child to do, follow the two-column "bug list" technique. In one column write down all those behaviors of your child that "bug" you. In the opposite column, write down a corresponding *positive* behavior to each negative behavior you listed. Focus your attention and your behavioral goals on these positive behaviors. We too often get locked into looking for what is wrong with our child rather than what is right with him. Make every effort to bite your tongue and *not* give your child negative attention when he does something negative. Instead, give him positive attention when he does something positive.

Here are some examples of the two-column technique to help you get started:

NEGATIVE BEHAVIOR	POSITIVE BEHAVIOR
Leaves messes	Picks up after himself
Puts off doing homework	Starts homework when told
Responds to teasing by hitting or name-calling	Walks away and ignores
Whines when told "No"	Accepts "No" without whining
Argues when loses a game	Accepts losing graciously

Use a Marble Jar

Tell your child that you are going to try to catch him using good impulse control. Every time you see him demonstrating good impulse control on his own, give him specific positive feedback and drop a marble in a jar. When the marbles reach a certain height marked by a red line on the jar, reward your child with a special activity or item. If you use this system with more than one child, make sure each child has his own specific color of marbles as well as his own jar. This prevents one child from padding his jar by taking marbles from a sibling's jar.

Classify Offenses and Consequences

This system can be extremely effective in providing structure and predictability to your discipline, and it can help you avoid shooting from the hip. Although it is effective with all school-age children, it is especially helpful when dealing with adolescents.

Classify your child's problematic behaviors into three categories: Big Deal offenses, Medium Deal offenses, and Little Deal offenses. Then decide what consequences are appropriate for each category. Some typical offenses and consequences to consider are the following:

Possible Big Deal Offenses:

- hitting or other forms of physical aggression
- stealing
- drinking, doing drugs
- having a party without permission
- coming home more than an hour late without calling

Possible Big Deal Consequences:

- fine of a significant amount of money
- do chores/project for a certain number of hours
- grounded for a week(s)
- no TV for a week
- no use of the car for a week
- no phone for a week

Possible Medium Deal Offenses:

- lying
- forgot/lost homework
- friends over without permission
- swearing using the "F" word
- sneaking to the mall

Possible Medium Deal Consequences:

- revoking permission for party, concert, or going out with friends
- deduction of medium amount of money from allowance
- no TV for a certain number of days
- deduction of certain number of points from point system, i.e., response cost
- do chores for a certain number of hours
- loss of telephone privileges

Little Deal Offenses:

- not making bed
- not putting toys/clothes away
- leaving bike outside
- wearing other family member's clothes
- going into siblings' room
- swearing using the "S'" word
- name-calling

Little Deal Consequences:

- time-out
- deduction of money from allowance
- can't watch certain TV show
- deduction of certain number of points from point system, i.e., response cost

This system categorizes offenses with corresponding consequences in a uniform and consistent manner. It helps you thoughtfully choose a consequence to impose each time for each class of offenses, thus avoiding thinking on your feet, shooting from the hip, and overreacting.

Use a Special Allowance System

Impulsive children are notorious for not managing money well and for wanting what they want when they want it. A systematic allowance system can deal with both of these problems. Every week give your child $1 for every year of age, rounding up or down to an even amount (e.g., a 7-year-old gets $6). Keep one-third of it for college savings, one-third for home savings for a special item/event that your child wants (e.g., new Nintendo cartridge, compact disc, etc.) and one-third for weekly spending money (e.g., candy, small toys, movie rental, junk at the check-out counter, etc.). The money should be kept in three separate containers. Discuss ahead of time what you as the parent will pay for, such as books, regular clothing, movies at the theater, etc. Once your child spends the one-third allotted for his weekly spending money, do not give him more or float him a loan. Take your child to the bank once every three months to deposit his college savings.

Give Self-Control Tickets

Give self-control tickets to your child whenever you see him controlling himself in a potentially impulsive situation. Tell your child that it is necessary that he learn to control his behavior and that each time he does, he will be given a ticket that he can use to buy a special reward. Give him specific examples of how he can earn these tickets. The tickets should be of different value depending upon the degree of self-control your child exhibits. For example, catching himself before he calls his sister a name earns a yellow one-point ticket, but stopping himself before he bonks his sister on the head earns a red five-point ticket. Let him cash in his tickets for a special item or privilege at the end of the day or end of the week, depending upon the child. The higher the number of tickets earned, the bigger the reward.

Enforce a Chore Time Line

Children with ADHD are great procrastinators, especially when it comes to doing something that they don't want to do. They can put off a chore all day or procrastinate to the last minute and then rush through it just to get it done. You may find that you constantly nag your child to do a simple chore, and the nagging probably escalates into an argument. It may lessen the power struggles around chores if you give your child a clear time limit for his chores. Tell him that he must complete a particular chore by a certain time, say 12:00 noon. Also tell him that if he does not complete the chore by this time, he will be given a specific consequence, for example, no television for the day or no playing with friends for the day. You might also tell him that if he completes the job, but does a sloppy job, the consequence will follow as well. Be sure to define ahead of time specifically what you mean by "sloppy job."

Reinforce Completion and Accuracy

When impulsive children complete what they were asked to do, they often rush through it so quickly that they don't do a good job. To slow your child down, give him points or tokens for completion and bonus points for doing a good or careful job.

Use Shaping Procedures

It is best to use shaping procedures for particularly difficult behaviors. This method involves beginning with a behavioral goal slightly above his current behavior (baseline) and then gradually increasing the goal and reinforcing small steps. For example, if your child has difficulty playing with friends for more than 15 minutes before problems arise, set a goal that he will follow the "play rules" and play peaceably for a 16-minute period, and then set a timer. If he has played appropriately for this 16- minute period, reward him (and his friend) with a special snack. Once your child has consistently accomplished this goal, gradually increase the time limit by a few minutes each time and reward him in the same manner until he has reached a final goal of playing appropriately for the whole play period.

Try Modified Response Cost

Children with ADHD are usually not accustomed to earning rewards for good behavior because of their high rate of negative behaviors. Also, they often lose interest or give up before they have worked hard or long enough to earn a reward. Therefore, they may work harder to keep a reward which they already have rather than to earn a reward which they don't yet have.

To create this situation, begin each day by giving your child a certain number of tokens or points which he has to work to keep by virtue of his positive behavior. Every time your child commits an offense of poor impulse control, he loses a certain number of tokens or points. If your child loses all of the tokens by the end of the day, there is a consequence. If a certain number of tokens remain at the end of the day, he can cash them in for a reward. If he got through the day without losing any points, he can earn some bonus points. For example, your child can start the day with 50 points, and he must work hard to keep them. Explain to him that he will lose one point each time he breaks a rule such as not making his bed, talking back to a parent, or teasing his sister. Be specific about all the ways he can lose points. At the end of the day, count the number of points he has left. If he has no points left, he must go to bed early. If he has 30 or more points, he earns $1. If he still has all 50 points at the end of the day, he earns $2 plus five additional bonus points to save for a special reward.

Try a "You Lose It" Box

Impulsive children often leave things lying around the house because it just takes too much time to pick them up. If items are left lying around after a certain time of the day, put them in a locked, "you lose it" box and keep them for seven days. The box could be a locked closet or the trunk of your car.

Set up a "Buy Back Store"

Another alternative to the messy room and things left on the floor is to take everything your child does not put away and store it in the basement. Tell your child that this is the "buy back store." When he wants something from the store, he can buy it back using tokens or points he earned for good behavior as his form of payment. If this system works for a while, he can gradually buy more than one item at a time from the store.

Charge for Unfinished Chores

Don't engage in nagging or arguing with your child to complete his regular household chores, such as making his bed or taking out the trash. Ask just once. If your child does not complete the chore by a certain time, charge him for doing the chore yourself (e.g., 30 cents for making beds). Submit a bill at the end of the week and deduct it from his allowance if necessary.

Use a Secret Signal

Talk with your child about his impulsive behaviors and agree on a secret signal that you will give him every time you see that he is *starting* to lose control or *is* acting impulsively. A secret signal could be a time-out signal with your hands, raising your finger, or saying a code word. To increase the power of this technique, it may be helpful to dispense a token or small reward every time your child responds appropriately to the secret signal. This system is especially good to use at someone else's house, the store or mall, etc., where he would be embarrassed by a reprimand.

This list is meant to stimulate your thinking. Some of these strategies will be more suited for you and your child than others. Based upon the principles in Part Three and knowing your child and his environment, you may devise other ways to structure your child. Or, you may find that some ideas work for awhile, then lose their effectiveness. Be creative! And always be proactive.

CHAPTER

15 Teaching Your Child to Structure Himself

All parents hope that eventually their child with ADHD will be able to control his own behavior. You know you can't be with him every minute of the day, modifying his environment and giving him rewards for good behavior. You don't want him to be too dependent on you for success, but you worry that he won't be able to get his act together without you. Granted, your child will gradually improve his self-control just through normal maturation, but chances are he will still lag behind his peers in behavior and emotional control. He will need to be taught some self-control skills that other kids just learn naturally.

Model and Teach Self-Talk

An important part of self-control is self-talk, that is, self-directed speech that is used to guide one's behavior. It is theorized that individuals with ADHD do not adequately develop this ability to regulate their own behavior, so you must teach self-talk to your impulsive child. One way is to talk to yourself out loud as you direct your own behavior, thus modeling self-talk to your child (e.g., *"Let's see. I need to pay attention to what I'm doing and go slowly so that I don't make a mistake here."*). Also, model for your child how he can talk to himself on an ongoing basis so that he can slow down and put on the brakes (*"OK, I need to stop and think of what I should do."*).

These methods work best if your child is also taught how to *self-monitor* his attempts at self-control (*"I stopped myself from calling my brother a name just now."*), *self-rate* his attempts (*"I think my self-control was a 6 on a 1 to 10 scale."*), and *self-reinforce* his efforts (*"I did a great job. Good for me."*).

Encourage Use of a Self-Control Calendar or Journal

A self-control calendar or journal can be an important, all-purpose way for your child to keep track of his problems or successes with impulse control. Older children can use a journal to write down their thoughts, frustrations or ideas about self-control. It can be used as a diary where your child records his progress toward gaining more self-control. A calendar can be used as a simple recording system where your child records the number of times he "kept his cool" each day and/or the number of times he "lost it." It can be used as a chart to record progress toward a goal. For example, if he keeps his cool 4 out of 7 days, he earns a reward.

Predict The Day

Positive prediction can be a powerful but subtle method to increase motivation. Ask your child to predict how well he is going to control impulses today (pointing out the specific goal behaviors), perhaps by using a 1 (low) to 10 (high) scale. Tell him to write his prediction on a piece of paper, in his journal or on his self-control calendar. Make sure he compares his written prediction with how well he actually did at the end of each day.

Rate The Day

At the end of the day, or at the end of a certain period of the day, ask your child to rate how well he did in controlling his impulses or "stopping and thinking." He can use a 1 to 10 scale and write his ratings on his daily self-control calendar. For younger children, parents can also rate their child's self-control for the same rating period. To promote accurate self-observation skills and honesty in reporting in your child, it may be helpful to award points/rewards if your child's ratings closely match yours.

Anticipate Problems Ahead of Time

If your child is planning to go somewhere new or someplace where you expect he may run into difficulties, sit down with him ahead of time and ask him to consider any potential problems. Ask him to talk about possible ways to avoid the problems or about possible solutions if the problems do arise.

Make Self-Control Posters

Young children may have fun designing and making their own self con-trol posters that can act as vivid reminders to practice impulse control. Examples include a large thermometer with the saying, "I KEPT MY COOL," or a red stop sign with the saying, "STOP AND THINK."

Devise a Self-Control Contract

Older children and adolescents tend to respond to behavioral goals if they are devised in an official and cooperative manner. Write a con-tract together with your child that states the behavioral goal for which your child will work, the reward that will follow if he achieves his goal, the consequence that will be enforced if he does not reach his goal, and the date when progress toward his goal will be reviewed. The contract should be signed and dated by all parties (see example in Appendix B).

Teach the Rubber Band Technique

This technique can be an effective self-reminder to help older children put the brakes on impulsive urges. Your child or adolescent can wear a rubber band on his wrist and snap it every time he feels like he is going to "lose his cool," say something that he shouldn't, etc.

Use Calming Breaths

The calming breath exercise is one of the most efficient techniques for achieving relaxation quickly. Teach your child to use this technique whenever he is aware of those body cues that tell him he is getting overly-excited or is about to lose control. First, show him how to breathe from his abdomen instead of from his upper chest: place one hand on the upper chest and one hand on the abdomen, inhale slowly and deeply through the nose (the abdominal hand should rise, not the chest hand, showing that the air is expanding the abdominal cavity), and then ex-hale slowly. Second, after he has practiced and mastered abdominal breathing, teach him to inhale slowly and count backwards from 20 to 1 on each exhale. He should practice calming breathing daily.

Read His Own Body Cues

Teach your child that when he is stressed out, anxious or angry, differ-ent parts of his body are tightening, creating more tension and mak-ing it almost impossible for him to put on the brakes. Show him how to be aware and feel the symptoms of stress, such as a clenched fist, rigid jaw, fast breathing, scowl on his face, tight shoulders, hard stomach, etc. Teach him to use his calming breaths to relax those different parts of his body. Tell him that when he relaxes his body, he is better able to think clearly and plan what to do.

Read Social Cues

Impulsive children often miss those important social cues that provide feedback and help guide their interpersonal behavior. Teach your child how to pay attention to and read the body language of others. For example, show him that when other children back away, it may mean that he is standing too close and intruding on their space; that he should listen for a pause in the other person's conversation before he speaks; and if he notices people start to fidget and look around when he is talking, it may mean he has been talking too much; etc.

Visualize an Imaginary Bubble

Intruding on the space of others, especially grabbing things, is a common problem with younger, impulsive children. Teach your child to visualize an imaginary bubble around other people, and if he enters the bubble without permission, it will pop. Therefore, he must keep his appropriate distance and always ask before he can enter another person's "bubble."

Use "To Do" Lists

Encourage older children and adolescents to organize their day by writing a "to do" list the night before. They can check off each activity as it is completed, and/or at the end of the day they can review the list to see how well they did.

Estimate and Measure Time to Do Tasks

Impulsive children often underestimate the time it takes to do tasks. Consequently, they rush through tasks because they think it's taking too long, or they avoid the tasks all together because they think it will take "forever." It is important, therefore, for these children to develop more realistic expectations about the time needed to perform tasks correctly.

Before doing a task, ask your child to predict how long he thinks it will take him to do a good job. Tell him to record this estimation in his self-control journal or calendar. After he completes the task, ask him to measure how long it actually took and to compare his estimate with the actual time. This will teach him to more realistically manage his time and may also help him break larger tasks into smaller, more manageable ones. This technique is especially helpful for students who tend to put off or rush through their homework.

Teaching your child to develop more self-control is probably the most challenging and difficult hurdle in his behavior management. More than any other, this is the area where he may know what to do, but has difficulty doing it. Keep in mind that his difficulty arises from his neurologically-based deficit and not his "badness." Chapter 16 helps you focus more on your child's "goodness," thereby enhancing his self-control.

CHAPTER 16

"Catching Him Being Good"

Parents often come to parent training sessions and announce in surprise that their child did "a nice thing" or "did something well." When asked if they gave their child this positive feedback, they often reply that they didn't; it hadn't occurred to them.

Unwittingly, parents play a part in strengthening noncompliant, oppositional behaviors by over-focusing on their child's negative behaviors. For example, how many times have you been in a store with your child and he starts to fuss, drawing attention from other people? Out of your embarrassment, you tell him that if he quiets down and stops fussing, you will let him pick out some candy at the cash register on your way out. In this case, you unwittingly rewarded your child's negative behavior, increasing the chances that it will happen again next time.

Often, because the disruptive, noncompliant behaviors of the child with ADHD are so noticeable and frustrating, parents will give attention to this behavior by telling the child to stop it, by redirecting, arguing, or yelling. This negative attention can be reinforcing to the child, particularly if that is the way he gets most of his attention from his parents. Chances are, much of his positive behavior goes unnoticed because it is overshadowed by the high degree of negative behaviors.

In fact, **research shows that adults spend significantly less time paying attention to the positive behavior of children with ADHD.** The majority of interactions are negative, involving redirecting, controlling, or commanding.

Why Parents Give Negative Attention

There are at least three understandable reasons why parents of children with ADHD give a disproportionate amount of negative attention.

1. **"Let sleeping dogs lie"**

    Consider the following scenario:

    You have loaded up the kids in the car and set out on vacation. You've driven for 50 miles, and all of the sudden it dawns on you that the kids aren't fighting or teasing each other. In fact, they're playing nicely together. What do you do? Do you turn around and say to the kids, *"I really like how you are playing quietly and keeping your voices down,"* or do you say nothing?

    Chances are, most parents would not say anything for fear that if they did, the kids would start to act up. They believe it's best to "let sleeping dogs lie."

    Indeed, if the pattern of negative attention has progressed far enough, your child *would* more than likely act up if you said anything positive. Why? His learning history has taught him that the way to keep parents paying attention to him is to engage in negative behavior, to act up. He probably knows by now that if he behaves, it will go unnoticed, and what fun is that? But if he goofs off, he will get lots of attention from you. Chances are, if he continued to behave appropriately after you gave him some initial positive feedback, you would probably not give him much more attention. But you certainly would give him continued attention if he started to act up again. Attention is attention, and that's what kids want, whether it's positive or negative.

2. **The "negative alert"**

    You may not be as aware of your child's positive behavior because you have been conditioned to be on the alert for his negative behavior. This phenomenon is exemplified by the parent who recently exclaimed at a workshop, *"I don't notice the good behavior because there isn't any. He's always doing something wrong."*

    Of course it is not likely that your child does something wrong continuously throughout the day. It may seem like that, however, especially if you have a distorted perception of what is "good behavior." Behavior is not black or white; a child is neither "all good" nor "all bad." Behavior varies along a continuum, depending upon your child's mood, attitude, health, skill level, environment, task, etc. So, as we have come to understand with ADHD, your child is more likely to pay attention if a particular task is stimulating and has inherent interest for him. If your perception is that your child is "good" only if he pays attention well *all* of the time, your perception of "good" is distorted and unrealistic. When guided by such distorted perceptions or expectations, you likely will not *see* any "good" behavior. Any occurrence of "good" behavior will go unnoticed because it does not fit into your mindframe.

3. **Learned avoidance**

Parents often begin to avoid their child with ADHD so that they can avoid the inevitable conflict that always seems to ensue. They are reluctant to take their child on an outing, play a game, or do a joint project. As a result of spending less time with their child, parents may not witness the positive behavior when it occurs.

Unfortunately, this phenomenon seems more prevalent with fathers. Fathers have often confessed to me that they find themselves staying at work later or going to the health club more because they want to avoid the family conflicts that arise from their child with ADHD. Unfortunately, this escape method usually creates more conflict in the family. Mom gets worn down and becomes less effective from carrying most of the load, and the child gets resentful and acts out because he doesn't get enough time with Dad.

The Impact of Negative Attention

The over-focus on negative behavior begets a self-fulfilling prophecy. If a child is viewed negatively by others, he will eventually view himself negatively, and consequently he will act out this identity.

Also, if a child feels he is viewed negatively by someone, it affects his desire to cooperate with that person. Cooperation is replaced by resentment and hostility.

The foundation for building compliance and cooperation in your child with ADHD is to increase the positive attention you give him. The cycle of negative attention cannot be turned around until your child learns that cooperation is valued. You need to give attention to cooperation. Your child needs to be recognized within the family more for his *cooperation* than for his noncompliance.

Parents are usually unaware of how much negative attention they give their child each day. Likewise, they are usually unaware of how little *positive* attention they give their child. Imagine if you were to strap a tape recorder to your hip, record your interactions with your child throughout the day, and play it back at the end of the day. You might be surprised at the "quality" of your interactions with your child, not only in terms of *what* you said, but also *how* you said it. As parents, we tend to go through the day as if operating on "automatic pilot" with our pre-programmed, negative reactions to our children. We may be so conditioned in our responses that we're not even aware of what is regarded as positive versus negative attention.

It is important that you pay attention to what you say to your child throughout the day. Avoid red flag words that signal negative attention, such as:

- don't
- stop
- quit it
- don't forget
- you never
- you always
- why...
- if you don't...

Likewise, it is essential that you make a conscious effort to speak to your child in a way that conveys positive attention. Some examples are:

- I like the way you...
- That's nice that you...
- You must feel proud that you...
- You are really good at...
- Thanks for...
- It's a big help when you...
- I noticed that you... Good job!

Steps for Creating Positive Attention

To start the process of change, pay attention to your interactions with your child for one day, relating to him in your usual way. On a sheet of paper, make two columns; one labeled "negative" and the other labeled "positive." Record with hatch marks in the negative column each time you give your child negative attention. Make a hatch mark

in the positive column each time you give your child positive attention. Add up the number of hatch marks in each column at the end of
the day. What is the ratio of positive to negative? The ratio should be
at least 10 positive to 1 negative.

There are five steps for creating positive attention:

1. **Focus on "start" rather than "stop" behaviors**

   To increase your positive attention, you must know what to look
   for. First, think in terms of what you want your child to *start* doing
   instead of what you want your child to *stop* doing. For example, if
   you find yourself often frustrated because your child argues with
   you whenever you tell him "No," think of what you want him to
   start doing. If you want him to accept "No" without arguing, look
   for this and praise him when he does it.

2. **Pay attention to small gradations of the goal behavior**

   Second, pay attention to even *small gradations* of what you ultimately want your child to do. For example, if one of your ultimate,
   realistic goals is for your child to pick up after himself, give him
   positive feedback with every small step toward that goal, such as
   when he puts one thing away. This shaping technique will provide
   more opportunity to give your child positive feedback. Remember,
   form realistic expectations about your child's behavior and his ability to change. Don't expect huge changes overnight. Be satisfied
   with little steps.

3. **Give yourself a daily quota for positive attention**

   Another step to help you focus your attention toward the positive
   is to give yourself a *daily quota* for the number of times you will
   give positive feedback to your child. For example, your goal could
   be 10 times today. As a way to self-monitor, you could put a hand-
   ful of beans or buttons in one pocket and transfer a bean to the
   opposite pocket every time you give positive feedback to your child.

4. **Reward spontaneous positive behavior**

   An ultimate goal for any parent of a child with ADHD is that the
   child will eventually do what he is supposed to do without having
   to be asked. Although this is not a realistic goal for all of your
   child's behavior, it is important to give attention to this spontaneous positive behavior whenever it happens. Let your child know
   that you're going to be on the lookout for times when he does positive things without being told (for example, when he hangs up his

jacket without your reminding him). Tell him that when you see this behavior, you will award him some bonus points that he can save and cash in for a special reward.

5. **Spend regular special time with your child**

   As described above, parents gradually spend less time with their oppositional child. Consequently, there are fewer opportunities to observe positive behavior and give appropriate feedback. The child eventually learns that the way to get some attention and keep his parents engaged is to act up. Parents need to reverse this trend and re-establish a positive relationship with their child. To this end, it is very important for you to regularly schedule "special time" with your child. Special time involves spending brief but regularly scheduled one-on-one time with your child and doing something that he enjoys. Special time may be playing a board game, reading a new or favorite story, going out for a doughnut, sledding, building with Legos, baking cookies together, etc.

There are some important points to follow for special time:

- Let your child choose the activity, within reason. Don't attempt to overly direct his choice.

- Try to schedule at least one or two special times a week, for about 20 to 30 minutes each time.

- Plan the activity ahead of time so that your child can look forward to it and learn to count on it.

- Make all attempts to protect this planned special time and treat it as a commitment to your child.

- Don't involve other siblings in the special time, otherwise it loses its value for your child with ADHD. If you have other children, they may want their own special time. This isn't a bad idea. All children can benefit from their own special time with a parent.

- Special time should not involve expensive or extravagant activities. This should definitely be avoided. The focus should be on the *quality of the time* together, not the extravagance of the event. If you get caught in the trap of spending a lot or doing a lot, it will break the bank, you will grow to resent special time, and you will end up back in the cycle of avoiding time with your child.

- This time should be as nondirective as possible to provide an opportunity for each of you to enjoy each other. Therefore, don't give your child commands or make attempts to control or teach.

- Ignore any small occurrences of negative behavior during this time. However, if your child should act up, give him one warning. If he does not stop after 15 seconds, tell him that he has chosen to end special time, so it is terminated for the day. Tell him that you will try again next time. Ignore all protestations.

SUMMARY

- Unfortunately, adults tend to give more attention to the negative behavior than to the positive behavior of their child with ADHD. This negative attention reinforces the child's negative behavior.

- Parents tend to give a disproportionate amount of negative attention for three reasons: They're afraid if they compliment their child for good behavior, he will start to "act up"; parents have distorted perceptions of what constitutes "good behavior"; and parents don't often see their child's good behavior because they eventually start to avoid him.

- If a child is viewed negatively by others, he will eventually view himself negatively and act out this identity.

- There are five steps for creating positive attention: Focus on start rather than stop behaviors; pay attention to small gradations of the goal behavior; give yourself a daily quota for positive attention; reward spontaneous positive behavior; and spend regular special time with your child.

Devising Behavior Modification Systems

Behavior modification is a highly effective system that uses positive rewards or negative consequences to change or improve behavior. When it comes to using rewards with children, however, parents frequently tell me that they are philosophically opposed to bribing their child to get him to do what he's supposed to do. They worry that their child will come to expect a reward for everything he does. They have nightmares of starting out by giving their child candy for emptying the trash and ending up making monthly payments on a condo to get him to do his homework.

Certainly, if we were dealing with a child *without* ADHD, concerns about bribery and conditional compliance would be valid. However, when we consider the fact that ADHD is a neurobiologically-based disorder of motivation, the importance of reward takes on a different meaning.

Children with ADHD lack internal motivation to do many types of tasks because it is difficult to stay stimulated, work through frustration, organize the steps to accomplish the task, ignore distractions, control impatience, and maintain attention. They do not respond to consequences, positive or negative, in the same way as other children. Their behavior is not easily controlled by reward or punishment.

A child who is *not* ADHD may be intrinsically motivated to help around the house, do homework, and obey his parents because it makes him feel good, and he likes to accomplish things. He can even persist and stay motivated when he encounters obstacles or frustration. Sometimes, praise from his parents may be the only extra push he needs. For the child with ADHD, however, this is usually not the case. The intrinsic motivation is *not* there, or if it is there, only sporadically. The threat of negative consequences usually does not motivate him either. Parental praise is often not powerful enough to make a difference. The child's behavior is not easily regulated by consequences.

Given this deficit in *internal* motivation in children with **ADHD**, parents need to manufacture the motivation *externally*. It just takes more to move these kids! This is accomplished by using formal, behavior modification reward programs, in which the child earns points, chips, stars, etc., for positive behavior, which he can then exchange for a rewarding item, event or privilege. **This is not bribery, this is compensating for a deficit in motivation.**

TOKEN SYSTEM

The most effective behavior modification approach for children with ADHD is the token system. In this system, the child earns points, chips, stars, etc., for specific positive behavior. After the child has earned a predetermined number of points, he can then cash them in for a reward (or primary reinforcer). This system can be used with children as young as four years of age or as old as mid-adolescence. Children eight years and younger typically respond to earning such tokens as chips, stars or smiley faces. Children nine years and older tend to respond more to earning points or receiving ratings recorded on a chart or in a notebook.

Advantages of a token system

There are several advantages to using a token system:
- Tokens can be dispensed immediately, thereby providing the needed immediate feedback and reinforcement that these children need.

- Tokens allow the dispensing of the reward at a later and more convenient time. After the child earns his predetermined number of tokens, he can count them up and cash them in at the end of a time period or end of the day.

- Tokens reduce satiation. If you were to give your child a piece of candy after each positive behavior, he soon would become too full (or sick!). This doesn't happen with tokens.

- Tokens increase motivation. Remember that rewards often lose their potency sooner with children with ADHD. Tokens can be cashed in for a variety of desirable items or activities, providing more choice and greater stimulation value to the rewards. So, if your child is tired of working toward one particular reward, he can choose another from his reward menu. Reward menus are discussed later in this chapter and examples are provided in Appendix B.

Feedback and Consequences

Before we discuss how to set up a behavior modification program, let's review the unique way in which children with ADHD respond to consequences. Generally, they respond to feedback and consequences differently because of their neurobiologically-based deficit in motivation. Accordingly, changes need to be made in the way feedback and consequences are given. Knowing this will help you to avoid some of the common pitfalls of behavior modification.

- **More <u>immediate</u> feedback and consequences**

  Children with ADHD require more immediate feedback and consequences for their behavior than children without ADHD. Therefore, when using a point or token system, dispense the point or token to your child immediately after he engages in the target behavior. *"That's great that you brushed your teeth as soon as you were told. You just earned another point."* Waiting until you have more time or until the end of the day causes the system to lose its effectiveness.

- **More <u>frequent</u> feedback and consequences**

  Children with ADHD require more frequent feedback and consequences than do other children. Therefore, be sure to watch for every occurrence of the target behavior and reinforce it immediately *"You just earned another point for holding your thoughts until I was through speaking. That's five times already this morning."* If children with ADHD expect a reward or feedback for positive behavior and don't get it, their behavior often deteriorates quickly. Don't become too intrusive when giving feedback, however. If you make a big deal every time your child behaves appropriately, he may become annoyed.

- **More <u>consistent</u> feedback and consequences**

  Feedback and reinforcement must be delivered consistently over time, across settings and among people. Inconsistency in using a token system is one of the main reasons why this system may fail with a child with ADHD. If you reward your child with a token for his positive behavior on one occasion, then you must reward the same behavior every time you see it occur. *"I'm going to watch carefully and give you a point every time I see you play gently with the dog."* Inconsistent, unpredictable or erratic feedback or rewards will only disorganize, confuse and frustrate your child.

Likewise, once you start a behavior modification program, you must use it consistently across settings. This means you use it not only at home, but at Grandma's, when shopping, at restaurants, and at friends'. *"I'm going to be giving you points for controlling your temper when we visit Grandma's house, just like you earn points for this at home."* Your child needs to know that the same rules for behavior apply wherever he is.

Parents also need to be consistent between themselves when using a behavior modification program. *"Both Dad and I are going to give you points every time we see you control your temper."* It does no good for only the mother to use this system. This disparity tells your child that acceptable behavior is appropriate only with certain people.

- **More <u>interesting and tangible</u> consequences**

  Whereas verbal praise or an expression of affection may be powerful enough for the child without ADHD, the child with ADHD has reduced sensitivity to these types of consequences. Therefore, rewards or punishments may have to be larger (*not* more expensive), more obvious, and more directly linked to the likes and dislikes of your child. More substantial consequences may involve such things as special snacks, material rewards, money, special privileges, or a small toy. Here are some examples of rewards that children tend to like:

  - Play a board game with a parent
  - Bake cookies
  - Select special dessert
  - Make popcorn
  - Stay up 15 minutes later
  - Rent a video
  - Rent a video game
  - Have a sleepover
  - Get to skip a certain chore
  - Earn a comic book
  - Lunch at a fast food restaurant
  - Have a friend over for dinner
  - Go to a movie
  - Buy a CD

DEVISING A HOME BEHAVIOR MODIFICATION PROGRAM

A behavior modification program at home can achieve significant results for many children — provided it is designed and implemented according to the following parameters.

Step 1: Select an appropriate goal

The first step is to select an appropriate goal or goals. Include your child in this process if he is six years or older because you will be more likely to get his vested interest, thereby increasing the chances for success.

There are four critical points to consider when selecting your goals:

- **Positive goals.** Choose a behavior you would like your child to *start doing* rather than *stop doing*. For example, if your child is often interrupting others at the dinner table, choose as your goal to *increase waiting before he speaks* rather than to *decrease interrupting*. Or, if your child often forgets to make his bed in the morning, choose as your goal that he *make his bed*. Choosing a positive goal is especially important for children with ADHD because they get so much negative attention to begin with. If you choose a negative goal (such as to *decrease* your child's arguing) you are now looking for the negative; essentially increasing your negative attention to him. We have already learned that excessive negative attention leads to excessive negative behavior.

  Sometimes it's difficult to think of goals in terms of the positive. To help you do this, let's go back to the "bug list" strategy, that is, list the things your child does that "bug" you. This includes the undesirable behaviors that you would like to see your child *stop* doing as well as the things around the house that he fails to do. For example, you would like him to stop arguing when you tell him "No" or make his bed before he goes to school.

  In the right-hand column, write down the positive alternative for each item on the "bug list." The positive alternative for the first behavior would be to *accept "No,"* and the positive alternative for the second behavior would be to *make his bed*. Choose your goals from the right-hand column. Following is an example of this two-column technique.

NEGATIVE BEHAVIOR	POSITIVE BEHAVIOR
Interrupts	Waits before talking
Refuses to do his homework	Starts his homework without fussing
Rushes carelessly through his work	Works carefully and accurately
Reacts to frustration by hitting or name-calling	Walks away and ignores
Argues when told "No"	Accepts "No" without arguing
Whines when asking for something	Uses a respectful voice with parents
Argues and grabs when playing games	Waits his turn and keeps hands to self
Leaves his dirty dishes on the table	Brings his dishes to the sink
Doesn't feed the goldfish	Feeds the goldfish
Refuses to take a shower	Takes a shower without fussing
Doesn't make his bed	Makes his bed
Doesn't brush his teeth	Brushes his teeth
Refuses to go to bed	Goes to bed when told

- **Limited goals.** Begin intervention with only one or two goals and add new ones slowly. Given the many problems that children with ADHD have, the inclination is to work on many behaviors simultaneously in order to improve behavior quickly. This will only overwhelm your child and increase the chances for failure.

- **Reinforcement at a level of success.** When initiating a behavior modification program, it is very important to begin at a level where your child can achieve success immediately. Success builds upon success. Setting a goal too high will prevent your child from experiencing success soon enough, and he will give up.

At first, your child should be rewarded for only small improvements in behavior. You can gradually "up the ante" as your child begins to feel successful. This process is called *shaping* because you are gradually shaping your child's behavior to reach the ultimate or big goal. For example, let's assume your goal is that your child play cooperatively with his sister. Currently, he pushes, bosses and yells almost every time he plays with her. It's not realistic to set as your goal that he must go through the whole week without conflict with his sister before he is rewarded. In this case, it would be more effective to reinforce him if he plays cooperatively for 10 minutes or perhaps for two short play periods a day. Gradually, you can increase the length of the play period, perhaps from 10 minutes to 15 minutes, then from 15 minutes to 20 minutes, and so on. Increase the goal, however, only after he has achieved consistent success at the lower level.

It is also important to break down larger goals into smaller, more achievable ones so that your child experiences success early on. For example, perhaps your desire is for your child to get better grades, and his grades right now are mostly D's. It's unrealistic to set as your goal that he will get A's or even B's right away (given his organizational difficulties and forgetfulness, he probably doesn't know how to achieve this goal). There are a number of intervening steps between low grades and reaching the honor roll. A better place to start is that he record his assignments in a notebook and then bring his schoolwork home every day. He should earn points and be rewarded for doing so. From there, the goal could be that he completes his assignments and hands them in every day. These are logical first steps that are more achievable and that help him eventually achieve the goal of good grades.

- **Short-term goals.** Children with ADHD have great difficulty working for long-term goals. They will usually lose focus, persistence and motivation before they ever reach their goal. Avoid beginning with goals that can only be reached after a number of weeks. For example, allowing your child to receive his reward after he earns 200 points when he averages only about five points a day will be too long term, and he will likely give up before he's reached his goal.

In the beginning, it's more effective to establish a *daily* goal and an *end-of-the-week* goal. For example, his daily goal may be to comply with his parents on the first request at least three times a day. If he meets his daily goal, he receives a small reward, perhaps the chance to play his favorite board game with Dad. His end-of-the-week goal could be to achieve his daily goal at least three out of the seven days. If he reaches his end-of-the-week goal, he chooses a larger reward, such as renting a video. The end-of-the week goal is important because it motivates your child to "keep up the good work" throughout the entire week.

Step 2: Determine how to measure the target behavior(s)

The target behavior can be measured by monitoring *individual occurrences* (frequency monitoring) of the target behavior or by monitoring *intervals of time* (interval monitoring) in which the behavior may occur.

Frequency monitoring is used to record behaviors that can be counted and that have a clearly definable beginning and end. Examples include: the number of times your child brings his homework home; the number of times your child accepts "No" from you without arguing; the number of times your child complies after the first request.

Interval monitoring is used with any behavior that happens over a period of time rather than in a single occurrence. Consequently, you monitor your child's behavior during an entire time period to see if he engages in the positive behavior. Examples of interval monitoring include: observing whether your child plays quietly in the house when friends are over; observing whether your child plays gently with his baby brother during play periods; or observing whether your child speaks respectfully to you when guests are in the home.

Step 3: Select the tokens to be used

The third step in devising an effective program is to decide what kind of token system you will use. Possible tokens can include marbles in a jar, stars or points on a chart, or chips or tickets in a bank. Be sure the token is age appropriate for your child. If tangible tokens such as marbles or tickets are used with very young children, keep them in jars away from your child to avoid swallowing or losing them. If more than one child in your family is earning some kind of token in a jar, give each child a different color. For example, Matt only gets red chips and Sarah only gets blue chips. Older children are often embarrassed by stars on a chart and may respond better to earning tickets, points or ratings on a 1 to 5 scale.

Step 4: Determine the rewards and cost in tokens

Sit down with your child and decide together what he will work for as his rewards. You may find that a certain reward works for a while, but then your child loses interest in it, and it is no longer reinforcing. This means you have to change the rewards relatively frequently.

A reward menu is an effective way to vary the rewards and to keep your child engaged in working toward his goals. A reward menu lists the various privileges or activities your child has chosen to work for and the value in tokens for each item.

The reward menu should contain about five to ten items, privileges or activities. A few should be short-term rewards for which your child will have to pay only a few tokens, such as having a special dessert, baking cookies, or getting to skip a certain chore. Some should be mid-term rewards that require more tokens, such as going to bed 30 minutes late, having a friend over for dinner, or renting a video. The rest of the privileges or activities should be bigger rewards which require the most tokens, such as contributing money toward an outfit, going to a movie, or having a sleepover.

Here's an example of a reward menu.

Item	Cost in Tokens
• Select special dessert	5
• Play a board game with a parent	5
• Make popcorn	5
• Earn a baseball card	5
• Bake cookies	10
• Get to skip a certain chore	10
• Stay up 30 minutes later	20
• Lunch at a fast food restaurant	20
• Have a friend over for dinner	20
• Rent a video	30
• Rent a video game	30
• Buy a CD	40
• Contribute money toward an outfit	40
• Have a sleepover	50
• Go to a movie	50

Step 5: Devise the recording system to monitor progress

Devise your recording system or chart for keeping track of your child's progress toward his goal(s). Your child may enjoy helping you design this. Keep the chart openly visible to your child throughout the day so that he can see how he is doing on an ongoing basis. A favorite place for charts tends to be the kitchen refrigerator. The system should be logistically realistic and not cumbersome, or you will be less likely to follow through. Some examples of charts are included in Appendix B.

WHAT ABOUT SIBLINGS?

Parents often ask how they deal with siblings who are upset because they are not getting special treats for their positive behavior. The best way to respond is to put them on a token system as well. Even children without ADHD can work on some aspect of their behavior.

BONUS POINTS

Although you don't want to set goals that are too high, you also don't want to inadvertently encourage "just getting by" when your child could actually perform better than his goal. To motivate your child past "just getting by," offer bonus points for performing past the set goal. For example, if the goal is to make his bed four out of seven days, award your child bonus points for every additional day that he makes his bed. Children often enjoy saving up bonus points to earn a bigger, more long-term reward.

RESPONSE COST

Children with ADHD are usually most successful with a combination of positive reinforcement and response cost. Response cost means that your child loses points or tokens that he previously earned if he commits an infraction. Response cost is most effective if your child loses approximately one-tenth to one-fifth of what was earned. For example, if he earned five points for accepting "No" without arguing, he loses one point for arguing when he is told "No."

MODIFIED RESPONSE COST

In Chapter 14 we discussed modified response cost. Because children with ADHD have histories of not earning rewards, they are often more motivated when they are working to keep what they already have rather than earning something they don't have. Try providing your child with the entire reward in points or tokens at the start of the day. He must then work to keep the points. Every time he breaks one of the agreed-upon rule(s), he loses a certain number of points. At the end of the day, he's given whatever is left. With this system there is the possibility that your child may end up "owing the bank." If this happens, it may be good to allow him opportunities to earn bonus points so that he can crawl out of the hole and consequently maintain his motivation.

PROFILES OF BEHAVIOR MODIFICATION AT WORK

Following are two case studies that profile how two sets of parents established specific target behaviors for their children with ADHD; set up the behavior modification systems; and successfully used the systems to manage the chosen target behaviors. The first case involves an interval monitoring system (monitoring behavior over time). The second case involves the more common, frequency monitoring system (monitoring individual occurrences of behavior).

CASE 1: "You're Not The Boss of Me"

Kevin was a 5-year-old boy with ADHD, Predominantly Hyperactive-Impulsive Type. He had a 2-year-old sister, Sue. Kevin's parents, Lynn and Dick, came to me for help in learning how to control their son's rambunctious, defiant, overly aggressive and bossy behavior. Kevin clearly had excessive difficulty regulating his behavior and his emotions, even for a 5-year-old. He rarely sat still long enough to color pictures or read books. He definitely preferred gross-motor activities like riding his bike, playing tag, kicking a ball, or speeding down a slide. His parents learned early that they couldn't take him to church or to restaurants because he would run around, make noises, or complain loudly that he wanted to go. He rarely did what his parents asked him to do without protesting, whining or yelling. He was still having tantrums at the age of five. He seemed unable to handle any degree of frustration, and an uncooperative toy usually ended up being thrown against the wall. If a parent tried to intervene, his frustration usually spiraled to ballistic proportions.

Although this behavior was exasperating enough, Kevin's parents were especially concerned about his relationship with his young sister. Before his sister was born, Kevin was the only child and the only grandchild on both sides of the family. He had grown accustomed to basking in all the attention that this privileged position bestowed upon him.

When Sue arrived on the scene, Kevin was not thrilled. Although he often said he loved his sister, his actions suggested otherwise to his parents. His favorite sister activity was to squeeze her head like a tomato whenever he gave her a "kiss." It was hard for Kevin to gauge the strength of his actions with his sister or to put the brakes on his own rambunctiousness. Consequently, he usually squeezed too hard, tickled too much, grabbed too strongly, held too tightly, and bumped into her too often.

True to form for **ADHD**, Kevin was exceptionally competitive, and he didn't like to share or lose. It was bad enough that he had to share his mom and dad with this short intruder, but to share his toys? This usually called for swift action on his part, like a bonk on the head and a push for good measure. Lynn and Dick were afraid to leave Kevin alone in the same room with his sister for fear she'd be flattened — either on purpose or unintentionally.

Lynn and Dick were also exasperated with Kevin's refusal to obey. It seemed as though it didn't matter what they asked him to do; he loudly refused with the indignant exclamation, "You're not the boss of me!" Kevin acted as though he had elevated himself to the position of parent, and his parents had lost their parental authority over their son. He routinely refused to brush his teeth, go to bed, put his toys away, come inside and eat, lower his voice, or turn off the TV.

Kevin's parents also lamented that their son did not understand the meaning of the word "No," especially when he wanted something. He had perfected the art of badgering and would not let up until his parents gave in, which they usually did in order to get some peace and quiet.

Understandably, Lynn and Dick were thoroughly frustrated and worn down. Clearly, there was a lot of work to do to turn Kevin's behavior around. The behavior management program for Kevin involved many components, beginning with Lynn and Dick: clarifying their expectations for Kevin's behavior given his ADHD; teaching them the art of positive attention, positive feedback, and positive redirection; helping them understand what situations/conditions seemed to set off Kevin and then acting proactively to avoid or modify these situations; scheduling regular special time for each parent; changing the structure in the house so that there were consistent schedules and routines, including the same bedtime ritual every night, regular snacks and mealtimes, reading times, and playtimes; and learning how to give effective commands. We also used *1-2-3: Magic*[1] for STOP behaviors ("Stop badgering") and START behaviors ("Come into the house for dinner"). *1-2-3: Magic!* is explained in depth in Chapter 18.

Step 1: Select an appropriate goal

I asked Lynn and Dick to follow the two-column technique so that we could decide on appropriate positive target behavior(s). Their "bug lists" (negative behaviors) and corresponding positive behaviors looked like this:

NEGATIVE BEHAVIOR	POSITIVE BEHAVIOR
Leaves his toys scattered	Picks up his toys
Hits, pushes and grabs when playing with his sister	Plays gently with his sister
Makes up stories	Tells the truth
Refuses to go to bed	Goes to bed at bedtime
Reacts to frustration by hitting or name-calling	Controls his temper
Argues when told "No"	Accepts "No" without arguing
Grabs when playing games	Keeps his hands to himself
Slams doors	Closes doors quietly
Bosses his playmates	Lets friends choose activities
Interrupts when parents are talking	Waits to talk
Refuses to share his toys	Shares his toys
Refuses to get dressed in the morning	Gets dressed in the morning

Given the level of Lynn and Dick's frustration and their desire to change Kevin's behavior fast, it was understandable that they wanted to tackle all of the behaviors in this right-hand column at the same time. However, setting many goals at the beginning would have overwhelmed Kevin and likely increased his defiance. Also, monitoring, charting and reinforcing a number of behaviors all at once would have been logistically cumbersome for Kevin's parents.

We chose as the target behavior: *Kevin will play gently with his sister.* This behavior was chosen first because of his parents' understandable concern for the safety of their daughter. Although we speculated that some of Kevin's rough behavior with his sister was fueled by possible feelings of displacement, it was also clear that he had diffi-culty putting the brakes on his over-rambunctious behavior. He sim-ply did not know when to stop. We also speculated that if Kevin learned to play harmoniously with his sister, there potentially could be some secondary benefits: he would get more positive attention from his par-ents; he would learn a degree of interpersonal self-control; and he would learn that his position in the family was secure even with a younger sister.

After the target behavior was selected, it was now important to specifically state the goal. Lynn and Dick estimated that Kevin tended to play aggressively with Sue almost every time he played with her, which was about ten times a day. Given this high rate of negative be-havior, it was critical that we start the goal at a level where Kevin could achieve success early on. Therefore, we stated as our specific goal: *Kevin will play gently with his sister at least once a day.*

After determining his daily goal, we focused on Kevin's weekly goal. Remember, a weekly goal is important as a means to sustain your child's behavior throughout the week. This double-reward system increases the power of reinforcement that is essential for children with ADHD. Not only does he earn a daily reward for good behavior, but if he can keep it up for a week, he also earns a bigger end-of-the-week reward.

Given Kevin's high rate of negative behavior with his sister, we again chose a weekly goal that we thought he could obtain fairly soon: *Kevin will achieve his daily goal (i.e., play gently with his sister) at least four times in one week.* These four acts of positive behavior could oc-cur over four separate days, or Kevin could engage in the positive behavior four times in one day or over two, three, four days, etc. It didn't matter.

It is of no use to establish a behavioral goal for your child if he doesn't know how to engage in the positive target behavior. In this case, Kevin's parents had to be sure Kevin knew what it meant to play gently. Once Kevin's behavioral goal was established, there-fore, his parents sat down with him to explain their concerns and share their wish that he and his sister could play gently together. Lynn and Dick were careful not to send the message to Kevin that he was a bad boy or that everything was his fault. They talked about his feelings about being a big brother and how it felt to have to share his mom and dad. They asked him if he knew what it meant to play gently with his sister, and they supplemented his response with concrete examples. They told him playing gently meant keep-ing his hands to himself; kissing his sister only if she said it was okay; touching her softly; letting her play with her own toys without grabbing them away from her; stopping when she said stop; not tickling, teasing, pushing, or hitting her. They spent some time role-playing with Kevin to show him what they meant.

Step 2: Determine how to measure the target behavior(s)

Lynn and Dick were somewhat confused about how to measure Kevin's play behavior with his sister. Were they to keep track of how many times he kissed her without squeezing her head? Or were they to monitor how many times he played with Sue without drawing blood? It would be difficult to monitor and reinforce the many individual positive behaviors that could occur during a play period. Therefore, *frequency monitoring* was not the best way to measure this target behavior. Because *playing gently with his sister* was something that occurred over a time period rather than something that occurred individually or in an instance, it was more appropriate to use *interval monitoring*. That is, Kevin would be rewarded for his behavior if he engaged in the positive target behavior for a specified interval of time, for example, a play period of 10 minutes. Lynn and Dick decided to use an interval monitoring system whereby they would monitor Kevin's gentle behavior with his sister for play periods of 10 minutes. We kept the initial interval to 10 minutes because we wanted Kevin to succeed. Success builds upon success. Failure breeds failure.

Step 3: Select the tokens to be used

Given Kevin's young age, we chose to use stars on a chart as the token. Kevin's mother purchased different colored self-adhesive stars at her local office supply store. To make it even more rewarding for Kevin, he was allowed to choose the color of the stars he wanted to put on his chart each time he reached his goal. He loved the look of alternating colors on his chart, so this was an additional motivator for him.

Step 4. Determine the rewards and cost in tokens

The token and reward system had to be simple and appropriate for Kevin's developmental level. Children five years of age are generally too young for a multi-item reward menu because they don't yet understand the concepts of cost or money. We allowed Kevin to select from just a few items, all equaling the value of one star (token), which he received every time he reached his daily goal, i.e., played gently with his sister for 10 minutes.

It was also important to discuss with Kevin what he wanted to earn as his possible rewards. Especially given his issues with control, it was essential that he felt like a partner in this program rather than a subordinate who had no input. After some discussion, Kevin and his parents agreed upon two rewards:

- popcorn
- Mom or Dad read him a story

Every time he played gently with his sister for a period of 10 minutes, he could choose either one. We limited the number of choices because children at this age can become overwhelmed if given too many choices.

Kevin also chose his end-of-the-week goal, which he earned if he played gently with his sister at least four times in one week. He chose to go to his favorite fast food restaurant with Mom or Dad, *without* his sister.

Step 5. Devise the recording system to monitor progress

Kevin and his mother worked together on making his star chart. It consisted of a sidewalk divided into four sections or grids. Every section of the sidewalk represented a play period of 10 minutes. At the end of the sidewalk was a drawing of a hamburger and french fries, representing Kevin's end-of-the-week goal of lunch. Every time Kevin played gently with his sister for 10 minutes, he earned a star on a section of the sidewalk. If he earned four stars by the end of the week, the sidewalk would be filled up, and he got his weekly reward. Kevin's parents chose Saturday as the end-of-the-week day. Therefore, if Kevin made his end-of-the-week goal, both he and his parents knew that Saturday was the day.

After Kevin reached his daily and end-of-the-week goals, and sustained them for three weeks, we upped the ante. The daily goal was increased to 15-minute play periods, and the end-of-the-week goal was increased to at least six times in one week. As time progressed, it was also necessary to change the daily rewards because Kevin was no longer motivated by popcorn or a story. Other daily rewards included a game with Dad and chocolate pudding for dessert. Lunch out with Mom and Dad, however, continued to be a favorite reward.

Kevin's Chart

DAILY GOAL: Kevin will play gently with his sister at least once a day.

WEEKLY GOAL: Kevin will play gently with his sister at least 4 times a week.

The daily and end-of-the-week goals were gradually increased as Kevin's play behavior improved. After about four months on this program, Kevin was able to play with his sister with relatively few incidents.

CASE 2: "The Morning Routine"

Nine-year-old Stephanie was diagnosed with ADHD, Predominantly Inattentive Type. She was Peg and Tim's youngest child. Her parents reported that their biggest frustration with Stephanie was her apparent inability or refusal to follow through with anything. They had come to learn that if they told their daughter to do something, it would be half done, if at all. Tim stated that she operated as if her "receiver was off the hook" because nothing seemed to register. One of their frustrations was convincing Stephanie that she needed to write down her homework assignments. No matter how many times they told her to use her assignment notebook, it wouldn't happen. Consequently, assignments were often forgotten or missing. Even when she did bring homework home, it was a recurring battle to get her to finish any of it. When she was supposed to be doing her homework in her bedroom, she usually spent that time daydreaming or doodling on her notebook. After an hour, very little homework was completed. Being grounded, losing TV time, or getting a bad grade did not seem to make a difference.

Stephanie's parents lamented that she seemed unable to follow through with even the easy stuff. After repeated reminders to pick up her backpack, feed the dog, set the table, empty the trash, or turn off the lights when she left a room, they rarely got done.

Another big hassle was the morning routine. Stephanie just could not seem to get out of bed, get groomed and dressed, eat breakfast, and get out the door in time for school. She often missed the bus in the morning so Peggy had to drive her. Peggy complained that she dreaded mornings because they usually escalated into shouting matches. She admitted that she became very anxious during these brawls, worried that the conflict would get drawn out too long and Stephanie would miss her bus. Peggy didn't want to end up driving Stephanie to school because that only reinforced her dawdling behavior. Peggy sighed that she always felt guilty send-ing her young daughter off to school when she was so upset; she worried that it would affect her whole school day.

We followed the five-step process to set up Stephanie's program.

Step 1: Select an appropriate goal

Peggy and Tim constructed their "bug list" and corresponding positive behaviors:

NEGATIVE BEHAVIOR	POSITIVE BEHAVIOR
Doesn't write down assignments	Writes down assignments
Forgets to make her bed	Makes her bed in the morning
Forgets to feed the dog	Feeds the dog twice a day
Doesn't bring her dirty clothes to the laundry room	Brings her clothes to the laundry room daily
Doesn't put her clothes away	Puts her clothes away in the right places
Refuses to wash her face	Washes her face in the morning and at night
Doesn't brush her teeth	Brushes her teeth after meals
Gets up late	Gets up when told
Misses the school bus in the morning	Makes the school bus
Yells at parents	Uses respectful tone of voice with parents
Argues when told "No"	Accepts "No" without arguing

Even though Peggy and Tim's initial complaint was about Stephanie's failure to bring home her assignments, they realized that the majority of negative behaviors on their list involved the morning routine. Therefore, that's where they agreed to focus their behavior management program.

Before we set up the program, we analyzed the morning situation to determine whether there were any factors or circumstances which interfered with Stephanie following through with the morning rou-tine. These situations would have to be changed or controlled before we set up the program. As we discussed the morning scenario in more detail, a number of situational problems came to light.

Stephanie was expected to get up by 7:00 to make the 7:45 bus. However, Stephanie's father had already left for work by then, and her mother didn't get up until 7:15. The expectation was that Stephanie would get herself up at 7:00 and begin the morning tasks without supervision. This is an unrealistic expectation for a 9-year-old child with ADHD. Remember, if we consider the impact of her ADHD on her level of responsibility, we should subtract about 30 percent from her chronological age and base our expectations on that adjusted age. Consequently, her ability to follow through with the morning self-help tasks was more like that of a 6-year-old. Also, given that children with ADHD tend to have poor time management skills and become disorganized by time pressures, allowing only 35 minutes to complete the morning routine and get on the bus was not enough.

Peggy also reported that when she did get up, she usually found Stephanie watching TV rather than getting ready for school. Of course, the television is much more stimulating than the prospect of washing one's face and going to school. It's guaranteed that Stephanie would gravitate toward the TV, and it became an entertaining way to avoid doing an unpleasant task such as brushing her teeth.

Further, it turned out that neither Stephanie nor her mother tended to do any preparation the night before for the following school day. Consequently, there was a mad rush each morning to cram in many tasks in a short period of time.

Based on this situational analysis, we made the following changes before we initiated the behavior modification program. Peggy agreed to be up and dressed before Stephanie was expected to get up. Although Peggy liked to press her snooze alarm and sleep in those few extra minutes, she realized that she needed to be ready, calm and available to supervise her daughter on an ongoing basis. Peggy and Tim also agreed that Stephanie needed to get up 20 minutes earlier to allow her to move at her relatively slower pace and still have time to accomplish all she needed to do.

Stephanie's parents also changed the role of the TV from a distraction to a reward. Stephanie was allowed to watch TV only *after* she completed all of the morning routine. Her mother would set a kitchen timer to signal when the TV had to be turned off to get Stephanie out the door. Stephanie and her parents also agreed to do more preparation the night before to alleviate the morning time crunch. This involved preparing Stephanie's cold lunch; selecting her outfit for the next day and hanging it on the outside of her closet; putting Stephanie's homework and any other necessary books or materials in her backpack; and placing the backpack by the back door where she left in the morning.

Following these changes, we proceeded to set up the behavior modification program.

Peggy and Tim stated that they had two goals: 1) they wanted to eliminate the morning arguments and send their daughter off to school with a calm and positive attitude, and 2) they wanted their daughter to get to the bus on time. They estimated that Stephanie tended to miss the bus an average of two to three times a week. The two situations were related; if Stephanie didn't complete the morning routine on time, she missed the bus. Therefore, the two goals were stated in the following way: (1) Stephanie would follow the morning routine, and (2) Stephanie would get to the bus on time.

Peggy and Tim agreed wholeheartedly (with Stephanie agreeing somewhat more reluctantly) that she should meet her goal of getting to the bus on time every school day. That is, Stephanie had to meet the bus on time five days out of five. Stephanie's parents were concerned that if they chose a lesser goal, such as four out of five days, Stephanie would view this as license to miss the bus once a week. Completing the morning routine was somewhat more complicated to figure out. We discuss it in the next step.

Step 2: Determine how to measure the target behavior(s)

Measuring whether or not Stephanie got to the bus on time was fairly straightforward; if she got on the bus before it took off, she met her goal; if she missed her bus, she did not meet her goal. Measuring whether she completed the morning routine was somewhat more complicated. There were many steps involved in completing the morning routine so that Stephanie *could* catch the bus on time. This routine made significant demands on her organization, memory and self-regulation — those skills that were challenged by her ADHD. This complicated goal had to be broken down into its component steps, and Stephanie would have to be reinforced in some way if she completed the steps. Therefore, we had to determine the steps involved.

We consulted with Stephanie and, in the process, her parents made an eye-opening discovery. Stephanie was fairly clueless about what was expected of her in the morning or what necessary steps were involved in getting out the door on time! She clearly was disorganized, and her parents were beginning to realize that Stephanie's problem was fundamentally ADHD-related rather than laziness or lack of caring. After Stephanie and her parents consulted, they agreed upon the following steps:

1) get out of bed at 6:40
2) make the bed
3) get dressed
4) wash face
5) brush teeth
6) comb hair
7) pick up room
8) bring dirty clothes to the laundry room
9) eat breakfast
10) put on shoes, coat, backpack, etc.
11) out the door at 7:40

It was decided that Stephanie would be monitored to see if she completed each of the steps above. This is a frequency monitoring system because her mother was monitoring Stephanie to see if she engaged in the individual target behaviors, e.g., out of bed at 6:40, wash face, etc. There were a total of 11 steps involved in the morning routine.

Peggy and Tim questioned whether they had to be so strict as to demand that their daughter complete all 11 steps all the time. After all, they estimated that at the present time she probably completed the entire morning routine only about two days out of five. We agreed that there had to be some room for flexibility and that we had to set her up to succeed. Consequently, we did not want to set the goal too high. We also acknowledged the fact that much of the arguing between Stephanie and Peggy in the morning resulted because Peggy was insisting that her daughter do all of the 11 steps, and Stephanie had a hard time doing them.

I asked Stephanie and her parents which of the 11 steps seemed to be the most difficult for Stephanie to complete. They agreed that the hardest steps were getting out of bed on time, making her bed, and bringing her clothes to the laundry room. We discussed the fact that it was critical that she get out of bed at 6:40 because it affected all the other steps. Stephanie's mother was also adamant that her daughter make her bed in the morning. Bringing her clothes to the laundry room, however, was not as critical. Therefore, we agreed to allow some flexibility with the dirty clothes but not with making the bed and getting up on time.

Next, we determined Stephanie's daily goal. Everyone agreed that she had to complete at least the mandatory 10 of the 11 steps in the morning routine. She would earn one point for each step completed.

The only step that was not mandatory was bringing her dirty clothes to the laundry room. Also, Stephanie was now going to be required to get on the bus every day, no flexibility was allowed for this one. She earned one point each time she got on the bus on time. Totaled together, the number of points she needed to earn in one day was 11 (one point for getting on the bus and 10 points for completing each mandatory step of the morning routine). Therefore, her *daily goal* was to earn 11 points. She could choose a small reward if she earned her 11 points in one day.

We also determined the end-of-the week goal that would motivate Stephanie to get through the week. Since she completed the morning routine only two days out of five before the start of this program, we decided that we would up the ante only slightly, by requiring Stephanie to complete the morning routine three out of five days. Therefore, her *end-of-the week goal* was to complete the morning routine 3 out of 5 days (totaling 30 points), and get on the bus five out of five days (totaling five points) for a weekly total of 35 points. This meant that she could choose an end-of-the-week reward if she earned at least 35 points by the end of the week. If she earned fewer than 35 points, she did not earn an end-of-the-week reward.

To encourage Stephanie to work a bit harder, she was allowed to earn bonus points. She could save up the bonus points to purchase a bigger reward. The bigger reward could only be purchased with bonus points, not daily points. Bonus points could be earned in the following ways:

Bring dirty clothes to the laundry room = 1 bonus point
Complete the morning routine 4/5 days = 2 bonus points
Complete the morning routine 5/5 days = 4 bonus points

Step 3: Select the tokens to be used

Stephanie felt she was too old for stars or smiley faces on a chart, and she didn't want to keep track of chips. She chose to go the more sophisticated route of recording her daily points on a calendar chart.

Step 4: Determine the rewards and cost in tokens

Stephanie liked the idea of cashing in points for special privileges or activities. She devised a reward menu with her parents:

If Meet Daily Goal :	Cost in Daily Points:
Watch a favorite TV show	11
Play a board game with Mom or Dad	11

If Meet End-Of-Week Goal:	
Rent a video	35
Mom fix favorite meal	35

If Earn Bonus Points:	Cost in Bonus Points:
Movie at a theater	20
Have a friend sleep over	20
Order Pizza	15
Have a friend over for dinner	15
Ice cream treat	10
Mom cook popcorn	10
Stay up 30 minutes later	5
Skip a household chore	5

Step 5: Devise the recording system to monitor progress

Stephanie decided to keep her chart in her room, but her mom took responsibility for recording the points. The total points for the morning routine were entered on the calendar each day, as well as points for getting to the bus. Any bonus points earned were also recorded. At the end of each day and at the end of the week, she added her total daily, end-of-the-week and bonus points.

Stephanie responded to this approach and improved her morning behavior. She liked the idea of not having to complete all of the steps to the morning routine, and it gave her an appropriate sense of control. Ironically, because now it was her choice and not her mother's demand that she bring her dirty clothes to the laundry room, she started to do this almost every morning. Receiving bonus points helped motivate her.

As Stephanie's behavior continued to improve, the goals were increased. After four weeks of success, she was expected to complete the morning routine every morning and make the bus on time. Stephanie usually missed the morning bus only about once a month. Because Stephanie had achieved success with the positive reinforcement system, it was appropriate to now add a punishment component to the system to get her on the bus every morning. Consequently, it was decided that Stephanie would have to pay her mother cab fare for those mornings that she had to drive Stephanie to school.

Stephanie's Chart

	Mon	Tues	Wed	Th	Fri
Get on bus					
Out of bed by 6:40					
Make bed					
Get dressed					
Wash face					
Brush teeth					
Comb hair					
Pick up room					
Clothes to laundry room					
Eat breakfast					
Shoes, coat, backpack					
Out the door by 7:40					

Total Daily Points   _____ _____ _____ _____ _____   _____ Total wkly Points

Daily Bonus Points   _____ _____ _____ _____ _____   _____ Total wkly Bonus Points

If It's Not Working

If you find that your system is not working, consider the following possibilities:

- You may have overlooked some critical steps in your goal. For example, if your goal is that your child complete his homework, and he's still not doing it, you may have overlooked some of the steps required to accomplish this goal. Does your child have a homework assignment book? Are assignments written in it and initialed by the teacher? Does he have all the materials and books he needs? What time of day does he do his homework? What room is he in when he does it? Do you check in with him frequently to see if he is on task and tracking? Are large homework assignments broken down into smaller chunks? Is he allowed some stretch breaks to wake him up when he's bored? You need to organize and monitor these steps and not assume that your child can do so on his own.

- You have too many goals. If you are asking your child to work on many goals at the same time, he may become overwhelmed, confused or defiant because he's feeling over-controlled.

- The system is too loose. That is, you may not be providing reinforcement to your child frequently enough. If your system is set up so that your child earns a reward after a relatively long period of time, he may not be able to hang in there long enough to earn the reward; if so, tighten it up. Revise the system so that he is rewarded more frequently.

- Your child is not part of the feedback loop. Don't fall into the pattern of marking points on your child's behavior chart, but failing to tell him when he's earned a point. Remember, these kids need ongoing feedback about their performance.

- The reward is not rewarding. Do you know what rewards your child wants to earn? Also, he may lose interest in working toward the chosen reward(s) after a while, so be prepared to revise the reward menu.

- You're inconsistent. If you make a commitment to use this system, be consistent. Don't promise to reward your child for reaching a goal, and then put off or not get around to giving him the reward. Don't monitor his behavior one day and not the next, or forget to mark his chart.

- Both parents aren't using the system. If only one parent is following through with the system, your child will be confused or learn that the goal behaviors aren't that important.

SUMMARY

- Since children with ADHD often lack internal motivation, parents have to provide the motivation externally. Formal behavior modification reward programs are one way to do this.

- The most effective behavior modification approach is the token system, in which the child earns points, chips, stars or tokens for specific positive behaviors and then exchanges them for a reward.

- Children with ADHD respond to feedback and consequences differently because of their neurologically-based deficit in motivation. Therefore, to be more effective, feedback and consequences have to be immediate, frequent, consistent and tangible.

- There are five steps to devising a home behavior modification program: 1) Select an appropriate goal; 2) Determine how to measure the target behavior; 3) Determine the type of token to be used; 4) Determine the rewards and the cost in tokens; and 5) Devise the recording system to monitor progress.

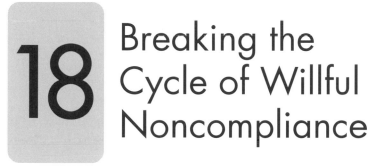

CHAPTER

18 Breaking the Cycle of Willful Noncompliance

As a parent of a child with ADHD, you are painfully familiar with the exasperation that builds when you try to get your child to do something. Invariably, the two of you get locked into a battle of words as you try to convince your child to listen to reason, and he tries to convince you that you're unreasonable. How many times have you made a simple request of your child, and he stubbornly refused? How many times have you told your child "No," and he kept asking? How many times have you tried to explain your reasoning to your child, and he argued circles around you? How many times have you asked your child to calm down, and he went ballistic?

NONCOMPLIANCE

There are probably many times throughout the day when you and your child get caught in the cycle of willful noncompliance. Here is an example which may be familiar to many of you. Imagine that your child wants you to drop what you're doing and drive him someplace. You tell him "No," and he starts whining and complaining, refusing to let up. The scene may go something like this:

CHILD: Mom, can you take me to the video store?

MOM: Sorry, son. I'm right in the middle of fixing dinner.

CHILD: Come on, Mom. It won't take long.

MOM: I can't leave now with all of this food cooking on the stove.

CHILD: We can go real fast, and you don't even have to get out of the car.

MOM: I said NO! It's dangerous to leave food on a hot stove.

CHILD: You just don't want me to have any fun.

MOM: I want you to have fun. I just can't go right now.

CHILD: You never do anything for me. It's always what **you** want.

MOM: What do you mean I don't want you to have fun? How about the movie I took you to yesterday, and the sleepover I let you have last week when you kept us up all night?

CHILD: That's different. I'm just asking for a little video. What's the big deal?

MOM: Why don't you ever accept NO? I'm so tired of telling you 10 times, NO. NO. NO.

CHILD: You're the worst Mom there is. All you do is yell, yell, yell. I hate you!

MOM: Don't you dare speak to me that way. You apologize right now!

CHILD: Why should I? You talk to me that way!

MOM: You are such an ungrateful child who thinks the world revolves around you. You seem to think that Dad and I should drop what we're doing and jump whenever you want something.

CHILD: You always expect me to do whatever you want. It doesn't matter what I want.

MOM: If you keep it up, you're going to be grounded from playing with your friends for a month, and you won't get any videos either!

CHILD: See if I care!

This fiasco started with a "No" from Mom, but quickly escalated to reasoning, arguing, name calling, blaming and threatening. This probably left Mom thoroughly frustrated and demoralized, and it likely threw her son into a tailspin that ruined his mood for the rest of the evening. These kinds of episodes whittle away at the self-esteem of your child and teach him that he has to comply only if he can be talked into it. Repeated episodes of this sort *may* help your child if he plans to join the debate team, but they certainly don't foster a healthy parent-child relationship.

Despite the anger and bad feelings that result from exchanges like these, they continue to happen time and time again. Why do parents continue to take the bait and get caught up in this frustrating and self-defeating cycle? Why do they continue doing "more of the same"? Before we answer these important questions, let's take a closer look at noncompliance. Once you understand it, you're better equipped to do something about it.

Why Should You Change Your Child's Noncompliance?

In addition to the fact that your child's noncompliance is thoroughly frustrating and wears you down, there are at least five reasons why you should try to change his noncompliance.

1. Noncompliance is the most frequent complaint lodged by parents of children with ADHD when they bring them to mental health centers.[1]

2. The majority of negative interactions among parents, children with ADHD, and their siblings involve noncompliance.[2]

3. Children who display noncompliance at home often display it in other settings, such as school, church, stores, restaurants and with peers.[3]

4. The noncompliance of the child with ADHD eventually has a pervasive negative effect on the rest of the family.[4,5]

   • Parents stop asking the child with ADHD to do chores, and either end up doing the chores themselves or asking another sibling to do them. This creates resentment on the part of the parent and hostility on the part of the other children.

   • Parents eventually spend less time with their attention-disordered child to avoid the inevitable conflicts that arise when they are together.

   • Parents argue between themselves over how to handle the child's noncompliance, creating marital stress.

   • Parents and the child with ADHD escalate more quickly in their mutual commanding, arguing, yelling or threatening because of their history of repeated conflict and the frustration that results.

5. Childhood noncompliance is a predictor for future adjustment. Noncompliance in childhood is often followed by academic prob-

lems,[6] delinquency, conduct problems,[7] and poor peer relationships in later childhood and adolescence.[8]

Examples of Noncompliant Behaviors

The most common types of noncompliant behaviors that are common in children with ADHD are:[9]

Arguing	Crying	Ignoring self-help tasks
Teasing	Lying	Destroying property
Talking back	Yelling	Physically fighting
Throwing tantrums	Ignoring requests	Failing to complete homework
Screaming	Whining	Physically resisting
Defying	Humiliating	Disrupting others' activities
Throwing objects	Swearing	Complaining
Running off	Stealing	Failing to complete chores

How many of these (or other) occur in your household? What do you think causes this noncompliance? What do you do *now* to deal with these behaviors?

CYCLE OF NONCOMPLIANCE

All children are noncompliant some of the time. Children with ADHD, however, are noncompliant a lot of the time. Noncompliance is a cycle. It is a cycle that is perpetuated by a parent and a child. Unfortunately, the cycle is not easily broken when you have a child with ADHD. The diagram explains why. It is adapted from Barkley's original flow chart showing the interactions between parents and defiant children.[10]

Most child noncompliance begins with a request from a parent. For example, you ask your child to pick up his room. If he complies, you say a silent prayer of thanks, and then he and you continue on to other things. Unfortunately, when children comply with tasks that parents expect them to do, parents usually don't give them positive feedback about their compliance. After all, kids are just supposed to do these things we parents tell them to do. *But as a result of insufficient positive feedback, over time the child will be less likely to comply in the future* (more about this later).

Let's go back to your request. Your child will be more likely to comply if the request involves an activity which he likes, that takes a minimal amount of effort, and has an immediate reward or pay off.

The majority of requests that you (and parents in general) give your child do not meet these necessary motivational requirements. The request is usually for something your child does not particularly enjoy doing, or for something he feels takes more effort than he prefers;

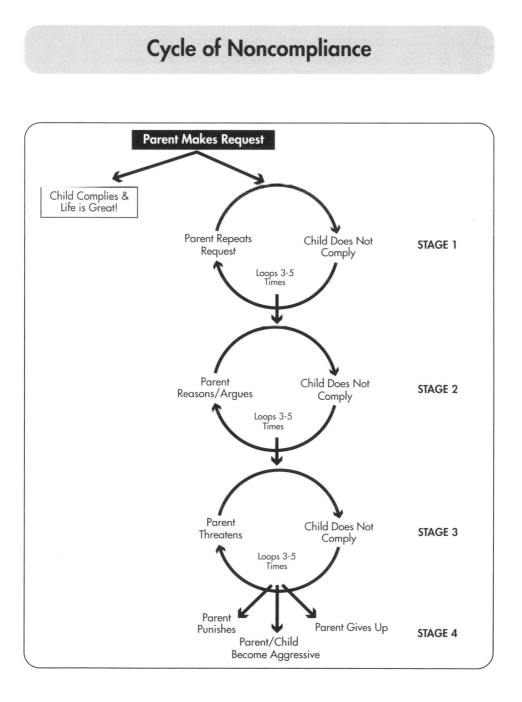

Cycle of Noncompliance

Parent Makes Request

Child Complies & Life is Great!

Parent Repeats Request

Child Does Not Comply

STAGE 1

Loops 3-5 Times

Parent Reasons/Argues

Child Does Not Comply

STAGE 2

Loops 3-5 Times

Parent Threatens

Child Does Not Comply

STAGE 3

Loops 3-5 Times

Parent Punishes

Parent/Child Become Aggressive

Parent Gives Up

STAGE 4

whatever it is, it's not as rewarding as doing what he was doing before you interrupted him. Consequently, your child does not comply with your initial request. In reaction, you **repeat** the request a number of times, but nothing happens, as illustrated in Stage 1 of the diagram.

You quickly go to the next stage (Stage 2), explaining to your child why he is being asked to do such an "unreasonable thing." You **reason and argue** with him in the hopes that maybe you'll phrase it just right this time so that he'll step back and say, "Well, gee Mom, now that you said it that way, I'll be more than happy to comply with your request." You find yourself caught in this cycle of repeated reasoning and arguing, looping around a number of times as your child refuses to comply.

The process escalates to the next stage — **threats.** *"Do it now. If you don't, you'll be grounded for a month!!"* This type of interaction may go on for a while as well, as shown in Stage 3.

The interaction may end in a number of different ways. You could **acquiesce** out of frustration and anger, maybe by leaving the room or just doing it yourself. You could **punish** by grounding him, sending him to time-out, or removing a privilege. Or maybe you or your child become verbally or physically **aggressive.** Perhaps you spank your child; call him names or swear; or your child yells, hits you, insults you, or swears at you (Stage 4).

There are times when a child finally complies. As one parent commented, *"I know I'm going to win eventually because I can be just as stubborn as she is."*

But the victory is usually only short-lived because the next time this parent asks her child to do something, the same cycle will be repeated. The battle may be won, but she is losing the war.

The power struggle goes on and continues over and over because you and your child are approaching the situation from two different perspectives. You are probably thinking long term: *"I'll get him to do it eventually, even if it kills me."* But remember, the child with ADHD does not think long term but only relates to what feels good right now, at the moment. Consequently, he is thinking: *"Aha! I just bought myself two more minutes of not having to do the stupid dishes,"* especially because what he is doing at the moment (watching TV, playing video games, etc.) is probably more rewarding than doing what you just asked him to do. Granted, almost any child would rather do something more rewarding or fun than do something hard or boring. But it is infinitely more difficult for the child with ADHD to do the hard or boring task. It's almost like a law of ADHD: When the child is faced with two alternatives, the more immediately rewarding, more stimulating, more fun event or activity will win out every time. Video games are always going to beat homework or doing the dishes!

Why the Cycle Continues

Parents often say, *"He spent more time battling over doing what I asked him to do than it would have taken to do the thing in the first place."* This may be true, but the cycle is so difficult to stop because it is strengthened by at least three factors: positive reinforcement, negative reinforcement and intermittent reinforcement.

- **Positive reinforcement**

  First, this cycle is positively reinforcing to your child because his moment-to-moment putting it off allows him to keep doing what he is doing. And you can bet that what he is doing is a lot more interesting and rewarding to him than the task you want him to do.

- **Negative reinforcement**

  Second, and more importantly, this cycle is perpetuated by negative reinforcement. A person's behavior is negatively reinforced if his behavior is successful in allowing him to avoid something unpleasant. In this case, the unpleasant thing is the task that you asked your child to do, or perhaps it is you, the messenger. Your child's procrastinating behaviors, which may include whining, ignoring, telling you he will do it "in a minute," or arguing, are successful in avoiding or at least putting off that unpleasant thing. If your child's avoidant behaviors are really successful, he perhaps can get out of doing the task all together by forcing you to give up and go away. As a result, these avoidant behaviors are negatively reinforced (and therefore strengthened), increasing the chances that he will engage in the same avoidant behaviors the next time he is asked to do something.

  Even if your child is punished for refusing to comply, he will likely engage in the same noncompliant behaviors next time if the punishment is delayed long enough that it does not have any effect on his immediate behavior. It is important to remember that children with ADHD are managed by the moment, and the moment-to-moment reality is that he is escaping, or at least putting off something that is not interesting or rewarding to him.

- **Intermittent reinforcement**

  You may be saying that your child does not get away with this behavior every time, and sometimes you can get your child to comply sooner. **The fact that your child is sometimes successful in avoiding the task, however, further strengthens the cycle of noncompliance.** This phenomenon operates on the same principle as a slot machine. When a gambler plays the slot machines, he obviously has no guarantee that he is going to win every time. The fact that he has won once or twice before motivates him onward in hopes that just maybe he will win again. Eventually he may even become "addicted" to playing the slot machines. This drive to play the machines becomes so powerful because it has been reinforced intermittently. He doesn't win every time, but there is the chance and the thrill that he may win the next time, or the next time, or the next time. Likewise, if your child with ADHD is intermittently successful in avoiding your requests, he will try avoidance again and again on the chance that maybe it will work this time like it worked before.

  It is critical to cut off the cycle at the very beginning, before it has the chance to play out. Avoid going down the path of reasoning, arguing, cajoling or threatening to get your child to comply. Every time you "take the bait" and go down this path, you are contributing to the cycle by delaying your child's compliance and unwittingly allowing him to avoid the unpleasant thing you asked him to do. You are negatively reinforcing your child to NOT comply!

  To break this cycle of noncompliance, simply refuse to argue with your child. Give up the notion that you can reason him into compliance! Instead, take proactive steps to cut off the cycle before it even begins. Here's an effective and simple method to do that.

1-2-3: MAGIC!

Dr. Thomas Phelan, an Illinois psychologist who specializes in ADHD, has developed a discipline method that can be especially effective with children with ADHD between the ages of two and ten. The name of the method is *1-2-3: Magic!*[11] It's a variation of a fundamental technique for all children, but with special rules and applications that make it especially effective for children with ADHD. In fact, Dr. Phelan named this technique *1-2-3: Magic!* because many parents who use it report that it works like magic.

This technique applies directly to the cycle of willful noncompliance. The critical component of *1-2-3: Magic!* is that it cuts off the cycle before it starts, before you and your child go down the path of negative reinforcement.

Dr. Phelan begins his explanation for the *1-2-3: Magic!* program by stating that parents usually approach their children with an unrealistic expectation: that children should respond to parents like *"little adults."* That is, they should listen to words and reason (often *excessive* words and reason), say " thank you" for helping them finally see it your way, and then act accordingly. How naive we are! Children are not little adults, and they will often test limits, disobey and argue. As parents we need to provide limits and help our children function within them. *1-2-3: Magic!* is an effective tool we can use.

Two Rules for *1-2-3: Magic!*

There are two important rules that ensure this strategy's effectiveness.

1. No-Emotion Rule

The "No-Emotion Rule" states that you should control yourself and not get upset. Any ranting and raving you do reinforces your child's delaying behaviors, because now you are putting on a good show. For example, if you persist with your reasoning and words until you are real upset, and then try to use "1-2-3," you have already started down the path of negative reinforcement. Too much time has elapsed between your initial request and your child's eventual compliance. You are going down that slippery slope, and it's very hard to crawl back up.

When upset, almost everyone tends to overreact. You may yell too much, threaten unrealistic or excessively harsh consequences, and say hurtful things that strengthen your child's resolve to "never give in." In a power play between a superior adult and a weaker child, this stubborn resolve elevates the child to a powerful position from which he can dig in his heels and wear you down. How many times have you thought to yourself, "My kid acts like he thinks he's the parent"? By overreacting and getting angry, you have inappropriately shifted the power to your child, and he's reluctant to give it up.

2. No-Talking Rule

The "No-Talking Rule" means the fewer the words, the better. The more you talk in your attempts to convince your child to comply, the more you are contributing to the negative reinforcement cycle by building in a delay filled with reasoning and lecturing. Spending a lot of time reasoning with your child tells him that he doesn't have to follow your request unless you can talk him into it.

When to Use *1-2-3: Magic!*

There are two classes of behaviors for which parents use the *1-2-3: Magic!* method:

1. Stop Behaviors

"Stop behaviors" are the relatively frequent and fairly benign behaviors you want your child to *stop* doing, such as:

- Arguing
- Whining
- Demanding
- Screaming
- Pestering

2. Start Behaviors

"Start behaviors" are those you want your child to *start* doing. Typically, they can be accomplished in just a few minutes, such as:

- Pick up toys
- Hang up coat
- Turn off television
- Brush teeth and hair
- Make bed

Other "start behaviors" that are more complicated and take more time to accomplish (such as cleaning rooms, doing homework, etc.) are best managed using charting and other behavior modification techniques described in Chapter 17.

How to Use *1-2-3: Magic!*

The process for *1-2-3: Magic!* is very straightforward. Give your child a start or stop command in language that is direct, simple, and without extra verbiage. If your child does not comply within five to ten seconds after this **initial directive,** start "1-2-3":

1. Without saying anything more, calmly hold up one finger and sternly say, **"That's 1."**

2. Wait 5 seconds *but say nothing more.* If your child does not comply, hold up two fingers and sternly say, **"That's 2."**

3. Wait 5 more seconds but continue to say nothing more. If your child still does not comply, hold up three fingers and sternly say, **"That's 3, take 5."** Your child must then go immediately to time-out (usually to his room) for five minutes. Five minutes of time-out is appropriate for children five years of age and younger. The general rule for older children is 1 minute per year of age. For example, a 10-year-old gets 10 minutes of time-out. If your child refuses to go to time-out, escort him. If he refuses to stay in time-out, stand by his door and put him back every time he comes out (do not say a word, however), or perhaps get a lock for the outside of the door.

Let's revisit the scene between the mother and her child at the beginning of this chapter and contrast it with how it would unfold if the mother used *1-2-3: Magic!*. The scene depicted an example of a "stop behavior": the mother wants her child to stop badgering. With *1-2-3: Magic!* the scene unfolds very differently than when the mother unsuccessfully tries to reason her child into compliance. Here's how it works.

CHILD:	Mom, can you take me to the video store?
MOM:	Sorry son. I'm right in the middle of fixing dinner.
CHILD:	Come on, Mom. It won't take long.
MOM:	That's 1.
CHILD:	We can go real fast and you don't even have to get out of the car.
MOM:	That's 2.
CHILD:	You just don't want me to have any fun.
MOM:	That's 3, take 5.

As you can see, this exchange took less than a minute, and all of the arguing, name-calling, blaming and anger that damages your child's self-esteem and leaves you feeling inept and upset was avoided. Sound simple? It is. But it's not easy. The critical factor is you must be consistent. Here are some key points.

1. Sit down with your child and explain that you will be using this technique from now on. Most children will test the limits initially, so their behavior may get worse before it gets better. Hang in there and ride out this storm. Once this method works, it's not unusual for children to respond and change their behavior before you get to the count of 3.

2. If your child acts aggressively (e.g., kicks his sister), you immediately say, "That's 3, take 5!" He must go directly to time-out. Do not count your child in these situations; it would essentially allow him three more chances to flatten his sister. The immediate "take 5" also applies to instances of verbal aggression.

3. If your child taunts you, talks back to you, or starts to count *you*, ignore it. This is his attempt to wear you down, which pulls you right back down the path of arguing and reasoning. If your child becomes verbally abusive, add additional minutes to his time-out, "You get another 10 minutes for the foul mouth."

4. If your child promises to comply after you've counted to "3," it's too late. He still must "take 5." Once you've started counting, be sure to see it through. Don't fall into the trap of counting to 2 and then turning soft, "That's '2,' ... now don't make me get to '3'..." Your child will see through this and realize that you don't mean what you say.

5. Make sure that both parents use this method and agree on when to use it.

6. Continue to use it even when you are visiting relatives, have house guests, or are at a friend's house. When you use it in public, tell your child that you will use some other location as the time-out room (such as your car or public bathroom) or that he will serve the time-out immediately when you get home.

7. If your child refuses to quiet down when he is in time-out, let him know that the time-out does not start until he is quiet. Set a timer for 5 minutes or more *after* your child has quieted down. If he tears apart his room while he's in time-out, you can try different strategies: take away the items he has tossed about for at least a week; leave the mess on the floor for a few days and then clean it up together; or change the time-out location to a different room (e.g., the laundry room).

8. Once your child has served his time-out, don't launch into lecturing him, "I told you if you didn't stop arguing with me you would go to time-out. When are you ever going to learn?" It's best to simply be

quiet. If you counted your child for refusing to comply with a start behavior (e.g., "Pick up your jacket."), it is all right to repeat the command after he has served his time (if you *reasonably* believe it is worth it). If he refuses again, repeat "1-2-3." This may go on for a while until he finally understands that you mean what you say.

Some Words of Caution

If you find that "1-2-3" is not working for you, perhaps you're committing some common errors:

- You are talking too much before you start counting.
- You are talking or trying to reason with your child between each count.
- You waited too long before you started to count.
- You got too upset before you started counting or when you were counting.
- You gave in to your child's pleading not to send him to time-out.
- You are using this method inconsistently, sporadically, or at a time when you should be using active listening (which is discussed in Chapter 19).

After using this method for a while, some parents complain that their child is not internalizing the "1-2-3"; that he's not stopping himself from whining, complaining or arguing; that he's still not choosing to comply. Remember the purpose of this method is not to teach kids with ADHD to internalize self-control (although for children with milder forms of ADHD, this may be a side benefit). It's meant to stop the cycle of noncompliance before it spirals out of control into arguing, yelling, threatening, shaming or even hitting. Other strategies are used to help internalize self-control.

Some parents complain that when they count, their child always reacts with the same type of manipulating behavior, such as refusing to go to his room, banging doors, or claiming he doesn't care if he goes to time-out. Children will use the same tactics repeatedly if they find they work. Your child may have found that banging doors is a sure-fire way to get you upset — so it works for him. He may have found that acting like he doesn't care makes you exasperated — so it works for him. Or he may have found that refusing to go to time-out makes you give up—so it works for him. If your child continues to use the same manipulating behaviors over and over again with you, it means that you are probably reinforcing that behavior. If you don't give in to the behavior, stay calm, and stick to the rules of "1-2-3," your child will eventually give up the manipulations.

Parents are fearful that when they count, they're cutting off their child's feelings and his right to express himself. They're worried that they will damage their child's self-esteem. In fact, just the opposite is true. There are many opportunities for your child to express himself — defying you is not one of them. Allowing the cycle of arguing, yelling and shaming to continue does *more* damage to your child's self-esteem and erodes your relationship with your child. The most significant value in stopping this cycle is that it decreases the frustration and the conflicts between you and your child, thereby helping preserve his self-esteem.

Finally, parents tell me that they are uncertain when to use "1-2-3" and when they should talk and listen to their child. The rule of thumb for using "1-2-3" is to use it if you are enforcing a rule or trying to get your child to comply with something you asked him to do. This is not always a clear distinction, but the following section on active listening may help you understand when it is more appropriate to listen and talk instead of counting.

To learn more about "1-2-3," you can read Dr. Phelan's book, *1-2-3: Magic! Training Your Preschoolers and Preteens to Do What You Want,* or view his excellent videotape, *1-2-3: Magic!.* Both are published by Child Management Press and can be ordered through the A.D.D. WareHouse (800-233-9273).

SUMMARY

- There are many reasons to change your child's noncompliance: 1) It is one of parents' most common complaints, 2) The majority of negative family interactions involves noncompliance, 3) Noncompliance usually spills over into settings outside the home, 4) Noncompliance has a pervasive negative effect on all family members, and 5) Excessive noncompliance is associated with adjustment problems in adolescence and adulthood.

- Noncompliance is a cycle that usually begins with a request from a parent. The parent repeats this request several times, leading to reasoning and arguing. This escalates to threats. The parent eventually gives up, punishes or becomes aggressive.

- The cycle of noncompliance is perpetuated primarily by negative reinforcement, i.e., a child does what he can to avoid the unpleasant request made by his parent. If he is successful in putting off or getting out of doing what he was asked, his behavior is negatively reinforced, guaranteeing that he will engage in the same behavior the next time. Parents negatively reinforce their child's noncompliance by getting stuck in repeating, reasoning, arguing and threatening.

- Parents can cut off the cycle of noncompliance by refusing to engage in it. 1-2-3: Magic! helps them do this.

- Using a new discipline technique such as 1-2-3: Magic! usually leads to an initial escalation in negative behavior by the child. This is normal and is the child's attempt to coerce the parents into backing down and going back to the old way. Unfortunately, this is when parents prematurely give up. If parents do not give into this behavior, they will likely find that the new method works, and the child's behavior improves.

19 Using Active Listening

1-2-3: Magic! is an effective intervention strategy for start and stop behaviors. However, there are times when it is not appropriate. Another method is active listening. Actually, this method should *always* guide your general style of listening and responding to your child. However, it should be actively employed at those times when your child needs to be heard rather than disciplined.

The most frequent complaint that I hear from children in therapy is, *"My parents don't listen to me."*

At these times, the most common response I hear from parents is, *"We want to listen, but he won't tell us what's bothering him."*

THE LANGUAGE OF UNACCEPTANCE

Children with behavior problems often close down; they stop talking honestly to their parents. Consider what this 14-year-old girl with ADHD told me during one of our sessions:

> *"There's no way I'd tell my parents what I just told you. They don't listen, they just lecture. They give me the same lecture over and over again, like I didn't hear it the first time. I'm so frustrated by their telling me what to do when all I want them to do is listen. I don't want to tell them how I feel, because I'll just end up feeling like an idiot again."*

What this child was saying is that she feels unacceptable to her parents. If she feels this way, she is not likely to expose her true self, to open up and talk. She is more likely to feel defensive and shameful and to want to build a wall to protect herself from her parents' unacceptance of her.

Children form their vision of themselves, in part, based upon how others (especially their parents) see them. Parents are like a mirror. What they reflect back to their child is how the child learns to see himself. Parents reflect their "view" of their child through their tone of voice, facial expressions, their actions toward their child, and what they say to their child.

As parents, we are well-intentioned. We want our children to turn out to be the best they can be. Out of our concern and love, we worry and sometimes even focus excessively on what we see as our children's shortcomings, problems and foibles. We direct, help, correct, cajole, teach, and yes, even punish, in our attempts to help our children change and function more successfully. Our well-meaning efforts are often interpreted as disapproval. Dr. Thomas Gordon, author of *Parent Effectiveness Training* [1] captures it well:

> *Most people have been brought up to believe that if you accept a child he will remain just the way he is; that the best way to help a child become something better in the future is to tell him what you don't accept about him now. ...Therefore, most parents rely heavily on the language of* **unacceptance** *in rearing children, believing this is the best way to help them. The soil that most parents provide for their children's growth is heavy with evaluation, judgment, criticism, preaching, moralizing, admonishing, and commanding — messages that convey unacceptance of the child as he is.* (Gordon, 1975, p.31.)

This *language of unacceptance* — what we say to our children in our attempts to change them — conveys a hidden message that negates the help we want to provide and undermines our good intentions.

Listen to what another child with **ADHD** said in therapy:

> *"My parents are always telling me that they can't trust me; that I never do what I say I 'm going to do. It's not like I try not to do it. I forget. Then my mom gets mad and yells and tells my dad. He gets real mad and usually says they are sick and tired of me always leaving things for them to do. They act like I don't have a brain and that I'm a loser. I don't care anymore because no matter what I do, it's not right. Why even try?"*

The language of unacceptance creates a self-fulfilling prophecy and causes behavior to get worse, not better. **If a child hears often enough how bad he is, he will become "bad."** Children often become what people tell them they are.

Communication Process

How does the language of unacceptance start, anyway? Consider this variation of Dr. Gordon's diagram of the communication process.[2]

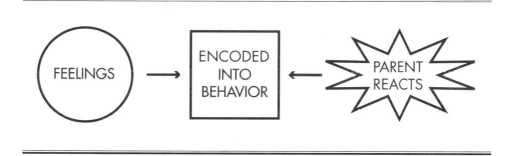

Children have innumerable feelings and needs; however, they are often unable to express them. Perhaps they don't want you to know how they feel about something. Or they may not have the psychological sophistication and insight to even know themselves. Often they don't have the emotional language to express how they feel. As a result, children frequently encode or convert their feelings and/or needs into some form of *behavior.* The behavior is what parents see — especially when it's dramatic and/or "in their face." Unfortunately, parents then react to the *behavior* instead of *actively listening to the underlying feeling or need* that generated the behavior.

This communication dynamic takes on special significance for children with ADHD. These children do not have good insight into their own behavior, nor are they well tuned into their own feelings. Those feelings also tend to be stronger because impulsivity makes it difficult to put the brakes on them. The children overreact and charge ahead like unstoppable locomotives, often not taking the time or possessing the needed self-control to think about their feelings before they act on them. Their feelings swell up, almost instantaneously, and explode before they know what happened. Their overreactive and uncontrolled behaviors distort and exaggerate the underlying feelings that drove their behaviors in the first place.

Parents react, almost in self defense, to this explosive behavior. While the behaviors take center stage and consume the parents' attention, the child's underlying feelings go unacknowledged. The behavior gets punished, and the feelings get ignored. Ignored feelings lead to stronger feelings. Stronger feelings lead to more explosive behaviors. And so the cycle continues.

A recent incident with one of my daughters illustrates this communication (or perhaps miscommunication) process and also provides an example of when it's more appropriate to use active listening instead of "1-2-3."

My husband and I make concerted efforts to have special times with each of our three children on a regular basis. For one special time with our then eight-year-old daughter Kate, she chose to go out for a doughnut and soft drink at the doughnut shop close to our home. We had a wonderful time, talking about silly things, watching people, and just enjoying each other's company.

Later that evening I asked my younger daughter Sarah what she would like to do for her special time with me, which happened to be scheduled for the following morning. Her eyes grew wide as saucers, she fidgeted with excitement, and then exclaimed that she would like to go to Camp Snoopy (an amusement park inside the Mall of America, which is in our community). Although this seemed like an extravagant special time, we were able to strike a compromise. She agreed that she would only go on two rides of her choice and that we would not buy any souvenirs. This seemed like an equitable plan, a win-win situation. It was not expensive or extravagant, it allowed her to choose her own activity for our special time, and it's a fun place to go with my daughter.

Before bedtime that evening, the family was sitting together talking about the day. Kate told about the special time she had had that afternoon and how she liked the chance to just sit and talk with Mom at the doughnut shop. Sarah then excitedly exclaimed that she was going to Camp Snoopy with Mom the next morning for her special time. I looked at the expression on Kate's face, and I saw trouble. She suddenly jumped up and shouted, "That's not fair! If you go to Camp Snoopy, you can't go on the Screaming Yellow Eagle, and if you do, I hope you puke!" My husband was aghast at such an outburst and demanded in response, "We don't talk like that in our family. You have no right to jump all over Sarah. Apologize to your sister, and do it now!"

Well, at this point, asking her to apologize was like asking her to shave her head. "No!" she shouted back defiantly.

Apparently thinking this was a "start behavior" (start apologizing), or maybe a "stop behavior" (stop defying me), my husband started to count, "That's 1." His face was turning red and his finger was shaking. I could tell this was headed nowhere fast. My husband had just been blindsided by our daughter's unexpected outburst. He impulsively reacted to her strong behavior and totally missed her feelings behind the behavior.

Based on what I knew of this situation, I saw that this was a time for active listening, not "1-2-3." To defuse the unfortunate cycle that was beginning, I switched to my active listening mode. I tried to understand what Kate must be feeling and what message she was trying to send through her behavior. I needed to interpret her behavior, not react to it. From her 8-year-old point of view, her perfect special time at the doughnut shop had just been ruined by her younger sister's proposed trip to Camp Snoopy. She was probably thinking, "Sure, all I got was a lousy doughnut and my little sister gets to ride on the Screaming Yellow Eagle — my favorite ride in the whole world!" I tried to reflect Kate's feelings back to her without adding my own message, opinion or direction. It was important that I let her know that I acknowledged her feelings and their importance (which did not mean I agreed with her behavior). By doing so, she would be more likely to calm down, we would probably prevent an escalation of emotions and hurt feelings, and she would be more open to resolving the situation.

What followed went something like this:

MOM: Gee, Kate, Sarah is going to Camp Snoopy, and all you got was a doughnut.

KATE: If I had known I could have picked Camp Snoopy, I would have done that.

MOM: How frustrating. Sure you would have picked Camp Snoopy if you'd known that was a choice.

KATE: You know that Camp Snoopy is my favorite place to go.

MOM: Camp Snoopy is your favorite place, isn't it.

KATE: I liked having a doughnut with you, Mom, but next time I'd like Camp Snoopy.

MOM: You'd like Camp Snoopy for our next special time.

KATE: Yeah. Can we go to Camp Snoopy next time?

MOM: You've got a deal. It's Camp Snoopy next time we have special time.

Kate calmed down and came to her own solution. This exchange ended with Kate actually giving her younger sister a hug. By *not* reacting to her behavior but instead listening to her feelings and reflecting them back to her, she felt understood. There was no need for her to stubbornly defend her feelings, because they weren't under attack. If she had been forced into defending herself, she couldn't have listened, and she wouldn't have changed.

There's another lesson from this example: parents should help each other out. My husband and I try to operate as a tag team; when one parent is stuck in a "more of the same" cycle or needs bailing out, the other parent can respectfully step in and redirect the process. In this instance, my husband's emotions took him to a *reactive* response. I was able to stand back and be proactive. In another situation, the roles might have been reversed.

TWELVE TYPICAL WAYS THAT PARENTS RESPOND TO CHILDREN THAT DON'T WORK

In the example above, I had to resist the temptation to demand that my daughter change her attitude, accept that life is not always fair, and understand that parents can't always measure every little thing they do with their kids to make sure everything is exactly equal. To have lambasted her with my message at that moment would have sent her the message that her feelings were not important or not acceptable. Feelings are an integral part of who we are. If our feelings are discounted, we are discounted.

The ways that we express unacceptance to our children can be very obvious or very subtle. We know that children with ADHD get more than their share of unacceptance. Is it any wonder that by the time they are in middle childhood, most of these children suffer from feelings of inferiority and low self-esteem?

In his book, *Parent Effectiveness Training.*, Dr. Thomas Gordon describes 12 typical ways that parents express unacceptance to their children. Dr. Gordon is a pioneer in active listening, and his classic book is must reading for all parents. Below, I have included Dr. Gordon's catalog of ineffective ways that parents respond to children. I have adapted his 12 examples of unacceptance to provide illustrations more typical of ADHD.

1. Ordering, Directing, Commanding

Children with ADHD get more than their share of ordering, directing and commanding as adults attempt to control their behavior.

"I don't care what other kids do, you have to do the yard work!"
"Don't talk to your mother like that!"
"Now you go back up there and tell your sister you're sorry!"
"Stop complaining!"

Although these children usually respond better to directives that are stated as a command rather than a request, the command should still be stated respectfully. *"Please start the first half of your homework, now."*

Harsh commands tell your child that his feelings or needs are not important; he must comply with what *you* feel or need. *"It's not my problem what your friends think; you're not going anywhere tonight."*

These messages communicate unacceptance of your child *as he is* at the moment. For example, *"Stop fidgeting around"* provides a negative message. It is more positive and helpful to redirect your child by telling him what he should do, not what he shouldn't do. *"You need to listen quietly."*

Threatening commands produce fear of your power. Your child hears a threat of getting hurt by someone bigger and stronger than he. *"Go to your room — and if you don't, I'll see to it that you get there."* This type of role modeling by parents will most certainly get acted out on the playground.

Children with ADHD are often in the defensive, "save face" mode as they try to salvage their self-esteem. Orders given in anger intensify this because they make your child feel resentful or angry, frequently causing him to express hostile feelings, throw a tantrum, fight back, resist, or test your will.

Parents often impulsively and harshly direct their children to avert a mishap. *"Don't pour that milk yourself."* *"I'll have to do that for you."* Unfortunately, directives like this communicate to your child that you don't trust his judgment or competence. In life, it's not spilling the milk that is so important, it's how it gets cleaned up!

2. Warning, Admonishing, Threatening

Parents often revert to warning, admonishing and threatening their child into compliance when repeated requests don't work.

"If you don't shape up, you'll never amount to anything!"
"Keep it up and you'll be grounded for a month!
"You better not do that if you know what's good for you!"

There are many problems with these messages. They can make your child feel fearful and submissive. *"If you do that, you'll be sorry."*

These messages can evoke resentment and hostility in the same way that ordering, directing and commanding do. *"If you come home late one more time, you'll never get the car again!"* Usually your child does not comply with such a threat, and now you're forced into having to follow-through with something you don't want to do or you never intended to do. Now your child knows you don't mean what you say.

These messages also invite your child to test the firmness of your threat. Children sometimes are tempted to do something that they have been warned against, just to see for themselves if the consequences promised will actually happen.

Also, when children hear a lot of such threats, they become immune to them and sometimes respond by saying, *"I don't care what happens, I still feel this way."*

These types of messages can communicate that you have no respect for your child's needs, wishes or preferences. *"If you don't stop playing that music, I'm going to throw the darn CD away."*

3. Exhorting, Moralizing, Preaching

Telling your child what he should or ought to do is the fastest way to cause parent deafness: your child tunes you out and stops listening.

"You shouldn't act like that."
"You ought to be more careful."
"You must always respect your elders"

Such messages cause feelings of guilt in your child — that he is bad as he struggles unsuccessfully to follow your many "shoulds," "oughts" and "musts." Children may also respond to such messages by resisting and defending their posture even more strongly.

Children with ADHD often doubt their own sense of competency. Preaching and moralizing may make your child feel you don't trust his judgment — that he is incompetent and had better accept what "others" deem is right. *"You should always do what your teachers say."*

4. Advising, Giving Solutions or Suggestions

This includes telling your child how to solve a problem, giving him advice or suggestions or providing answers or solutions for him.

"Why don't you just do it their way and see how it feels?"
"Just sleep on it, and you'll feel better in the morning."
"That's not even worth worrying about; just forget it."
"Go make friends with some other girls."

Such messages are often felt by a child as evidence that the parent does not have confidence in the child's judgment or ability to find his own solution. *"I'd better call your friend's parents and explain the situation to them."*

They may influence your child to become dependent on you and stop thinking for himself. *"Tell me what I should do, Dad"*

Sometimes children strongly resent parents' ideas or advice. *"Let me figure this out myself." "This is probably a dumb idea; otherwise, Dad would have suggested it"*

Advice sometimes communicates your attitudes of superiority to your child. *"Your mother and I know what's best."* Your child can also acquire a feeling of inferiority. *"Why didn't I think of that?" "See, I never know what to do."*

Advice can make your child feel you don't understand him at all. *"You wouldn't suggest that if you really knew how I felt."*

Advice sometimes results in children devoting all their time reacting to their parents' ideas to the exclusion of developing their own ideas. Given their tendency to act before they think, it is important to encourage children with ADHD to come up with their own solutions to problems. *"What do you think you should do to avoid a conflict with Andrew?"* This practice stimulates your child's critical thinking skills.

5. Lecturing, Teaching, Giving Logical Arguments

This includes trying to influence your child with facts, counterarguments, logic, information, or your own opinion:

"Your teen-age years should be the happiest of your life."
"School can be the most wonderful experience you'll ever have."
"Children must learn how to get along with each other."

"If kids learn to take responsibility around the house, they'll grow up to be responsible adults."
"When I was your age, I had twice as much to do as you."

The act of trying to teach your child often makes him feel you are making him look inferior, subordinate or inadequate. *"You always think you know everything."*

Children, like adults, seldom like to be shown that they are wrong. The highly defensive child with **ADHD** will defend his position to the bitter end. *"You're wrong, I'm right." "You can't convince me." "You think you know everything!"*

Children generally hate parental lectures. It also leads to parent deafness. *"They go on and on and expect me to just sit there and listen. I've heard it a hundred times before. I just stop listening."*

Also, remember that children with **ADHD** usually know the rules that they break, but their impulsivity overrules the rules. When parents insist on teaching them, they resent the implication that they are uninformed. *"I know all of that — you don't need to keep telling me."*

When children are humiliated or badgered with repeated lecturing, they often resort to desperate methods to discount parental facts. *"Well, you're just too old to know what's going on." "You just don't understand." "Things are different now." "You're such a dweeb."*

Characteristically, the impulsive, impatient child often ignores facts. *"I don't care." "So what, it won't happen to me."*

6. Judging, Criticizing, Disagreeing, Blaming

Negative judgments, criticism or blame are probably what children with **ADHD** hear more than other messages:

"That's so childish."
"Don't be silly."
"You're wrong."
"You act like you don't have a brain in your head."

These messages, more than any of the others, make children feel inadequate, inferior, stupid, unworthy, or bad. A child's self-concept is shaped by parental judgment and evaluation. As you judge your child, so will your child judge himself. *"I heard so often that I was bad, I began to feel I must be bad."*

Negative criticism evokes counter-criticism by your child. *"I've seen you do the same thing." "You're not so hot yourself."*

Evaluation strongly influences children to keep their feelings to themselves or to hide things from their parents. *"If I told them, they'd just criticize me."* Children, like adults, hate to be judged negatively. They respond with defensiveness, simply to protect their own self-image. Children with ADHD are masters at this. Often they become angry and feel hatred toward the evaluating parent, even if the judgment is correct.

Frequent evaluation and criticism can make children feel that they are no good and that their parents don't love them.

7. Praising, Agreeing

This involves offering an insincere positive evaluation or judgment or agreeing when the facts don't support agreement:

> *"Well, I think you played a good game."*
> *"You can run just as fast as he can."*
> *"You're right. She's just jealous."*

Contrary to the common belief that praise is always beneficial to children, it can have very negative effects when used incorrectly. A positive evaluation that does not fit your child's self-image may evoke hostility, *"I am not pretty, I'm ugly." "I hate my hair." "I did not play well, I was lousy." "I don't have a lot of friends."*

Praise can feel manipulative to your child — a subtle way of influencing him to do what you want. *"You're just saying that so I'll study harder."*

Children sometimes infer that their parents don't understand them when they praise. *"You wouldn't say that if you knew how I really felt about myself."*

Children are often embarrassed and uncomfortable when praise is given, especially in front of their friends. *"Dad, be quiet!"*

Children who are praised excessively grow to not trust praise because they know it is not genuine. *"Sure, you're just saying that." "You know darn well I didn't do a good job."*

This whole issue of praise is a very sensitive one for children with ADHD. Throughout this book I have underscored the importance of giving frequent positive feedback to your child. The reason for this is at least two-fold: First, children with ADHD are not good self-observers of their own behavior. Therefore, specific, positive feedback about their behavior tunes them into it. *"I see you are working more slowly so that you don't make mistakes."* Second, children with ADHD usually do not get a lot of positive attention, but they do get a disproportionate amount of negative attention. Statements like, *"You are always interrupting,"* create a bruised self-esteem and a negative identity.

The feedback that's important for children with **ADHD** is different from the "empty praise" we often give our children in our misguided attempts to build self-esteem. Feedback given to these children should describe specific behavior in a positive and accurate way, but must not add a value judgment. For example, *"I like you much better when you sit still and pay attention,"* sends your child the message that he's likable only if he's sitting still and paying attention.

One final note about praise: In a family where praise is used frequently, the absence of praise can be interpreted by your child as criticism. *"You didn't say anything nice about how I picked up my room, so you must not like it."* This underscores the importance of consistent attention to your child's appropriate behavior.

8. Name-calling, Ridiculing, Shaming

This involves making your child feel foolish, putting him into a category, or shaming him:

> *"You're a spoiled brat."*
> *"Look here, smarty."*
> *"You're acting like a wild animal."*
> *"Shame on you."*
> *"You should know better."*

Such messages take a devastating toll on the self-image of your child. They make him feel unworthy, bad and unloved. Over time, he will incorporate such messages into his self-image, creating a shame-based identity that will stay with him into adulthood.

Typically, children respond to such messages by giving back the same message. *"And you're a big nag." "Look who's calling me lazy!"*

When a child gets such a shaming message from a parent who is trying to influence him, he is much less likely to change by looking at himself realistically. Instead, he can zero in on the parent's unfair message and excuse himself. *"My room isn't messy. You complain about me no matter what I do."* This is especially true for children with **ADHD** who are more prone to project blame onto others rather than accept responsibility for their own behavior.

9. Interpreting, Analyzing, Diagnosing

These responses include telling your child what his motives are or analyzing why he is doing or saying something:

"You're just jealous of Jenny."
"You're saying that to bug me."
"You really don't believe that at all."
"You feel that way because you're not doing well in school."

Such messages communicate to your child that you have him "figured out," know what his motives are or why he is behaving the way he is. Such parental psychoanalyzing can be threatening and frustrating to your child.

If your analysis or interpretation happens to be accurate, your child may feel embarrassed at being so exposed. *"You don't do your homework because you don't really want to succeed."* *"You are doing that just to get attention."*

If your analysis or interpretation is wrong, as it more often is, your child will become angry at being accused unjustly. *"I am not jealous — that's ridiculous."*

Children often pick up an attitude of superiority on the part of the parent. *"You think you know so much."* Parents who frequently analyze their children communicate that they feel superior, wiser, and more clever.

The "I know why" and "I can see through you" messages frequently cut off further communication from your child at the moment. They also teach your child to refrain from sharing problems with you. This is one of the most common dynamics I see between parents and children in therapy, particularly with adolescents.

10. Reassuring, Sympathizing, Consoling, Supporting

No parent likes to see their child in emotional pain. When you know your child is hurting, understandably you try to make him feel better. You might do this by talking him out of his feelings, trying to make his feelings go away, or denying the strength of his feelings:

"You'll feel differently tomorrow."
"All kids go through this sometime."
"Don't worry, things will get better."
"I used to think that, too."
"I know, school can be hard for all of us sometimes."

Such messages are not as helpful as you may believe. To reassure your child when he is upset about something may simply convince him that you don't understand. *"You wouldn't say that if you knew how scared I am."*

Sometimes, parents reassure and console because they are not comfortable when their child is hurt, upset, or discouraged. So they are quick to reassure, sympathize, console, etc. Unfortunately, such messages tell your child that you want him to stop feeling the way he does.*"Don't feel bad, things will turn out all right."* He will eventually believe that his legitimate feelings are wrong or bad. Because feelings are an integral part of who we are, your child will grow to believe that *he* is bad for feeling a certain way.

Discounting or sympathizing often stops further communication because your child senses you want him to stop feeling the way he does.

Finally, children can see through parents' reassurances as attempts to change them. The result is distrust of the parent. *"You're just saying that to make me feel better."*

11. Probing, Questioning, Interrogating

These responses include trying to find reasons, motives, causes, or more information to help solve a problem:

> *"When did you start feeling this way?"*
> *"Why do you suppose you hate school?"*
> *"Do the kids ever tell you why they don't want to play with you?"*
> *"Who put that idea into your head?"*
> *"Just what do you think you'll do if you don't go to college?"*

On the surface, probing and questioning seem like good methods to solve problems with your children. In fact we use them as adults with one another in a wide variety of situations at home, in business, etc. With children, however, the dynamic is different because the relationship is not one of equals. Our children may receive many different messages when we question and probe.

To ask questions may convey to your child your lack of trust, your suspicion or doubt. *"Did you wash your hands like I told you?"* Children also perceive some questions as attempts "to get them out on a limb," only to have it sawed off by the parent. *"How long did you study? Only an hour. Well, then you deserve a C on that exam."*

Children often feel threatened by questions, especially when they don't understand why the parent is questioning them. Note how often children say, *"Why are you asking that?"* or *"What are you getting at?"*

If you question your child when he is sharing a problem with you, he may suspect that you are gathering data to solve his problem for him, rather than letting him find his own solution. *"When did you start feeling this way? Does it have anything to do with school?"* Children frequently don't want their parents to find answers to their problems: *"If I tell my parents, they will only tell me what they think I should do."*

When you question someone who is sharing a problem with you, each question limits the person's freedom to talk about whatever he wants to — in a sense each question dictates his next message. If you ask, "When did you notice this feeling?", you are telling the person to talk only about the onset of the feeling and nothing else. This is why being cross-examined, as by a lawyer, is so terribly uncomfortable — you feel you must tell your story exactly as demanded by the questions. Interrogation is not a good method to facilitate another's communication. Rather, it can severely limit the freedom of the other person.

Interrogating children with ADHD is particularly counterproductive because the underlying premise is faulty. We typically ask children about their actions to find out why they did what they did, to understand the reasoning behind their actions. This implies there *was* a reason(s) when in fact there may not have been one. Remember that children with ADHD are often driven by impulse, not by reason. They act first, think later. You can get caught in an endless loop that goes nowhere. Demanding a reason for why your child did what he did may likely be an exercise in futility ... and frustrating for you both.

12. Withdrawing, Distracting, Humoring, Diverting

This collection of strategies involves trying to get your child away from the problem, withdrawing from the problem yourself, distracting your child, kidding him out of it, or pushing the problem aside.

"Just forget about it."
"Let's not talk about it at the table."
"Come on — let's talk about something more pleasant."
"Why don't you try burning the school building down?"
"We've been through this all before."
"It'll take care of itself."
"It'll all work out."

Such messages can communicate to your child that you are not interested in him, don't respect his feelings, or are downright rejecting him. Consider humoring, for example. Children are generally very serious and intent when they need to talk about something. When you respond with kidding, you can make them feel hurt and rejected.

Putting off children or diverting their feelings may, for the moment, appear successful, but a person's feelings do not always go away. They often crop up later. Problems put off are seldom problems solved.

Children, like adults, want to be heard and understood with respect. If their parents brush them aside, they soon learn to take their important feelings and problems elsewhere.

ACTIVE LISTENING: LANGUAGE OF ACCEPTANCE

Active listening is the alternative to the 12 counterproductive types of responses. With active listening, you attempt to *interpret* your child's behavior rather than *react* to it. You do this by trying to understand your child's feelings and the needs behind his behavior. Then you reflect his feelings back to him without opinion, evaluation, direction, blaming, discounting, etc. You do not send your own message by using one of the 12 typical responses we have discussed (e.g., directing, warning, preaching, blaming, analyzing, etc.). You reflect back only the message that your child is sending you. By doing this, you keep communication open. You decrease the likelihood that your child will react rigidly and defensively, shutting down and shutting you out. When a child is in a rigid, defensive mode, he is not able to change.

Children with ADHD are more prone to rigidity and defensiveness than most children. It is hard for them to change their way of thinking or of viewing the world. Before they are adolescents, they have already built a self-protective wall to defend themselves from the barrage of negative feedback and failure they have experienced. Dealing with these children in a rigid manner only increases their rigidity and strengthens their defensiveness. It halts communication and decreases the chances for change.

In contrast, there are many benefits to using active listening. It sends a clear message of acceptance to a child who often feels unaccepted by virtue of his behavioral difficulties. It keeps communication open between you and your child because it helps decrease his rigidity and defensiveness. It helps your child become more aware of his feelings. (This is especially beneficial for the child with ADHD who lacks personal insight.) Finally, it helps your child's problem-solving skills, because it gives him the necessary freedom to talk through his problems so that often he can develop his own solutions.

Active listening is not easy. Parents often tell me that this way of talking to their children feels unnatural and requires too much thinking. This is understandable, because the way we usually respond to our children is through "automatic talk," by using some of the "typical twelve." **It is hard to stop and think about what you are going to say before you say it, but that is essentially what we are asking our impulsive children with ADHD to do;** *stop being so impulsive and think before you act!* **What we ultimately accomplish by using active listening with our children is to model reflectiveness: thinking before we act.**

Like any new skill, you have to practice and exercise it before it becomes automatic. The more you practice active listening, the more natural it will feel.

The following example demonstrates the power of active listening. The first interaction involves the parent's language of unacceptance, using some of the "typical twelve." Note the contrast in the second interaction, using active listening.

Interaction #1:

CHILD: Ryan wouldn't let us build our fort today. We always have to do what he wants to do.

MOTHER: Well, why don't you listen to his ideas once and a while. You've got to learn to give and take if you want to get along in this world. (ADVISING, MORALIZING)

CHILD: He always has dumb ideas, and everyone thinks he's too bossy.

MOTHER: Well, then just play by yourself and don't have any friends. You're so stubborn. (OFFERING A SOLUTION, NAME-CALLING)

CHILD: He's the one who's stubborn. Why do I have to always give in?

MOTHER: You're overreacting because you're tired. You stayed up too late last night. Just get some rest and you won't be so upset. (INTERPRETING, JUDGING, REASSURING.)

CHILD: I'm not overreacting and I'm not tired. Ryan just thinks he's so great.

MOTHER: Now just stop complaining! If you don't start trying to get along with other kids, you just won't be allowed to play with anyone. (ORDERING, THREATENING)

CHILD: Oh, forget it. You never listen.

Interaction #2:

CHILD: Ryan wouldn't let us build a fort today. We always have to do what he wants to do.

MOTHER: You're angry with Ryan. (ACTIVE LISTENING)
CHILD: I know. I'm so sick of playing with him. I don't ever want to play with him again.
MOTHER: Right now you don't care to ever do anything with Ryan. (ACTIVE LISTENING)
CHILD: Yeah. But then if I don't play with him, we won't ever finish building our fort. It's in his yard.
MOTHER: You would hate to not finish your fort. (ACTIVE LISTENING)
CHILD: Yeah. I guess I'll have to try getting along with him. But it's so hard to play with him when he thinks he's always right.
MOTHER: Even though you might want to try to get along with him, it's hard when he thinks he always has the answers. (ACTIVE LISTENING)
CHILD: We used to get along better, when he would do what I wanted to do.
MOTHER: Now Ryan wants to do more of what he wants to do. (ACTIVE LISTENING)
CHILD: He sure does. He only has some ideas that I like.
MOTHER: Some of his ideas stink, but some of his ideas aren't so bad. (ACTIVE LISTENING)
CHILD: Yeah, I guess so. Like it was his idea to put a secret back door in our fort. I probably wouldn't have thought of that. Everyone does think our fort is pretty cool. Maybe sometimes he has good ideas. I suppose I could try to give in more.
MOTHER: You think that sometimes it's worth listening to his ideas. Sounds like maybe you'll try listening to him a bit more. (ACTIVE LISTENING)

There is a striking difference between these two interactions. In the first example, the child digs in his heels in reaction to his mother's failure to truly listen to him. His mom was so intent on sending her own message that she completely failed to listen to her son's feelings. As she continued to advise, moralize, offer solutions, interpret, and reassure her son, he grew more stubborn. He was forced into a position of defending himself because he felt under attack. The focus of the original problem with his playmate was lost. It shifted to proving how he was right and his mother was wrong. As a result, he eventually shut down, and communication stopped.

In the second scenario, however, the mother refrained from sending her own message or pointing out to her son the "error in his thinking." As she listened to him, she reflected back what she heard him saying, using some of her own words to avoid the appearance of mocking him or being insincere. She listened unemotionally and acceptingly and reflected his *feelings message* back to him. In response, her son remained open and nondefensive. As his mother engaged in the language of acceptance, he had the freedom to think more flexibly, to take a look at his own thinking, and to eventually problem-solve his way to his own solution.

SUMMARY

- Parents often engage in the language of unacceptance (including ordering, warning, moralizing, advising, lecturing, blaming, shaming, analyzing, consoling, interrogating, and withdrawing) in their attempts to help their children change and function more successfully.

- Parents shut down communication when they react to their child's exaggerated behavior rather than actively listen to the underlying feelings and needs that generated the behavior.

- Active listening has many benefits: It keeps communication open; it decreases the child's rigidity and defensiveness; it helps him become more aware of his feelings; and it helps him talk through his problems so that he can reach his own solutions.

Part Five

Medication Management

Perhaps the greatest area of controversy and misinformation about ADHD is the use of medication. Parents are often reluctant to try medication for their child because of the "horror stories" that they hear from neighbors, relatives or strangers. "Ritalin turned my kid into a zombie." "Ritalin permanently stunts your growth." Parents may read an article in a popular magazine or watch a report on television describing the dangers of Ritalin. "Ritalin is highly addictive." "Ritalin will make your kid dependent on drugs." Parents may attend a seminar or read an advertisement about "safe and effective alternative treatments to drugs" (such as herbs, pine bark extract, biofeedback, or vitamins) and conclude that drugs such as Ritalin are dangerous and a "crutch" that parents use to control their kids. Unfortunately, such hearsay, myths and inaccurate reports lead parents to make decisions about medication based on emotion and fear rather than science and fact.

Many adults also struggle with their own characteristic ambivalence and opinions about drug therapy. Mothers, in particular, often feel defensive and even guilty about going forward with medication. They may be haunted by a nagging insecurity that suggests that if they were a "good mother," they would be able to control their child and not have to resort to the "easy way out." They worry about possible side effects and any long-term harm that may result from medication. Fathers often seem less conflicted but more skeptical that ADHD is anything more than immaturity and laziness, so why confuse matters with drug treatment? Grandparents may think the problem is simply working mothers, absent fathers and wimpy parenting.

It is true that medication does not work for everyone, nor is it indicated for everyone with ADHD. Medication can be very safe and effective in managing the symptoms of ADHD when used as prescribed and under careful medical supervision. When it does work, it can make dramatic and positive changes in an individual's life.

It is also important to understand that medication is used to manage the symptoms of ADHD, not to cure it. Nor should medication be the only form of treatment for the child with ADHD. These children exhibit a number of physical, cognitive, academic, behavioral, and social difficulties. It is unrealistic to assume that medication alone will manage all of this effectively. Medication is only one possible piece of a comprehensive, multi-modal treatment for ADHD.

Stimulants

Stimulants are the most commonly prescribed medications for ADHD. Research has found that 73-77 percent of children with ADHD who take stimulants have a positive response.[1] Perhaps the greatest benefit of stimulants is that they maximize the effects of other treatments. That is, stimulants help to manage ADHD-related symptoms so that the individual can more effectively engage in, and benefit from, other forms of intervention, such as social skills training, behavioral self-control training, and family or individual therapy.

Stimulants were first prescribed for children with behavior and learning problems in 1937 when it was discovered that stimulants had a calming effect on hyperactive children. Researchers are not completely certain why stimulants work. It appears that stimulants increase the production of certain neurotransmitters in the brain (particularly dopamine and norepinephrine), thereby increasing arousal in the part of the brain responsible for inhibiting behavior and sustaining attention and effort. In a sense, stimulants increase the brake fluid in the brain, which consequently improves the individual's ability to regulate and control his behavior.

The most common stimulant is **Ritalin**, generically known as methylphenidate. Other stimulants used in the treatment of ADHD are **Dexedrine** (dextroamphetamine), **Cylert** (pemoline) and **Adderall.** In the text, we refer to these four stimulants by their trademark names.

RITALIN

Ritalin is used approximately nine times more frequently than other drugs prescribed for ADHD. It is one of the most researched drugs on the market. Ritalin is a Schedule II controlled substance, which means that the FDA imposes strict regulations concerning its prescription and distribution. The drug can only be obtained with a written prescription from a physician; therefore, parents cannot call into the pharmacy for a refill. This requires that parents closely monitor their supply and plan ahead for refills.

Ritalin comes in regular 5 mg, 10 mg, and 20 mg tablets, and in a 20 mg slow-release form known as Ritalin-SR. The regular form of Ritalin takes about 30 to 45 minutes to take effect, and lasts an average of three to four hours. It reaches its maximum effectiveness approximately two hours after ingestion and then decreases in effectiveness over the next few hours. Most physicians will start young children at a 5 mg dose (preschoolers usually start at a 2.5 mg dose). Because the duration of action of Ritalin is so short, it is usually taken twice during the day — around breakfast time and again around noon. Children who wake up early in the morning or who metabolize the medication fairly quickly may require a third dose to get them through the end of the school day. These children may take their first dose around 7:00 to 7:30, their second dose around 10:30 to 11:00, and a third dose around 2:30 or 3:00. For those children who have an event or activity after school which requires that they focus and control themselves (such as homework, scouts, music lessons, or sports), a third dose (usually lower) can be taken around 4:00. If this is the case, however, parents should monitor their child to determine whether this later dose makes it difficult for their child to settle down for bedtime. If this is a problem, the third dose may have to be eliminated.

Ritalin-SR (slow release) tends to last approximately seven to ten hours. Therefore, when taken before school, a second dose at noontime is not needed. It requires 45 to 60 minutes to have an effect, and it generally reaches peak effectiveness approximately four hours after ingestion. Ritalin-SR is the equivalent of taking two, 10 mg doses daily. This longer-acting drug is often preferred when children (especially adolescents) resist taking medication at school, as they must with traditional Ritalin. A "rebound" effect (deterioration in conduct as the short-acting drugs wear off) is also reduced or avoided with SR.

Many clinicians and parents report that Ritalin-SR is not as predictable in its effects, and for some children, not as effective as the traditional Ritalin. Research studies investigating Ritalin-SR have also produced disappointing results.[2] A major problem appears to be its unpredictable rate of metabolism in different children. Some individuals metabolize the drug predominantly in the morning hours, resulting in an over-medicated condition in the morning and an under-medicated condition in the afternoon. Another drawback of SR is that it only comes in 20 mg form, making it difficult to fine-tune the dosage. Also, a 20 mg dose may be too high, particularly for younger preschool children.

Ritalin can also be obtained in its generic methylphenidate form (remember to specify to the pharmacist whether you want Ritalin or the generic brand). Although this form of the drug is slightly less expensive, there are often problems with its effectiveness, because the precise dosage of each pill is less exact than with the Ritalin brand of the drug.[3,4] As a result, you can obtain a "bad batch" of the generic medicine, evidenced by an increase in ADHD symptoms and decreased school performance. If there is a dramatic difference in your child's response to his medication after obtaining a refill or new prescription of methylphenidate, call your physician or pharmacist. Always explore the option of obtaining a new prescription before jumping to the conclusion that your child is getting worse, that he needs a higher dose, or that medication no longer works for him.

The recommended daily maximum for Ritalin is 60 mg, although most children rarely exceed more than 40 mg per day. Ritalin is typically prescribed for children six years of age and older.

The specific dose of medication for a child is determined individually. There is no consistent relationship between weight, height or age and the clinical response to medication. A medication trial period of four to six weeks is often used to determine the most effective dosage. A child usually starts with a low 5 mg dose, and it is increased in intervals of 2.5 or 5 mg per week until the most beneficial dosage is achieved. It is recommended that the medication be monitored closely by a physician or psychologist for benefits and side effects during this trial period.

Medication monitoring is best done by asking teachers and parents to complete various behavioral rating scales *before* the child begins medication to obtain baseline readings of unmedicated behavior, and then again for a period of a few weeks while the medication dose is being adjusted to obtain readings of medicated behavior. The most ideal method is to collect these ratings during a period of time when the child takes the medication alternated with a placebo pill. In order to get objective ratings, raters should be unaware of medicated versus placebo conditions. Some of the rating scales used for medication monitoring include the parent and teacher versions of the *Conners' Rating Scale*, the *DSM-IV ADHD Rating Scale*, and the *Academic Performance Rating Scale* (see Appendix D). The pre- and post-medication ratings from these questionnaires are compared to determine the most beneficial dose. Asking the child if the medication is working is usually not a reliable indicator of the medication's effectiveness. Children with ADHD typically are not good judges of medication effectiveness. It is important, however, to listen to the child's complaints of any side effects.

DEXEDRINE

Dexedrine is the second most commonly used stimulant for the treatment of ADHD. It is also a Schedule II drug with strict regulations. Because it is an amphetamine, it comes with a strong warning about the potential for abuse and drug dependence (*not* physiological addiction) with prolonged use. Dexedrine is available in a short-acting 5 mg form. This tablet requires approximately 15-30 minutes to become effective. It reaches its maximum effectiveness at two to three hours, and the period of effect tends to last about four hours.

There is also a longer-acting sustained release form, Dexedrine Spansule, that is available in 5 mg, 10 mg and 15 mg capsules. It requires about 45-60 minutes to become effective and lasts approximately 8 to 12 hours. Like Ritalin SR 20, it avoids the rebound effect sometimes experienced with shorter-acting drugs.

A liquid form, Dexedrine Elixir, is also available. It is used primarily for preschool children. One teaspoon of the Elixir is equivalent to 5 mg.

Dexedrine has greater potency than Ritalin, so it is often prescribed in lower doses. Although research studies indicate that Dexedrine is as effective as Ritalin in the treatment of ADHD, it may have a slightly higher incidence of side effects, including height and weight suppression and perhaps a slightly greater suppression of appetite. There may also be a greater tendency for sadness. Generally, overall effectiveness, side effects, precautions for use, and procedure for determining therapeutic level are the same as for Ritalin. Dexedrine is approved for use by the FDA for children as young as three years of age. Therefore, some physicians prefer it for younger children.

CYLERT

Cylert is the third primary stimulant prescribed for the treatment of ADHD. It was first introduced into the American market in 1975. Cylert is a Schedule IV drug which has fewer restrictions. Parents, therefore, can phone their pharmacist for a refill. It is not used as often as Ritalin or Dexedrine because it takes about six to eight weeks before it becomes fully effective. This is a considerable disadvantage compared to Ritalin and Dexedrine, which begin to show effects within minutes and reach maximum effectiveness within two hours. Likewise, children must go off the drug gradually to avoid the development of flu-like symptoms. Studies indicate that, in general, Cylert may not be as effective as the other stimulants.

The advantage of Cylert is that its duration of effect is eight hours, which is considerably longer than the four-hour duration of Ritalin and Dexedrine. This allows children to eliminate the noontime dose which can become important for older children who resist going to the nurse's office during the school day. Cylert is usually taken once a day, most often in the morning. The initial dose is typically 37.5 mg which is then increased by 18.75 mg every three to five days until the best response is found. The maximum dose is usually 112.5 mg. Some children may take a second, half-dose at the end of the school day if the single morning dose loses its effectiveness in the afternoon. However, insomnia may be a resultant side effect.

ADDERALL

Adderall was originally marketed under a different name for treatment of obesity in adults. Recently, it has been found to be effective for some individuals with ADHD. This drug is very similar to Ritalin and Dexedrine in its benefits and side effects. It contains a combination of amphetamine salts and is available in double-scored (for easy cutting) 10 mg and 20 mg tablets. The usual starting dose is 2.5 mg daily for children three to five years old and 5 mg, one to two times daily for individuals six years and older. The maximum dosage usually does not exceed 40 mg a day. Adderall lasts 8 to 12 hours, eliminating the need for a noontime dose. It is also less expensive than the other stimulants. There is usually no medical problem if the medication is stopped suddenly, but it is preferable to do so gradually, over a week or so.

Although preliminary reports about Adderall are optimistic for its use with ADHD, the evidence of its effectiveness comes primarily from clinical case studies, not well-controlled studies.[5] Until more research is conducted, parents should be especially diligent in having their physician monitor the use of Adderall.

BENEFITS OF STIMULANTS

The benefits of stimulants fall into two main categories: cognitive and behavioral. Many different positive effects have been reported from the research. Not all children who take stimulants show all of these positive cognitive and behavioral benefits. **Each child's response to**

medication is unique to that child. Most likely, if medication is effective, a child will show *some* of the positive responses listed below.

Cognitive Effects

The possible beneficial *cognitive* effects of stimulants include the following:

- Increased attention span
- Increased persistence of effort
- Decreased impulsivity
- Increased fine-motor coordination
- Improved reaction time
- Improved handwriting
- Improved short-term memory
- Improved organizational skills
- Less absent-mindedness
- More careful and deliberate approach to tasks
- Increased short-term performance in reading, spelling, and math

Behavioral Effects

The possible beneficial *behavioral* effects of stimulants include the following:

- Decreased rates of off-task and out-of-seat behavior
- More purposeful and goal-oriented activity
- Decreased disruptiveness/blurting out
- Less excessive talking
- Better regulation of activity level
- Better conformance to rules
- More patience (e.g., waiting turn in line)
- More keeping hands to self
- Decreased aggression
- Improved frustration tolerance
- Fewer accidents and bodily harm
- Better direction-following

- Better follow-through with routines
- Less dawdling
- Less hoarding of food
- Improved social interactions
- Decreased stealing in elementary school
- Fewer car accidents as adolescents and adults
- Higher self-esteem

In general, stimulants will have their greatest effect on tasks or in situations that make demands for sustained attention, organization, persistence of effort, and control of impulses. Consequently, you may find that the medication has a more positive effect on your child's functioning in the classroom (the school hours are also the time when children are typically medicated). Teachers often comment that the student is less disruptive, does not blurt out as much, is more compliant and more productive. He may be better able to pay attention and to control those impulses that would draw him off task. As a result, he may stick with tasks longer and complete more schoolwork. He might be less restless and less hyper. He is likely more able to control the frustrations and emotions that interfere with his persistence so he can work through the frustrations of homework (if he is still medicated after school). You might also find that he works more carefully and less impulsively on written work, resulting in a side benefit of improved handwriting and fewer errors. He may be more organized and therefore better able to keep track of things.

There is some controversy over whether the short-term improvements in academic performance with medication (improved handwriting, increased productivity as measured in the number of problems completed, increased accuracy, etc.) translate to greater long-term gains in academic achievement. Academic achievement refers to the level of difficulty of academic material that is mastered by the child over longer-term use of the medication. Stimulants help the student stay on task, control impulses, manage frustration, persist longer, and produce more, thus improving his classroom performance. Intuitively, it would seem that because stimulants produce significant improvement in academic accuracy and productivity, then long-term academic achievement would also improve. More research is needed to determine whether these short-term improvements lead to long-term scholastic success.

With the use of medication, improvement in the child's social interactions is frequently reported. His increased ability to control impulses can be seen in reduced aggression, fewer anger outbursts, less intrusiveness, and less excessive talking. You might find that your child has better follow-through on some tasks and seems more focused and less forgetful. Perhaps most importantly, general compliance may improve, leading to more positive interactions between parent and child. This, of course, may have a positive effect on the child's self-esteem, which is perhaps the greatest benefit of all.

SIDE EFFECTS OF STIMULANTS

There are side effects with any medication. Side effects with stimulants occur when areas of the brain other than the targeted area are stimulated. Approximately 20-50 percent of children treated with Ritalin will manifest some unwanted side effect.[6] It is common, however, for side effects to decrease over the first two weeks of starting the medication. It is usually advised that a child *not* suspend his medication on weekends because of the increased chances of start-up side effects on Monday when he's back on medication for school.

The hundreds of studies that have been conducted to examine the side effects of Ritalin have found few, if any, long-term side effects. Most side effects are mild, short-term and self-correcting. In addition, some side effects (particularly irritability, anxiousness and crying) have also been reported during placebo conditions, suggesting that some side effects are not the result of medication but may represent problems associated with the child's ADHD itself.

Unlike Ritalin and Dexedrine, there is some concern that Cylert may cause changes in liver function after several months of treatment. This is a rare side effect, however, occurring in only 1-2 percent of children. As a result of this concern, it is suggested that before starting Cylert, blood tests to monitor liver function be performed and then repeated throughout its use. Cylert should not be used for individuals with liver disease or a family history of hepatitis. Other, less serious side effects with Cylert may be licking of the lips and picking of the fingertips.

Short-Term Side Effects

The short-term side effects of stimulants include the following:

- Decreased appetite
- Insomnia
- Height/weight suppression

- Irritability
- Sadness/tearfulness
- Headaches/stomachaches/nausea
- Drowsiness
- Reduced social interaction
- Dizziness
- Daydreaming/staring
- Nail biting
- Increased heart rate and blood pressure
- Tics
- Rebound

The most common side effects of stimulants are reduction in appetite (with accompanying weight loss) and difficulty with sleeping.[7] Many parents manage the problem of reduced appetite by giving their child the first dose after he has eaten breakfast. Lunch may be more affected, so you can moderate the problem somewhat by packing a lunchbox with food that your child especially likes. Smaller, nutritious snacks throughout the day may also help your child counteract any loss of appetite.

Insomnia is usually characterized by difficulty falling asleep, so your child may fall asleep an hour or two later than usual. If this is a problem, you can consult with your physician about lowering the dose. Irregular sleep cycles and difficulty falling asleep, however, are common with children with ADHD, whether or not they are on medication.

Irritability with sadness or proneness to crying are also more frequently reported side effects.[8] These symptoms may spontaneously diminish after a few weeks if they are related to medication. If they persist, it may suggest that these symptoms are expressions of underlying anxiety or depression that are exacerbated by the Ritalin. If this is the case, the dose should be lowered, or a different medication (perhaps a tricyclic antidepressant) should be considered. These medications are discussed in the following chapter.

Headaches and stomachaches may also be reported, but they tend to be mild and typically diminish after a few weeks of taking the medication. They can be counteracted by beginning medication at lower doses.

If a child is drowsy, has reduced social interaction, feels dizzy, seems to daydream or stare, or bites his nails a lot, the dose is probably too high and should be reduced.

Some children may experience a minor increase in heart rate or blood pressure with stimulants. The increase is small enough, however, that the vast majority of children are not at any risk.

Fewer than one percent of children with ADHD may show a body tic or nervous mannerism on stimulants.[9] Tics may take the form of eye blinking, squinting, lip twitching, shoulder shrugging, throat clearing, nose wrinkling, sniffing or coughing. In most cases, these tics are benign and usually do not get worse. However, decreasing the dose or withdrawing the medication completely will usually cause the tics to subside within one to two weeks. If there is a family history of tics or Tourette's syndrome (TS), stimulants are usually avoided, or the child is started on a very low dose. If tics develop, the medication should be stopped immediately.

"Rebound" is an increase in ADHD-related symptoms when the medication is wearing off, typically in the late afternoon or early evening. It is estimated that perhaps only a third of children who take stimulants experience rebound, and the severity of the rebound varies greatly across children.[10] Those who do experience rebound may manifest it for only a few weeks. To counteract rebound, a third, lower dose of medication can be administered in the late afternoon, or your child's noontime dose may be decreased to a half-dose. If your child is administered a third dose, be sure that this extra dose does not interfere with his falling asleep at night. If it does, discontinue the third dose. Rebound does not appear to be a side effect of the longer-acting medications (Ritalin SR, Dexedrine Spansule and Cylert).

MISCONCEPTIONS ABOUT SIDE EFFECTS OF STIMULANTS

The four potentially serious side effects of stimulants that seem to get the most attention are tics, Tourette's syndrome, growth suppression, an increased likelihood of drug and alcohol addiction, and addiction to Ritalin.

1. Tourette's Syndrome

There is no clear evidence that Ritalin causes Tourette's syndrome. Tourette's, a neurologically-based chronic tic disorder that causes involuntary vocal and motor tics, usually develops between four and seven years of age. It is a genetic disorder that appears to affect more boys than girls by a ratio of about 3 to 1. About half of all children with Tourette's have ADHD, but only about one percent of children with ADHD have Tourette's.[11,12] Motor tics are first evident as facial tics that may slowly progress to other parts of the body, such as shoulders, arms, and legs. Vocal tics may include throat clearing, sniffing, coughing, barking sounds, or profanities in advanced stages. Symptoms tend to increase in adolescence but may improve during early adulthood for some individuals.

Although well-controlled research studies do not support the notion that Ritalin causes Tourette's, it may unmask this disorder. If the Tourette's is already there, but the symptoms are not evident, Ritalin may possibly uncover them. This is because Ritalin increases the flow of the neurotransmitter dopamine, and individuals with Tourette's have too much dopamine in parts of their brain. About one in three children with Tourette's who are treated with stimulants become worse. In these cases, the medication should be discontinued immediately. Most children with Tourette's do not worsen, and one in three shows a reduction in symptoms with stimulants.

2. Growth Suppression

Early studies in the 1970s suggested that children treated with stimulants for one to three years did not grow as fast.[13,14] Furthermore, when they were off their medication in the summer, they grew faster than expected. From these studies it was believed that Ritalin suppressed growth, and that children should take "medication holidays" on weekends and in the summer to give them a break from these perceived ill effects.

More recent and better-controlled studies that followed children as long as eight years found that there was no adverse effect on height or weight even when the children were taking the medication every day. Although some more current studies suggest that growth in height and weight may be slightly suppressed over the first 16 to 18 months of taking medication, growth spontaneously corrects itself, and there are no long-term adverse effects. This temporary suppression appears to be dose-related and is found more frequently with Dexedrine.[15]

3. Substance Abuse

There are no studies that conclusively support the belief that treating children with stimulants increases the likelihood of subsequent drug addiction, alcohol abuse or criminal activity.[16] It may be true that individuals with more severe ADHD (that is, with greater impulsivity, more aggression and poor interpersonal relationships) are more prone to antisocial acts and drug use. These behaviors, however, are more directly related to the disorder itself rather than to stimulant medication. Long-term studies, in fact, reveal a more positive outcome for those individuals who engaged in a multi-modal treatment that included medication. More research is needed to rule out the possibility of increased substance abuse with stimulant use.

4. Ritalin Addiction

Parents often ask if their child can become addicted to Ritalin after long-term use. Ritalin is not addictive in the doses prescribed for ADHD. Both Ritalin and Dexedrine are short-acting medications which have no appreciable build-up in the bloodstream because they metabolize completely and relatively quickly. If used as prescribed, these medications will not cause physiological addiction.

PREDICTORS OF YOUR CHILD'S RESPONSE TO STIMULANTS

There is no certain way to predict how a child will respond to medication. In general, the greater the inattention, impulsivity and hyperactivity, the better the response to stimulant medication, assuming an absence of anxiety or depressive symptoms.

It has also been found that a lower percentage (approximately 55 to 65 percent) of children with ADHD, Predominantly Inattentive Type respond as dramatically to stimulant medication as those who manifest more prominent hyperactive-impulsive symptoms. It has also been found that these children may require a lower dose for positive effects.[17]

It may take weeks, or even months, to determine the right dosage, so it is important to not discontinue medication prematurely if it doesn't seem to be working immediately. Also, the mechanics and the site of action within the central nervous system for each of the stimulants appear to be different. Therefore, if your child does not respond to one stimulant, he may respond to a different stimulant. Sometimes a stimulant will be more effective with the addition of another medication, such as an antidepressant. This is especially true for those individuals who have ADHD and coexisting depression or anxiety.

There are some people who are extremely sensitive to any medication. For example, they do not easily tolerate aspirin or cold medicine, and/or they become extra "antsy" on caffeine. It is important to recognize this sensitivity and not automatically terminate medication, thinking that it won't work. Instead, try a much lower dose.

One final note on your child's response to medication. Some researchers suggest that if the child's behavior and social interactions are the targets of treatment, medication doses should be at moderate levels. However, if the targets of treatment are cognitive skills and learning, lower doses are more effective.[18] There is not total agreement among researchers concerning this theory, however.

WHEN STIMULANTS SHOULD NOT BE USED

There are some factors that suggest treatment with stimulant medication is not advisable. These factors include:

- Tics/Tourette's
- History of thought disorder
- Psychosis
- Anxiety
- Depression
- Age less than four years
- Seizure disorder

Various symptoms which often mimic attention disorders, such as anxiety, depression, or thought disorder, can be exacerbated with stimulants. Also, remember that stimulants can provoke motor tics in a small percentage of individuals. Children under four years of age may manifest more adverse side effects with the use of stimulants, and positive effects of these drugs are less predictive at this young age. It is also known that children with Pervasive Developmental Disorder (otherwise known as autism) usually do not respond well to stimulants. Additionally, children with seizure disorders may have more behavior problems on stimulants.

HOW LONG SHOULD A CHILD BE MEDICATED?

It is estimated that the average length of time a child is on medication is two to three years, but this varies depending on the child and the situation. There are no strict guidelines. Generally, the less severe the ADHD, the shorter the length of time that the child is on medication. Some children's symptoms may improve with maturation and behavioral intervention. These children may reach a point after a year or two where they no longer need the medication. Those with more severe symptoms may require medication for a longer duration, perhaps into adulthood.

If a child has a teacher who is a "good fit," he *may* do well enough that he doesn't need the medication for a particular school year. However, he may require a resumption of the medication the following year if the teacher-student fit is not as good, or if the academic and organizational demands increase (e.g., from elementary to middle school or middle school to junior high).

As children get older, usually in middle school or junior high, they may discontinue taking medication, not because they no longer benefit from it, but because they resist taking it. They may feel embarrassed going to the nurse's office at school; they may be tired of taking the medication; or they may now resist the diagnosis and any intervention connected to it. Unfortunately, during the period of their lives when they may need medication the most, they may refuse to take it.

Children may also resist taking their medication if they have frequently heard the refrain from adults, "I can tell you haven't taken your medication today because of the way you're acting." Such comments may make the child defensive about "needing" a pill in order to act in an acceptable way by adult standards.

It usually does not work to force an older child to take medication when he does not want it. Children invariably find a way around it, such as "forgetting" to take it, discarding it when you're not looking, or just actively refusing. At this point, some children will accept the compromise to switch to a long-acting form of medication to avoid having to go to the nurse's office at noon.

Some children will agree to take the medication only on an "as needed basis," such as when they have to study for a big test or when they have to attend some important function. Ritalin and Dexedrine (but not Cylert) can be taken on an as-needed basis because of their quick action. You should consult with your physician, however, before agreeing to this unique regimen. Other children will agree to stay on the medication during the school year if they can discontinue it during the summer. If your child is not going to summer school or camp, and his symptoms are not too severe, this compromise may be appropriate.

A child should be reevaluated for the continued effectiveness of the medication at least once a year. This reevaluation is best conducted during the school year when we can more effectively determine if the medication is or is not having a desired effect. It is recommended that a child begin the new school year with medication. This is typically a stressful time of the year, and it is important to get off to a good start. The medication can then be discontinued about six weeks into the school year for one or two weeks to compare his behavior on and off medication.

To determine continued medication effectiveness, the child's teacher(s) are usually asked to complete one or two short, behavioral questionnaires while the child is on medication, and then again during a week (or two) when he is off the medication. The ratings on these sets of questionnaires are compared to determine if there is measurably improved functioning on medication. If there is, the medication is continued. If the ratings on and off medication show little or no significant improvement on medication, a decision may be made to increase the dose or change to a different medication. However, if the ratings indicate that the child's behavior is appropriate both on and off medication, or if behavior and/or side effects worsen on medication, the medication may be discontinued.

SUMMARY

- Stimulants (especially Ritalin) are the most commonly prescribed medications for ADHD. They appear to work by increasing the production of dopamine and norepinephrine in the brain, thereby increasing arousal in the part of the brain responsible for regulating behavior.

- Common beneficial effects of stimulants include increased attention and persistence, improved compliance and direction following, decreased off-task behavior and disruptiveness, improved frustration tolerance, and higher self-esteem.

- The most common side effects of stimulants include decreased appetite, insomnia, headaches, stomachaches, and irritability with sadness.

- The most common misconceptions about stimulants are that they cause Tourette's syndrome, permanently stunt growth, lead to increased substance abuse, and are addictive.

21

Other Medications Used to Manage ADHD

TRICYCLIC ANTIDEPRESSANTS

Tricyclics antidepressants have also been used successfully in the treatment of ADHD. These medications were originally used to treat depression, but they have been found to be also effective for treating migraine headaches, bedwetting, anxiety, panic, obsessive compulsive disorders, and eating disorders.

The two most commonly used tricyclic antidepressants are **Tofranil** (imipramine) and **Norpramin or Petrofrane** (desipramine). There are other tricyclic antidepressants used with ADHD, including Elavil (amitriptyline), Anafranil (clomipramine) and Aventyl or Pamelor (nortriptyline), but their effectiveness with ADHD has not been studied as thoroughly. Therefore, this chapter focuses on imipramine and desipramine.

It is believed that these drugs, like stimulants, increase the availability of dopamine and norepinephrine in the frontal area of the brain. An advantage of the antidepressants is that their effects generally last the whole day, so they are better for controlling symptoms during the late afternoons and early evenings. They can be given in a single daily dose or in a divided dose in the morning and evening.

Unlike the stimulants, antidepressants build up in the bloodstream over a period of time. Consequently, it may take two to three weeks to achieve full benefit of the medication, although some effects can be seen as early as the first day. Since these drugs do build up in the bloodstream, they should not be stopped abruptly. They should be gradually discontinued over a few weeks to prevent withdrawal symptoms, such as nausea and headache. Also, skipping a dose may result in headaches, nausea, stomachaches, crying, irritability, or nervousness. Some physicians prefer to do blood tests to determine if a therapeutic level of medication is in the bloodstream. This is usually done when the child is at the typical dose for his height and weight, but his symptoms are not improving adequately or side effects are problematic. Some children may develop a tolerance to tricyclics after a year or two and no longer derive benefits. Consequently, the tricyclics are usually not considered long-term medications like the stimulants. However, some children may resume the medication a few months later, after their bodies have had a break from the drug.

When to Prescribe Tricyclic Antidepressants

Tricyclics are prescribed when:
- stimulants are found to be ineffective or contraindicated;

- the side effects from stimulants are intolerable;

- low self-esteem or a mood disorder are evident;

- the child is found to be anxious; or

- the child has tics or Tourette's (for which desipramine is prescribed).

The tricyclic antidepressants are generally considered a second-line medication for the treatment of ADHD. They are used when an individual has not responded to stimulants, the side effects from the stimulants are intolerable, or when there is an accompanying mood disorder or excessive anxiety along with ADHD. Studies suggest that the tricyclics are not as effective as the stimulants in improving attention and concentration and reducing hyperactivity. However, they may be effective in improving mood by decreasing irritability, modulating anger outbursts, and decreasing anxiety or sadness.[1] Therefore, if a child's anxiety or depression symptoms are of more concern than the ADHD-related symptoms, it may be advisable to start with a tricyclic antidepressant. A stimulant can be combined later.

Although **imipramine** was first developed to treat depression, it is frequently used with children to treat enuresis (bedwetting). It is also effective with individuals who suffer from anxiety, insomnia, or a mood disturbance along with their ADHD. Imipramine is first administered in low doses and gradually increased. The dosage for younger children ranges from 20 mg to 60 mg per day. Adolescents can receive between 30 mg and 100 mg per day maximum.

Desipramine is usually administered in 25 mg to 100 mg doses. It is available in 150 mg tablets, but this dose is not recommended for children. Desipramine is also prescribed when tics or Tourette's syndrome are evident. Unlike the stimulants and imipramine, desipramine does not exacerbate tics. Desipramine has not been approved by the FDA for children under 12 years of age, although some researchers have found it beneficial with younger children. There is concern, however, that there is an increased risk of cardiac toxicity in younger children.

Side Effects of Tricyclic Antidepressants

Side effects are usually not evident at lower doses of the tricyclics. At higher doses, children may develop:

- dry mouth,
- constipation,
- skin rash,
- drowsiness,
- urine retention,
- impaired fine-motor coordination,
- blurred vision,
- cardiac problems, and/or
- seizures.

Some children may experience dry mouth with antidepressants. If this is a side effect, it can be helped by giving the child hard candy such as lemon drops or sugar-free gum because they stimulate saliva. If the child experiences constipation, the amount of fiber in his diet should be increased or he should be given a stool softener. A skin rash may develop in a small percentage of children and is usually an allergic reaction to the food coloring in the pill. Some children may experience difficulty urinating. Others may be somewhat drowsy. Imipramine's side effects may also include impairment of fine motor coordination (such as reduced quality of handwriting), memory loss or blurred vision. Desipramine tends to have fewer side effects than imipramine. Insomnia and reduced appetite are not side effects of either.

There is concern that at higher doses the tricyclics may exacerbate cardiac problems because they can slow down the transmission of the electrical signal in the heart. Therefore, the tricyclics should not be used for individuals with a personal or family history of heart problems, conduction defects, or heart rhythm irregularities. It is advisable that individuals who are prescribed tricyclics initially be given an electrocardiogram (EKG) to measure heart activity. If there are abnormal findings on the EKG, a child should not be placed on these drugs. If tricyclics are prescribed, routine follow-up heart rate monitoring should be conducted.

These medications may increase the risk of seizures, especially if the child has a history of seizure disorder. In these cases, tricyclics should not be prescribed.

A rare side effect with tricyclic antidepressants is the possibility of a psychotic reaction characterized by mental confusion, excessive talking, unusual thinking, significantly increased activity level, and possibly hallucinations. If any of these symptoms are observed, the child's physician should be called immediately and the medication discontinued.

PROZAC

Prozac (fluoxetine) is an antidepressant more commonly used by adults for depression and anxiety. As yet, not many studies have investigated the usefulness of Prozac for children. However, some researchers have found that it can be helpful for children with ADHD who also suffer from depression and anxiety, or who are excessively aggressive. Prozac is less helpful for increasing attention span.

The initial dose of Prozac is typically 2.5 to 5 mg administered once a day. Each week the dose is increased in increments of 2.5 mg doses until beneficial effects, with minimal side effects, are found. Usually the highest dose per day of Prozac for children is 20 mg. It is usual to discontinue the medication once a year to determine if it is still needed.

Unlike the tricyclic antidepressants, Prozac does not cause a potential slowing of heartbeat. Possible side effects of Prozac include headaches, nausea, weight loss or gain, anxiety, sleep disturbance, or excessive sweating. Some parents have reported increased aggression in their child while on Prozac. Others report that their child seemed more irritable, restless or tense. Physicians usually suggest a lowering of the dose to reduce these symptoms.

Although Prozac shows much promise, more research is needed to better understand its usefulness with ADHD.

CLONIDINE

Clonidine (Catapres) is an anti high-blood-pressure medication that has recently been used to treat ADHD. It is also used to treat manic depression, obsessive compulsive disorder, schizophrenia, migraine headaches, panic disorder, and anorexia nervosa. Clonidine has been shown to reduce excitability and hyperactivity in children with ADHD. It has been especially useful for children with Tourette's because it does not seem to aggravate tics. For some children, it increases frustration tolerance and decreases aggressive/impulsive behavior and outbursts. Clonidine is often used if a child has not had a positive reaction to stimulants, if he is exceptionally defiant, or if he has a conduct disorder. However, clonidine is not as effective as the stimulants in improving attention and work productivity.

Clonidine is usually administered in a low dose of 0.05 mg and then gradually increased by 0.05 mg doses. The drug is typically taken at each mealtime and then again at bedtime for a total of four times a day. The full effects of this medication are usually seen in two to four months although some change can be seen in the first few weeks of initiating the drug.

In addition to a pill form, clonidine is available in a skin patch, Catapres-TTS. The patch, which can be worn for five days, is applied to a part of the body that is out of easy reach for a child, such as the hips or lower back. The patch is waterproof, so a child can bathe with it on. Physicians usually prefer to begin clonidine with the traditional pill form and then switch to the patch after a therapeutic dose is determined. A child should not discontinue clonidine abruptly, because it could result in a rapid increase in blood pressure, anxiety, an irregular heartbeat, sleep problems, headaches, or stomachaches.

Clonidine may have a sedative side effect which can last up to four weeks after initiating the medication. Some children do not overcome this sedation effect, so the medication has to be discontinued. Other side effects may include a slight drop in blood pressure or a mild decrease in heart rate, neither of which is considered serious. Nonetheless, an individual should be monitored for blood pressure and heart rate every few months while taking clonidine. Some individuals complain of dizziness, nausea, stomachaches, or headaches after starting this medication, but these side effects usually subside after a few weeks. Dry mouth, constipation or water retention may also occur. Rare side effects may include depression, anxiety, weight fluctuation or sleep disturbance.

The following table contains a summary of the medications most commonly used to treat ADHD.

Medication Chart to Treat Attention Deficit Disorders

DRUG	FORM	DOSING	COMMON SIDE EFFECTS	DURATION OF BEHAVIORAL EFFECTS	PROS	PRECAUTIONS
RITALIN® Methylphenidate	Tablets 5 mg 10 mg 20 mg	Start with a morning dose of 5 mg/day and increase up to 0.3-0.7 mg/kg of body weight. 2.5-60mg/day*	Insomnia, decreased appetite, weight loss, headache, irritability, stomachache.	3-4 hours	Works quickly (within 30-60 minutes); effective in 70 % of patients; good safety record.	Not recommended in patients with marked anxiety, motor tics or with family history of Tourette's syndrome.
RITALIN-SR® Methylphenidate	Tablet 20 mg	Start with a morning dose of 20 mg and increase up to 0.3-0.7 mg/kg of body weight. Sometimes 5 or 10 mg standard tablet added in morning for quick start. Up to 60 mg/day*	Insomnia, decreased appetite, weight loss, headache, irritability, stomachache.	About 7 hours	Particularly useful for adolescents with ADHD to avoid noontime dose; good safety record.	Slow onset of action (1-2 hours); not recommended in patients with marked anxiety, motor tics or with family history of Tourette's syndrome.
DEXEDRINE® Dextroamphetamine	Tablet Spansules 5 mg 5 mg 10 mg 15 mg Elixir	Start with a morning dose of 5 mg and increase up to 0.3-0.7 mg/kg of body weight. Give in divided doses 2-3 times per day. 2.5-40 mg/day*	Insomnia, decreased appetite, weight loss, headache, irritability, stomachache.	3-4 hours (tablet) 8-10 hours (spansule)	Works quickly (within 30-60 minutes); may avoid noontime dose in spansule form; good safety record.	Not recommended in patients with marked anxiety, motor tics or with family history of Tourette's syndrome.
CYLERT® Pemoline	Tablets (Long Acting) 18.75 mg 37.5 mg 75 mg 37.5 mg chewable	Start with a dose of 18.75-37.5 mg and increase up to 112.5 mg as needed in a single morning dose. 18.75-112.5 mg/day* have been reported.	Insomnia, agitation, headaches, stomachaches; infrequently, abnormal liver function tests.	12-24 hours	Given only once a day	May take 2-4 weeks for clinical response; regular blood tests needed to check liver function.

TOFRANIL® Imipramine Hydrochloride	Tablets 10 mg 25 mg 50 mg	Start with a dose of 10 mg in evening if weight <50 lbs. and increase 10 mg every 3-5 days as needed: start with a dose of 25 mg in evening if weight is >50 lbs. and increase 25 mg every 3-5 days as needed. Given in single or divided doses, morning and evening. 25-150 mg/day*	Dry mouth, decreased appetite, headache, stomachache, dizziness, constipation, mild tachycardia.	12-24 hours	Helpful for ADHD patients with comorbid depression or anxiety; lasts throughout day.	May take 2-4 weeks for clinical response; to detect pre-existing cardiac conduction defect, a baseline ECG may be recommended. Discontinue gradually.
NORPRAMIN® Desipramine Hydrochloride	Tablets 10 mg 25 mg 50 mg 75 mg 100 mg 150 mg	Start with a dose of 10 mg in evening if weight <50 lbs. and increase 10 mg every 3-5 days as needed: start with a dose of 25 mg in evening if weight is >50 lbs. and increase 25 mg every 3-5 days as needed. Given in single or divided doses, morning and evening. 25-150 mg/day*	Dry mouth, decreased appetite, headache, stomachache, dizziness constipation, mild tachycardia.	12-24 hours	Helpful for ADHD patients with comorbid depression or anxiety; lasts throughout day.	May take 2-4 weeks for clinical response; to detect pre-existing cardiac conduction defect, a baseline ECG may be recommended. Discontinue gradually.
CATAPRES® Clonidine Hydrochloride	Tablets Patches .1 mg TTS-1 .2 mg TTS-2 .3 mg TTS-3	Start with a dose of .025-.05 mg/day in evening and increase by similar dose every 3-7 days as needed. Given in divided doses 3-4 times per day. 0.15-.3 mg/day*	Sleepiness, hypotension, headache, dizziness, stomachache, nausea, dry mouth, localized skin reactions with patch.	3-6 hours (oral form) 5 days (skin patch)	Helpful for ADHD patients with comorbid tic disorder or severe hyperactivity and/or aggression.	Sudden discontinuation could result in rebound hypertension; to avoid daytime tiredness starting dose given at bedtime and increased slowly.

* Daily dose range

From *Medication and Classroom Guide* by H.C. Parker. Published by Specialty Press, Inc. d/b/a A.D.D. Warehouse copyright © 1997. Reprinted by permission of the publisher.

SUMMARY

- Tricyclic antidepressants are a second-line medication used for the treatment of ADHD. They are prescribed when stimulants are found to be ineffective or their side effects are intolerable; low self-esteem or a mood disorder is evident; the child is exceptionally anxious; or the child has tics or Tourette's syndrome.

- Common side effects of tricyclic antidepressants include dry mouth, constipation, skin rash, drowsiness, and urine retention.

- Prozac can be beneficial for children with ADHD who also suffer from depression, anxiety or excessive aggressiveness. Possible side effects include headaches, nausea, weight loss or gain, and sleep disturbance.

- Clonidine, an anti-hypertensive, is prescribed for children with ADHD who also have Tourette's syndrome or who are exceptionally defiant or aggressive. Sedation is the most common side effect.

Part Six

How to Be an Effective Advocate for Your Child at School

You must be an active and effective advocate for your child at school. Understandably, you would like school personnel to understand ADHD and realize its impact on your child's functioning. You would also like your child's teacher to "take the bull by the horns" and make appropriate modifications for him. However, many parents have come to know that they cannot take a passive role in the education of their child with ADHD. Too often, appropriate interventions for these students don't materialize in schools. The reasons are many: large classroom size, the ever-changing demands on teachers from all sides, the complexities and frustrations of dealing with ADHD, and/or the belief still held by some educators that ADHD is not a valid disability. Whatever the reasons, parents are often left confused, resentful and angry.

It is important to form an active partnership with your child's teacher(s) to ensure that the most appropriate modifications and interventions are put in place for your child. Also remember that you should not be lulled into the false conclusion that because one school year went well, the following year is going to go just as well. There is rarely any break in the task of overseeing your child's educational program. Every year is different. The "goodness of fit" between a teacher and your child is probably the most critical factor in his success, and it changes from year to year. Also, the demands for organizing, completing homework, creating written work, and functioning independently increase every year. It is essential to treat each school year as a new challenge and a new responsibility.

Always be vigilant! Learn from the experiences of past years, such as what has worked for your child and what hasn't. Remember what situations posed more problems for him and what situations made life easier. Take your ever-increasing knowledge base — learned from hard experience, successes and failures — and share it with your child's teachers in a collaborative effort to maximize his chances for success.

Work hard to avoid an antagonistic relationship with your child's teacher. When parents work with teachers in a collaborative manner, the year goes much more smoothly. Teachers are generally grateful to receive information about ADHD if it is offered with the intention of wanting to work together to help your child rather than to somehow suggest to the teacher that he/she is uninformed.

There are many things involved in being an active and effective advocate for your child at school:

1. Understanding the effects of ADHD in the classroom
2. Understanding appropriate classroom modifications
3. Knowing the laws and your rights
4. Keeping records of your child
5. Preparing for the IEP or Section 504 meeting
6. Providing input into the selection of your child's teacher
7. Scheduling a meeting with your child's teacher(s) at the beginning and end of the school year
8. Establishing communication between school and home

The next seven chapters discuss these strategies. Select the ones that best fit you and your child's needs, experiences and strengths. Use them to create and execute a plan for success.

Understanding the Effects of ADHD in the Classroom

No one knows your child better than you. You must be the expert. That means you must totally understand how your child functions at home, *and* at school. Therefore, it is important to educate yourself in the dynamics of ADHD in the classroom.

Students with ADHD typically encounter their greatest challenges at school. Consider these statistics:[1,2,3]

- Over 90% of students with ADHD have problems in school

- 58% have received at least one failing grade by adolescence

- 20-25% have been suspended from school

- 11% have been expelled

- 50% have been retained in a grade at least once

- 20-35% will have at least one identified learning disability through high school

- Over 40% are in programs for learning disabilities or emotional/ behavior disorders

- 20-25% have a reading disorder

- 35% will not graduate from high school (four times the national drop-out rate)

- 20% go on to college (compared to 40-45% of the normal population)

- 5% graduate from college (compared to 20-25% of the normal population)

These sobering statistics tell us that there is indeed something about ADHD and the classroom that just does not mix. ADHD is an educational disorder, and children with ADHD are at risk in the classroom. However, there is good news. Studies show that the risks are reduced when special education and/or related services (e.g., behavior programming, classroom organization and management, and curriculum modifications) are implemented.

WHY ARE ADHD AND THE CLASSROOM SO INCOMPATIBLE?

What is it about ADHD that makes it so incompatible with the classroom? Remember the neurobiological basis of ADHD: there is reduced brain activity or understimulation in the prefrontal portions of the brain. This understimulation affects such functions as alertness, attention, concentration, impulse control, emotional control, organization, frustration tolerance, motivation, response to consequences, and persistence of effort over time. When these functions are impaired, there is a tremendous, negative impact on your child in school, where he is required to sit still, pay attention, work independently, work for long periods of time, stay organized, stay motivated, ignore distractions, and control impulses. ADHD interferes with your child's ability to effectively or consistently meet such behavioral and cognitive demands. As a result, he may often be in trouble academically and/or behaviorally in the classroom.

Let's look again at the diagram of the Brain Stimulation Curves from Chapter 3. It explains the disorder and also illustrates what has to happen in the classroom for intervention strategies to be effective.

The inverted U curve at the top represents the functioning of an individual who does not have an attention deficit. As his neurologic stimulation increases and he is engaged in a task, there is a corresponding increase in sustained attention, impulse and behavioral control, motivation and persistence. The individual is able to sustain these functions long enough to function effectively and "get the job done."

In contrast, the curve for the person with ADHD has many ups and downs. The downs, or "valleys," correspond to neurobiological understimulation. They represent periods of reduced attention, poor impulse control, low motivation, poor persistence, fragile emotional control, and low frustration tolerance. These "valleys" fluctuate over time, depending upon such factors as the nature of a particular task, the complexity or difficulty of that task, the length of time the person has to stay engaged, fatigue, and the amount and immediacy of feedback or reinforcement.

What is often confusing to teachers is this picture of variability and inconsistency. Your child with ADHD may pay attention, control his impulses and activity level, and work productively one day (or one hour) but not the next, as shown by the peaks and valleys in the graph.

Brain Stimulation Curves

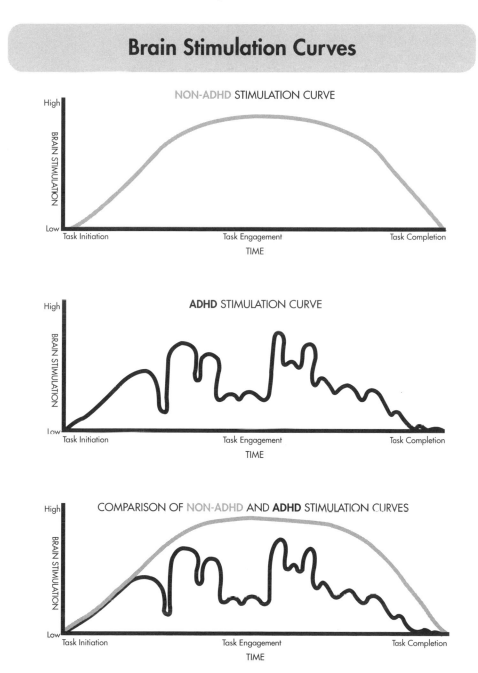

A teacher may erroneously conclude that because your child stays attentive and completes a task sometimes, he should be able to do it all the time. When he does not, he is characterized as "lazy," "unmotivated," or "not trying." Behavior that is actually a result of neurobiological understimulation (and therefore is not effectively within your child's control) is erroneously interpreted as willful, causing teachers (and parents) to say, "I know he could do it if he really wanted to," or "He can't be ADHD because I've seen him do the work when he feels like it."

This working model of ADHD underscores the importance of *appropriate* stimulation. The task for educators is to "raise the valleys" by providing students with ADHD with an appropriate level of stimulation to keep them effectively engaged. "Raising the valleys" includes such modifications as shortening work periods, allowing work breaks, decreasing monotony, decreasing repetition, increasing task variation, providing hands-on learning experiences, allowing needed physical movement, and providing immediate and consistent reinforcement and feedback for appropriate behavior.

If the student is in an environment or engaged in a task that does not provide appropriate stimulation, he will essentially provide his own stimulation by finding other objects, people or activities in the environment that are more stimulating. He will "bug his neighbor," fidget with his pencil, dig through his desk, leave his seat to sharpen his pencil or get a drink of water, or tune into whatever's going on outside the classroom window. Or he will rush through his work to get to something more stimulating such as recess, lunch or talking to a neighbor. In all of these situations, the student has difficulty "putting the brakes on" his impulse to seek stimulation. He is consequently drawn off task.

A child who is bored in the classroom, who cannot keep up with the pace of instruction, who cannot effectively control his impulses, and who experiences repeated academic failures, becomes discouraged, defensive, and finally, demoralized.

ADHD IN THE DAY OF A STUDENT

Many parents repeatedly go through the morning struggle of getting their child out of bed and out the door for school in the morning. Later, they face the nightly battle of first getting their child to admit that he *has* homework and then getting him to do it. Why such resistance? Quite simply, many children with ADHD find school to be a negative experience and therefore resist going to school in the morning and doing more schoolwork once they get home.

How does this resistance develop? Let's take a look at the problem through the eyes of Jeff, a student with ADHD.

Jeff, a fourth-grader with ADHD, hates to get up in the morning. When he hears his mother telling him he's going to be late for school if he doesn't get up now, he is filled with a sense of dread that builds into resentment and then anger. He says to himself, "How would my mom like to go to a job every day where the boss always tells her what she is doing wrong like my teacher does to me? I bet she wouldn't be too eager to get out of bed either."

Jeff drags himself out of bed and into the kitchen for breakfast. His mother reminds him again that he better get a move on; she is sick and tired of always having to push him in the morning. After breakfast, he stops to play with the dog and gets sidetracked by the television. He hears his mother calling from the kitchen, "Jeff, are you getting washed and dressed?" Jeff absentmindedly calls back, "Yeah," and continues to watch cartoons. When his mother comes to check on him, she is furious that he is parked in front of the television and hasn't even gotten dressed yet. She tells him to get going because he only has 10 minutes before the bus comes.

Jeff goes to his room to get dressed, moving at a pace that is irritatingly slower than the time pressures demand. His mother calls out in exasperation that he has only 5 minutes to finish getting dressed, brush his teeth and comb his hair. Jeff's siblings are already getting their jackets on and are ready to go out the door. Jeff is still upstairs. His mother rushes to his room to find that Jeff still doesn't have his socks on. She grabs a pair of socks from his drawer and demands that he put them on, fast.

As they run downstairs together, Jeff's mother asks him if he has his backpack and homework. Jeff has no idea where his backpack is and then remembers that he forgot to study his spelling words for his test today. That familiar rush of dread comes over him again. Jeff's mother races around trying to find the backpack while Jeff is rushing to get his jacket on. He runs out the door, jacket unzipped, without his backpack. His mother frantically runs after him to give him his backpack before he gets on the bus.

Jeff gets on the bus and elbows his way to a seat. His adrenaline is still flowing from the mad rush out the door; a rush that happens every day. The loud yelling and pushing on the bus further stimulate Jeff, who is easily irritated. He has a hard time putting the brakes on his already revved-up emotions. So when another student bumps into him and Jeff falls back, he sees red. He impulsively reacts by pushing the boy back and calling him a name. The bus driver reprimands Jeff and reports him to the principal. One more incident on the bus and he will be suspended from the bus for three days.

Things don't get much better once Jeff is in the classroom. It's hard for him to settle into the routine of the classroom because he is still upset about the chaotic start to his day at home and the trouble on the bus. His patience is limited, and his temper is short. Jeff's teacher tells the students to gather their materials, open their books, begin working on pages 35 through 45, and when they are finished with that, to start on their journals. Jeff is digging through his desk all the while, trying to find a pencil.

Once he finds his pencil, he forgets what his teacher told him to do. He leans over and asks another student. His teacher tells him to get back to work. Jeff looks at the assigned work and immediately feels overwhelmed by the quantity. He tells himself there is no way he can do all that. He goes to sharpen his pencil, hoping maybe that will get him going. On his way to the pencil sharpener, he takes a detour to the doorway to see what the noise in the hallway is all about. He becomes engrossed by the sight of the third-graders lining up for a field trip and asks one of them where they are going. Jeff's teacher sees that he is out of his seat and tells him to get back to work.

Jeff goes back to his desk, tapping other students on the shoulder along the way. One student yells at Jeff to stop bugging him. Jeff was thinking about the field trip as he made his way back to his desk and was not even aware that he was tapping students' shoulders. His teacher puts his name on the board and gives him a stern warning. Jeff sits back in his seat, with an unsharpened pencil.

As the morning wears on, Jeff becomes increasingly antsy and bored. He has a hard time staying focused on his teacher's lectures. His mind wanders to subjects that are more stimulating, such as getting to level seven on his new Sega® game or thinking about working on his tree fort after school. All of a sudden he hears the teacher call his name, and he has no idea what she asked him. His teacher tells him to pay attention, and the student sitting next to Jeff starts to giggle because Jeff has gotten into trouble one more time. Jeff gets angry at what he perceives to be the other student's teasing and yells at him to mind his own business. A check mark goes up on the board after Jeff's name.

As his teacher talks on, Jeff's self-control grows thin and his boredom increases. He needs some kind of stimulation; anything would be better than listening to his teacher "talk all day" or sitting and doing worksheets. Jeff begins to flick paper clips at the girl sitting in front of him, doing what feels good at the moment. The girl calls out, complaining to the teacher. The teacher walks back to Jeff, sternly reprimands him, takes away the paper clips, and puts another check by his name, reminding him that one more check and he's off to the principal's office.

Jeff thankfully welcomes recess so that he can get out of that "boring" classroom and have some fun. He joins the other students as they play kickball. Before too long, Jeff is yelling at another student who said Jeff was tagged out. Jeff is highly competitive and doesn't like the thought of losing. His anger rushes over him like a crashing wave, and he throws the ball at the other student, hitting him in the head. The playground monitor expels Jeff from the game and sends him to the principal. He receives the same lecture from the principal that he's heard a thousand times from adults: he had better start following the rules and thinking about the consequences of his behavior. He is suspended from the playground for the next three days.

Back in the classroom, Jeff has a hard time settling down again. His teacher tells him to stop milling around and to get to his desk. He is still agitated about the kickball game and feels penned in by the classroom. His impulsivity escalates. As his teacher carries on a classroom discussion, Jeff blurts out answers. His teacher tells him to raise his hand, and he tries hard for the next few questions, but he has a difficult time waiting to be called upon. He blurts out again. Other students angrily chastise him to stop "hogging all the answers." Jeff's defenses immediately go up and he tells another student to "shut up." The third check goes up by Jeff's name, and he is sent to the principal's office for the second time in one day. He is given another lecture plus a note to bring home to his parents to sign and return the next day. Jeff gets back to his classroom just in time to stuff his papers into his backpack and get on the bus.

When Jeff gets home, his mother asks him if anything happened at school today. He is tired of this constant question and gives his usual response, "No." His mother asks him if he has any homework. The last thing Jeff wants to do right now is to sit at a table and do more schoolwork; it's too boring and takes too long. He would rather be watching television, playing with his video games, or building his tree fort. He has come to know that homework turns into a battle every night with his mother, and he doesn't want to go through that tonight. He tells his mother he did his work at school.

Jeff's mother looks in his backpack and sees a clump of crumpled up worksheets, some of which were due last week, some of which are due the following day. She also sees the note from the principal. She is angry, concerned, frustrated, and humiliated. Jeff again feels attacked, and his defenses go up immediately. His mother tells him that he can't watch television or play with anyone until his homework is done. The problem is, Jeff forgot his books at school. He feels demoralized — everyone is mad at him. He dreads the thought of going back to school the next day just to go through this all over again. He has no idea how to change things. No one understands, including him. So what's the use of trying?

Adults can perhaps better understand how a child with ADHD may feel about school if they imagine themselves going to work every day and experiencing this level of negative attention, failure, frustration, and boredom. As an adult, they would probably quit and find another more rewarding job. Students with ADHD don't have this option. Since they can't quit by leaving and finding another school, they quit by feeling overwhelmed, falling further behind, and eventually giving up. Once they are in high school, they may drop out.

SUMMARY

- The child with ADHD is at risk in the classroom because the things that bring success there are the very things that are among his greatest challenges: sitting still, paying attention, working for long periods of time, etc.

- The pattern of understimulation in ADHD is not an even one, so inconsistency is commonplace.

- Modifications in the school setting (e.g., shorter work periods) can dramatically help the student with ADHD. Without them, he will experience boredom, frustration and failure, all of which add up to a negative school experience that may lead to dropping out, figuratively in the younger years and literally in the high school years.

Understanding Appropriate Classroom Modifications

To be an effective advocate for your child, you must understand the types of classroom interventions and adaptations that are appropriate for a child with ADHD. The complex nature of ADHD typically requires modifications in many areas. This chapter is designed to be a tool for parents to use in working with school personnel. There are many possible modifications, only some of which will be appropriate for your child's teacher. However, by understanding the large number of options, you can be a better advocate for your child.

The modifications are organized by eight areas of intervention: Goal-Setting, Reinforcement and Feedback, Attention, Impulsivity, Distractibility, Structure, Organization, and Motivation. Note: for ease of readability, this chapter is written in a format as suggestions for a teacher rather than a parent. Also, some of the techniques offered for parents in other chapters are repeated so that this chapter is self-contained.

1. ESTABLISH APPROPRIATE GOALS

The student with ADHD has to manage many problems in the classroom. Appropriate goals are an important tool for him, along with specific steps to achieve these goals.

- **Student Involvement**

  When a student is having behavioral difficulties, discuss those difficulties with him. Ask for his perception of the problem and his suggestions for solutions. Together, set up a behavioral goal(s) upon which to focus and an incentive program to help reach the goals. Soliciting the student's input in this process increases his motivation and commitment.

- **Positive Goals**

  Choose behavior(s) you would like the student to start doing rather than stop doing. For example, if the student is often off-task, choose as your goal to increase on-task behavior rather than to decrease off-task behavior.

- **Short-Term Goals**

  Students with ADHD have great difficulty working for long-term goals. They usually lose focus, persistence and motivation before they ever reach the goal. Avoid beginning with end-of-the-week or even end-of-the-day goals with younger students and end-of-the-quarter goals with older students. For example, with a younger student, working on on-task behavior may have to start with half-hour, then hourly, then half-day goals. Gradually increase the goal to full day, and so on. For older students, a similar breakdown may apply, depending on the problem behaviors.

- **Limited Goals**

  Begin intervention with only one or two goals and add new ones slowly. Given the many   problems that the student with ADHD has in the classroom, the inclination is to establish many goals simultaneously in order to improve behavior quickly. This only serves to overwhelm the student and increase the chances for failure.

- **Reinforcement at a Level of Success**

  When initiating a positive reinforcement program in the classroom, begin at a level where the student can achieve success immediately. Setting a goal too high will prevent the student from experiencing success soon enough, and he will give up. At first, reinforcement should be provided when the student is at, or slightly above, baseline. Increase the goal level very gradually and in small steps (e.g., first complete five out of ten, then eight out of ten, then ten out of ten math problems).

2. PROVIDE REINFORCEMENT AND FEEDBACK

Students with ADHD are more sensitive to (and dependent on) reinforcement and feedback than other students. Basically, reinforcement and feedback help stimulate the motivation and persistence and direct the focus that students with ADHD inherently lack.

- **Problems with Traditional Assertive Discipline**

  Traditional forms of assertive discipline (e.g., name on the board, check mark after his name when he breaks a rule, trip to the principal's office after three check marks, etc.) are often ineffective with students with ADHD and can exacerbate the problems . Generally, students with ADHD function more successfully with consistent and specific feedback and positive reinforcement (such as a token system) coupled with a response-cost procedure (in which the consequence for negative behavior is to forfeit tokens or points previously earned).

- **Immediate and Frequent Feedback and Consequences**

  Students with ADHD require more immediate feedback and consequences than do other students to maintain control over their behavior. Feedback should be clear and specific and should be given as soon as possible after the target behavior. Feedback and consequences given only at the end of the day or after long intervals will be less effective and less likely to control ADHD symptoms. Not surprisingly, students with ADHD also require more frequent feedback and consequences than other students.

- **Consistent Feedback and Consequences**

  Inconsistency in behavior interventions is one of the main reasons a behavior management program with a student with ADHD may fail. It is imperative that all teachers and parents working with the student work together to apply the devised behavior management strategies consistently over time, across settings, and across people.

- **Salient Feedback and Consequences**

  Research suggests that students with ADHD are less sensitive to rewards and therefore require stronger rewards/consequences to control their behavior, motivate them, and sustain positive activity and productivity. Whereas verbal praise may be sufficient for most students, it may be too weak of a consequence for the student with ADHD.

- **Positive Before Negative**

  It is critical to avoid the natural tendency to point out and then punish the student with ADHD for what he is doing wrong. To change an undesirable behavior in a student with ADHD, first redefine the problem behavior into its positive alternative. For example, if the problem is off-task behavior, redefine the focus as on-task behavior. Then focus on and reward occurrences of this positive behavior for at least one week before implementing a "punishment" component. The ratio of positive (reward) to negative (punishment) should be about 2:1.

- **Token System**

  Students with ADHD need a specialized positive reinforcement system to keep them on track. The most effective is a token system. With this system, the student earns points or tokens for appropriate behavior. After obtaining a predetermined number of points or tokens, the student can cash them in for a desired item or activity. The advantages of a token system are that tokens can be dispensed immediately, thus providing needed immediate feedback and reinforcement; they allow the dispensing of the primary reinforcer (reward or privilege) at a later and more convenient time (e.g., after class rather than during class); they reduce satiation (unlike edible reinforcers); and they increase motivation because they can be cashed in for various desirable items or activities.

- **Response Cost**

  Students with ADHD are most successful with a combination of positive reinforcement and response cost. Response cost means that the student loses what he previously earned (points, tokens, etc.) if he commits an infraction. Response cost is most effective if the student loses approximately one-tenth to one-fifth of what was earned. For example, if he earns five points for completing an assignment, he loses one point for not completing one.

- **Modified Response Cost**

  Because students with ADHD have histories of not earning rewards, they are often more motivated when they are working to keep what they already have rather than earning something they do not have. This strategy provides the student with the entire reward in points, tokens, etc., at the start of the day. He must then work to keep the points. Every time he commits an infraction of the agreed-upon rule(s), he loses a certain number of points. At the end of the day, he is given whatever is left, which he can cash in for a reward.

- **Frequent Changes in Reinforcers**

  Reinforcers lose their value sooner for the student with ADHD, so they should be changed relatively frequently. Also, it's good to let the student have input in choosing both positive and negative reinforcers (i.e., what he would work for and work to avoid). A reward menu with the objects or events the student has chosen to work for and the value in tokens for each item (refer to Appendix B), is an effective way to vary the reinforcers and to keep the student engaged in working toward his goals.

- **Daily Report Card**

  Students with ADHD need ongoing monitoring of their academic and behavior goals on a *daily* basis. A daily report card system does exactly that (refer to Appendix C). Teachers monitor various classroom behaviors (e.g., begins tasks, completes assigned tasks, etc.) by frequently giving written ratings (e.g., 1 to 5) on a reporting sheet (for younger students, an index card can be taped to the corner of his desk). This sheet or card is sent home on a daily basis. The teacher's ratings are then converted by parents into either positive or negative consequences (e.g., getting to stay up an extra 15 minutes for reaching a goal; losing television privileges for failing to reach a goal, etc.). For many children these consequences are more meaningful and effective than those readily available in school (e.g., stickers and extra recess time). This system also frees the teacher from the often-cumbersome responsibility of counting up points and dispensing rewards at the end of a busy and hectic school day. Implicit in using such a system, of course, is the need for ongoing communication, cooperation and collaboration between parents and school personnel.

- **Progress Charts**

  Students with ADHD need a concrete tracking system to monitor their behavior. Charts can list many things: behavior or academic goals; points earned toward the goals; rewards for achieving the goals; and consequences for failing to achieve the goals. Charts should be simple, and the student should have ongoing access to his chart so he can monitor his own progress. Sometimes younger students enjoy making their own charts.

- **Notebook System**

  Daily comments, observations or concerns of the teacher are written in a notebook that is sent home with the student on a daily basis. The parents read the comments and also add any questions or observations that they feel would be helpful for the teacher. It may be necessary to award the student a point each day for remembering to bring the notebook to and from school and also to establish a consequence for "forgetting" it.

- **End-of-the-Week Rewards**

  The student with ADHD has problems with motivation and impulsivity; therefore, maintaining work toward a daily goal throughout the week may by too long term. End-of-the-week goals with rewards can help sustain daily performance. For example, if the student reaches his daily goal four out of five days, give him an additional reward or some bonus points to save toward a bigger reward, such as a class party.

- **Specific Verbal Praise**

  Students with ADHD are often unaware of their behaviors. Therefore, when the student does something that you like, avoid general verbal praise. Instead state exactly what he did that you liked (e.g., "You went to your desk immediately and started your worksheet."). This focuses the student on his behavior plus helps him know what the appropriate behavior is. Bear in mind that verbal praise for the student with ADHD is most effective if it is also paired with a tangible reinforcement system.

- **Secret Signal**

  Develop a secret signal with the child to signal to him that he needs to make a behavior change. This is a respectful way of telling him to stop inappropriate behavior. A touch of your nose or cheek or a touch on the student's shoulder signals your message without drawing attention to him or embarrassing him in front of his peers.

- **Positive Redirection**

  When the student with ADHD is exhibiting an unwanted behavior in the classroom, instead of pointing out to him what he should *not* be doing, tell him what he *should* be doing. This helps him understand what is expected and avoids the common dilemma of the student with ADHD discontinuing one unwanted behavior but replacing it with a different one.

3. INCREASE ATTENTION AND ON-TASK BEHAVIOR

A primary deficit underlying ADHD is the inability to remain on-task and pay attention. To function effectively in the classroom, the student must master various attentional skills such as paying attention to what is important while ignoring what is not important, sustaining attention over time, dividing attention between simultaneous tasks (e.g., listening and note-taking), and being vigilant or ready to respond when necessary.

- **Eye Contact**

    Establish eye contact with the student with ADHD before giving him directions. If his eyes are diverted during direction-giving, he is less likely to recall and follow instructions. Be sure to face the student when writing on the board and avoid standing behind him when teaching.

- **Simplified Instructions**

    We are often unaware of the complexity of the instructions we give children. This is especially problematic for students with ADHD. Try to keep instructions short and simple. Do not hand out several worksheets and give all of the instructions at one time. Hand out one worksheet and give the instructions for only that worksheet. Repeat the instructions frequently throughout the task. It may be helpful to have the child repeat the instructions aloud before he begins a new task. This should be done as inconspicuously as possible to avoid embarrassing him. Or, assign a peer to whom the child can turn for help if he forgets an instruction.

- **Decreased Monotony**

    The behavior of students with ADHD tends to worsen with repetitive, routine activities. The more novelty that can be introduced into the learning situation, the better their attention will be. Also provide frequent structured breaks to maintain the student's effective arousal.

- **Morning Academics**

  Students with ADHD usually function optimally during the morning hours. Therefore, it is better to schedule more demanding academic instruction in the morning rather than the afternoon.

- **Reduced Workload**

  It is difficult for students with ADHD to sustain their attention to assigned tasks. Therefore, adjusting the child's classroom workload should be considered. One way to do this is to have the student complete a smaller subset of assigned items. For instance, instead of doing all 20 items, the student might be asked to complete the first 10 items only or perhaps just the odd-numbered ones. As long as the assigned number is sufficient for learning the material, learning will be enhanced. Similar adjustments can be made with homework.

- **Shortened Tasks**

  Remember that students with ADHD need to see an endpoint in order to stay focused and motivated. It is crucial, therefore, that assigned tasks be broken down into smaller segments that can be accomplished in a relatively short time. For example, a 20-item task might be presented as four, separate five-item tasks. After each set of five items is completed, the next five items are presented. Or, instead of working on math problems for 30 minutes, break the task into three, 10-minute periods or two, 15-minute periods. Tell the student how to recognize the endpoint (e.g., draw a line under the last item, put a red mark or red clock at the end, or set a timer).

- **Computer-Aided Instruction**

  In situations where students with ADHD do not respond well to traditional teaching techniques, academic instruction using the computer can be an excellent alternative. It affords them greater stimulation, self-pacing and more immediate feedback, thereby increasing their motivation for completing assignments.

- **Simplified but Stimulating Worksheets**

  Worksheets should be simple in appearance but designed to maintain the student's attention. Limited amounts of print, wide spacing, lines to separate material, and blocking out or folding under portions of the worksheet are a few ways to help reduce visual distractions. Using color for emphasis and squares or other highlights around important information help the student focus.

- **Timer-Managed Compliance**

  Using a timer is an effective way to keep the student with ADHD on task and working for the appropriate amount of time. Tell him ahead of time what he is to do during the time interval and then set the timer for a period that matches his attention abilities. If he engages in behavior that is incompatible with academic work, stop the timer, again tell him what he should be doing, and reset the timer. If he engages in target behavior throughout the preset time interval, he receives a predetermined number of points.

- **Sanctioned Movement**

  Standard classroom expectations are that students remain seated and limit excess body movement for relatively long periods of time. Students with ADHD often lose attention in this situation because they cannot effectively modulate arousal or energy levels to stay engaged in a task. Therefore, allowing the student to get up and stretch in between segments increases his arousal and helps him maintain attention.

- **Active Participation**

  Many students with ADHD will maintain focus and attention longer if they are actively and frequently engaged in the lesson. Therefore, avoid teaching by lecture only. Devise lessons that allow active involvement, movement or some sort of motoric participation. Use rhythm and music to learn rote facts. Teach history through drama. Learn science in the out-of-doors. Allow the student to come to the front of the class and point to answers on a chart or write his answers on the board.

- **Learning Partners**

  One of the most problematic situations for the student with ADHD is doing independent written work at his desk. This is when inattention and disruptive behaviors increase. Pairing the student with a peer who has good independent work habits will encourage him to be more on-task and attentive.

- **Active Listening**

  Opportunities for active listening should be provided. Active listening opportunities can be structured similar to a guided reading lesson. "Who," "what," "where," and/or "why" questions should be identified or listed before the lesson or story begins and then answered when the activity is completed. Also, avoid using predictable strategies for calling on students to participate (e.g., calling on a row at a time). Such predictability encourages the student with ADHD to not pay attention.

- **Task Review**

  Structure tasks to incorporate review. Announce to the class before beginning a lesson: "We will spend a few minutes on the directions and 10 minutes doing the task. Then you will spend 10 minutes reviewing your work." Also write these steps on the board. To keep the student actively involved, have him either rewrite what he feels are correct answers, or make a check by them. Help the student keep his own file of work at school. Review the file with him weekly and ask him to analyze his progress.

- **Self-Correcting Materials**

  The student with ADHD should be given many opportunities to immediately compare his answers with the correct ones. This not only helps maintain his attention but also provides pacing and feedback, which are critical for his success. Mathematics is an area where it is possible to provide students with numerous opportunities to develop the ability to self-correct their work.

- **Attention Tape**

  The attention tape is an effective, self-monitoring procedure used to improve attention-to-task. It consists of a tape that plays short beeps at irregular intervals. Every time the beep sounds, the student records on a monitoring sheet whether or not he was paying attention, was on-task, etc. This procedure should not be used with students younger than second grade. A commercial version of this system, *Listen, Look, and Think: A Self-Regulation Program for Children*, developed by Dr. Harvey Parker, is available through the A.D.D. WareHouse (1-800-233-9273). Other self-regulation systems available through the A.D.D. WareHouse include the MotivAider® developed by Dr. Steve Levinson, and the *Attention Training System Starter Package* developed by Dr. Michael Gordon.

- **Match Procedure**

    Self-monitoring procedures are most effective when they are combined with an accuracy component. If a student is monitoring his behavior on a self-monitoring sheet, his teacher can monitor the behavior during the same time period on his/her own rating sheet. With an attention tape, both can check the student's behavior with each beep. At the end of a 25-to 30-minute period, the teacher compares his/her ratings with the student's and awards bonus points if his self-ratings match or approximate the teacher's ratings.

4. DECREASE IMPULSIVITY

Impulsivity, or the inability to effectively inhibit or regulate one's behavior and thus "think before acting," is a major deficit underlying ADHD. Essentially, these students cannot easily wait and regulate their behavior to meet the demands of a situation. Consequently, planning does not occur before behavior. These students are "managed by the moment."

- **Decreased Time Pressure and Competition**

    Whenever possible, it is generally best to avoid excessive time pressure and highly-competitive classroom situations. Both make it even more difficult for students with ADHD to control themselves. Time pressures often increase impulsivity and cause careless responses. One way pressure can be reduced is by not allowing other students in the room to turn in their papers immediately upon completion. This noticeable movement of students' turning in papers may inadvertently encourage the student with ADHD to race to be the first one to hand in his paper. Or his peers' speediness could fluster or frustrate him enough to not complete or even attempt the task.

- **Extra Time for Work Completion**

    Students with ADHD usually take more time to complete tasks because they often don't get the directions, don't know how to start, have many starts and stops, etc. They are distracted, more easily frustrated, disorganized, and lose motivation sooner. Given all of these impediments, they will often need to be given more time to complete their work. It is not advisable to send large amounts of uncompleted classwork home as homework. This often increases the student's resistance to doing homework and creates significant family conflict. A better alternative is to decrease the amount of classwork or allow the student more time within the school day to get his work done.

- **Work Review**

  Teach the student with ADHD how to review his assignments to check for errors. This helps decrease his tendency to impulsively rush through his work.

- **"Stop, Think, Say, Do"**

  Students with ADHD can be taught a "stop, think, say, do" strategy to reduce impulsivity. In this approach, children are taught to "stop" before acting; "think" about what they are going to do; "say" quietly what they are going to do; and then "do" what they have said. To be most effective, teachers and parents should consistently model this approach in everyday situations.

- **Self-Talk**

  Teach the student to "talk" (he should whisper if in the classroom) himself through rote tasks, such as solving math problems or writing letters. This not only decreases impulsivity but also enhances focus.

- **Reinforcement of Accuracy and Completion**

  Although the student with ADHD should be expected to complete reasonable assignments, emphasis should also be placed on reinforcing and rewarding accuracy. This is helpful to reduce impulsive responses. As an example, reinforce each completed item on a worksheet with a green star and each accurate item with a red star. Or reinforce each completed answer with a point and offer 10 bonus points if the work is completed without error. The points can then be traded in for a tangible reward.

- **Reduction of Carelessness in Math**

  Students with ADHD often rush through their math assignments, making careless mistakes. Here are two suggestions: Ask the student to circle the math sign to ensure that he pays attention to it. Allow him to use graph paper to help keep his figures aligned.

- **Card System for Asking for Help**

  Impulsive students often make excessive demands upon the teacher's time. The card system is a way to control and monitor unnecessary requests for help or attention. Give the student a certain number of cards which he must use to signal the teacher that he has a question, wants to check in, or needs feedback. He should give the teacher the card after he uses it, thus making him aware of his remaining number of requests and encouraging him to make requests wisely. This system can be used not only for limiting the number of requests, but it can also be used to increase requests by those students who are reluctant to ask for help or feedback.

- **Turtle Technique for Aggression**

  Some children with ADHD are prone to aggression because of poor emotional controls and low frustration tolerance. The "turtle technique" uses visual imagery in a respectful way to prevent loss of control when you see the potential for it happening. Signal the student by calling out "Turtle." When he hears this signal, he should pull in his arms and legs close to his body, put his head down on the desk, and imagine that he is a turtle withdrawing into his shell. Use this technique when you perceive an aggressive interchange about to occur, when the child becomes frustrated, or when he is angry and about to throw a tantrum.

5. REDUCE DISTRACTIBILITY

Students with ADHD shift from one activity to another and work for shorter periods of time due to their inability to sustain effort, especially when tasks are long or boring. As a result, they are easily drawn to things in their environment that are more interesting, more stimulating, or more action-oriented. Consequently, it is very helpful to structure learning tasks so that they are more interesting than the surrounding environment.

- **Special Seating**

  To help ensure that students with ADHD will not be easily drawn off task, it is best to seat them in classroom locations away from tempting distractions such as windows, hallways or other distracting children. Additional consideration should be given to a location where the teacher(s) will best be able to monitor whether or not the students are paying attention to oral instructions, assigned work, etc. If the student with ADHD is placed near the front of the classroom, it is best to seat him in the seat second from the front, behind an organized, attentive student, so that he is provided a good role model.

- **Separate Desks**

  Avoid classroom arrangements where the students' desks are connected. This draws the student with ADHD off-task too easily and increases the temptation to bother his neighbor. Try to increase the distance between desks so that the students cannot touch each other.

- **Limiting Distractions**

  We are often unaware of how many auditory and visual distractions there are in the classroom. Materials that enrich a classroom can lead to a distracting or over-stimulating environment if items are poorly placed. Take special caution not to place visual distractions in the line of sight between the teacher and the student with ADHD.

- **Removal of Playthings**

  Students with ADHD often bring extraneous items or playthings to the classroom and fidget with them, causing distraction. It is important to place a ban on the student's bringing these items into the class. You may have to conduct an "item inspection" before class begins and instruct the student to leave these things outside the door. It is also important to ask parents to monitor what their child brings to school.

- **Monitoring Anxiety/Frustration**

  It is often difficult for the student with ADHD to bring closure to upsetting situations or feelings, thus making him more vulnerable to his own internal distractions. Try to note whether the student appears upset or bothered. Perhaps meet with the student privately and discreetly, acknowledge that he appears upset, and offer support. Such acknowledgement may provide the release he needs to feel better and get back on track.

- **Individualized Testing**

  Due to the problem that students with ADHD have with distractibility and reduced persistence, group achievement tests (e.g., Stanford Achievement Test and Iowa Tests of Basic Skills) may need to be administered either individually or in a resource classroom. Test administration may also need to be untimed with frequent breaks because of problems staying on task. Tests administered under these conditions will likely be a more accurate reflection of the student's academic skills. High school students may need to request exemption from *timed* college entrance tests. (Check with your school counselor).

6. INCREASE STRUCTURE

The student with ADHD does not easily internalize the structure needed to be successful in the classroom. Therefore, establishing external structure for him is imperative. Structure, however, should not be confused with strictness, which means inflexibility and failure to respond to individual needs. This leads to unnecessary power struggles.

- **Posting the Day's Schedule**

  Post the day's schedule on the board and review it at the beginning of the day with the class. Ask the class to repeat aloud each activity as it is reviewed. Make a point to highlight any changes in the normal schedule.

- **Review the Week's Schedule**

  At the beginning of the week, review the schedule for the week on a posted weekly calendar. Highlight any changes or important upcoming events.

- **Small-Group Instruction**

  Students with ADHD cannot easily maintain attention and motivation without external structure and reinforcement. They perform better when given academic instruction in one-to-one or small-group settings. This also maximizes teacher monitoring of their performance.

- **Controlled Transitions**

  Transitions are difficult for students with ADHD. They move most easily from formal to informal, focused to unfocused, and structured to unstructured situations. Therefore, keep informal transitions to a minimum, provide extra structure during transitional periods, and reinforce the child for successfully completing a transition and settling into a formal situation again.

- **Consistent Routines**

  Establish a regular routine in the classroom. Begin the day with the same routine or task. Also, begin new tasks with some readiness signal (e.g., ring a bell, count to 10, sing a "readiness song," etc.). This signals the class that it is time to change tasks, settle down, and begin working.

- **Teacher Monitoring of Independent Work**

  Students with ADHD require external structure, particularly when confronted with tasks that involve working independently. It is important to direct and focus the student's attention at the beginning of a task and monitor his attention throughout the task. Allowing the student to work without monitoring may lead to increased disruption, off-task behaviors or impulsive rushing through assignments.

- **Regular Review of Rules**

  Students with ADHD are often deficient in their capacity for adhering to rules. Teachers can help by reviewing rules and guidelines regularly. Index cards with general instructions (e.g., stay in your seat) may be used as well, possibly taped to the corner of the child's desk.

7. EMPHASIZE ORGANIZATION

Given the many demands, tasks, transitions, directions, worksheets, assignments, etc., involved in the classroom, organization is a must for academic success. The student's neurobiologically-based deficit in executive functioning interferes with his ability to effectively and consistently organize, plan and generally keep his act together.

- **Beginning-of-Day Organization**

  Spend the first 15 minutes of the day helping the student with ADHD and the rest of the class get organized. Ask students to clean their desks, clear the tops of their desks, throw away trash, sharpen their pencils, put loose papers in the correct folders, check for notes from parents, hand in homework, etc. Review the day's schedule, highlighting any changes or special activities. Perhaps have the students recite the schedule as it is reviewed.

- **After-Lunch Re-orientation**

  The behavior and organization of the student with ADHD typically deteriorate in the afternoon. Also, going from an unstructured lunch hour to a structured and formal classroom is a very difficult transition for him. Help the student ease into the afternoon by reviewing the schedule, reviewing behavior goals and accomplishments, and encouraging continued on-task and cooperative behavior.

- **End-of-Day Organization**

  At the end of the school day, it is helpful for either the classroom teacher or a resource teacher to check in with the student. Have him review his daily record of behavior and goals, and check to see if he has his assignment sheet and necessary books or anything else he needs to take home.

- **Consistent Routines**

  Students with ADHD function considerably better with consistent routines. Be careful not to unnecessarily vary the sequence of daily activities. If variation is necessary, give ample warning by taking the student aside and explaining the reason for the change, when it will occur, and specifically what the change will be.

- **Weekly Assignments Sheets**

  The problem of forgetting assignments is a common one for students with ADHD. Weekly assignment sheets that contain all the assignments for the period keep the student focused on what is due in the upcoming week and helps parents keep track of the student's assignments as well.

- **Folder for Finished/Unfinished Work**

  Help organize the student with ADHD by requiring him to provide separate, color-coded folders for finished and unfinished work or for each class. Be sure that he keeps the folders in the same place every day.

- **Organized Notebook**

  The *Notebook Organizer* is a carefully planned notebook to help the student with ADHD stay organized. It is available through the A.D.D. WareHouse Catalog, 1-800-233-9273. This is a three-ring binder which contains three pocket folders: *Work Due* (includes all homework, incomplete classwork, papers to be signed, etc.); *Work Done* (includes all completed work and signed papers to be returned to school); and *Work To Save* (includes completed work to be filed). The student should tape his assignment sheet on the inside of the *Notebook Organizer*. This program is appropriate for all grades.

- **Extra Books**

  Students with ADHD often forget to bring home the necessary materials to complete their homework. If possible, allow the student to keep an extra set of school books at home or help parents order their own copies for home.

- **Regular Desk Inspection**

  Students with ADHD often seem to "lose" homework, notes intended for their parents, and other important papers in their cluttered desks. Require that the student clean out and organize his desk once a week and then inspect it on a regular basis.

- **Cleared Desk Tops**

  Make sure the student has cleared his desk of any unnecessary materials before you begin instruction or he begins individual seatwork. Clutter on his desk will draw him off task and disorganize him.

8. INCREASE MOTIVATION

ADHD is regarded as a motivational deficit. Simply stated, it takes more to motivate the student with ADHD and keep him engaged, particularly for tasks which are not inherently interesting or stimulating to him. To keep him motivated, you need to provide enriching activities, frequent rewards and external structure. Things to avoid are repetition, monotony and excessively long work periods.

- **Ample Opportunity for Success**

  For students with ADHD, who typically have low self-esteem and/or anxiety problems, efforts should be made to provide them with lots of opportunities for experiencing academic success. Assignments should be started at a level well within their capabilities, so they have an opportunity to "warm up" prior to taking on more difficult tasks. Also, attempts should be made to praise and to reward not only their accomplishments, but also the effort that they expend to attain those accomplishments. In addition, they should be taught that mistakes are an opportunity for learning, rather than an indication of failure or ineptitude. These strategies increase the likelihood that students with ADHD will view schoolwork in a more positive light, thereby increasing their motivation to learn.

- **Reduced Homework Loads**

  The special difficulties of the student with ADHD often interfere with or prevent him from completing the same homework load as his peers. To give a sense of accomplishment and success, it may be necessary to reduce the student's homework load to an amount that is manageable for his processing style and frustration level. Once he has achieved a sense of mastery and accomplishment, the homework can be gradually increased.

- **Reduced Frustration with Written Assignments**

  Approximately 80 percent of students with ADHD experience difficulty with written work. Although many students with ADHD can verbalize their thoughts during spontaneous speech, they cannot easily generate ideas when confronted with tasks that require that they organize their thoughts, sustain attention and motivation, and work for relatively long periods of time in order to complete an integrated thought process. Additionally, many students with ADHD have reduced fine-motor skills that interfere with writing. The end result is that they usually resist written work or rush through it. To help the student, allow a visual instead of a written presentation if appropriate, or encourage the student to type or use a word processor, or let him record his thoughts into a tape recorder to transcribe later and make necessary corrections.

- **Bonus Points**

    Although we do not want to establish goals that are too high for the student with ADHD, we also do not want to inadvertently encourage "just getting by" when the student could actually perform better than his goal. To motivate the student past "just getting by," offer bonus points for performing past the set goal. For example, if the goal is to complete seven out of ten math problems, award the student one additional point for every math problem completed above seven.

- **Test Re-Taking**

    Students with ADHD are typically "poor test takers" because tests usually reflect what they cannot do (e.g., concentrate, ignore distractions, work carefully under time pressures, process quickly and accurately, etc.) rather than reflect their abilities. A history of poor test performance demoralizes students with ADHD, and they lose their motivation to even study for tests. Allowing students to re-take tests if they have poor performance on the first testing can be an effective way to help them maintain their motivation.

- **Peer-Dispensed Rewards**

    Too often, the ADHD student is singled out in the classroom for his inappropriate behaviors. To counteract this, establish a "climate" in the classroom whereby all students encourage and reinforce each other's appropriate behavior. Give all the students, including the student with ADHD, the capacity to dispense points to one another for an occurrence of acceptable behavior. Keep track of the points and tally them at the end of the day. Chart the classroom's behavior progress.

- **Group Token System**

    Award tokens to the class when all the students behave appropriately for a period of time (e.g., 15 to 20 minutes). Mark the time period with a timer. If the class behaves appropriately during the time period, the class gets the token. If the class does not behave appropriately, the teacher gets the token. Add up the "class" and "teacher" tokens at the end of the day and the end of the week. If the class has more tokens than the teacher, the students earn a special end-of-the week reward.

- **Team Points**

  To promote cooperative behavior, divide the class into teams. Team points are awarded when students provide academic assistance or emotional support to another team member. When the team earns a certain number of points, the team is awarded a special privilege. Note: Do not have the teams compete against each other. The more winners, the better!

- **Individual Reward Program With Private Contract**

  Teachers can set up a private contract with the student with ADHD. Tell the student that you know he has trouble with certain behaviors, such as sitting and concentrating on his work. Inform him that he has been chosen for a special program designed to help him do these things better. List the rules that he must follow to achieve success in these behaviors. Then tell him that at the end of short time periods, such as every 10 or 15 minutes, you will come over to his desk and give him a reward ticket if he has been following those rules. After school, allow him to trade in his tickets for a special prize or allow him to take the tickets home and receive a special prize or privilege there.

SUMMARY

- The possible modifications in the classroom can be grouped into eight areas: goal-setting, reinforcement and feedback, attention, impulsivity, distractibility, structure, organization, and motivation.

- The list of modifications is extensive, and only a portion will be feasible and appropriate for your child. Parents and teachers should work together to determine which ones make the most sense.

- Teachers have many demands placed upon them. Ideally, the modifications will be seen not as additional things to do, but rather as ways to minimize disruption, create a more positive atmosphere, and overall improve the learning experience for all the students as well as the teacher.

CHAPTER

24 Knowing the Laws and Your Rights

Parents have known for a long time that their children with **ADHD** struggle in the classroom academically, behaviorally and socially. Many parents have also experienced the frustration and heartache of being unable to bring about changes for their child in the classroom. Their requests to school personnel for modifications, understanding and tolerance may fall on deaf ears. Instead of help, they too often receive a response that suggests their child is a "troublemaker," lacks parental direction and discipline, or is "lazy" or "hopeless." Furthermore, parents are sometimes told that if teachers make "exceptions" for their child, it would be unfair to all the rest of the students who are not given "special treatment"; or that with so many other students in the classroom, it is impossible for teachers to do extra work for their child.

Students with **ADHD** require more work from their teachers and, understandably, teachers may become frustrated and even resentful. Teachers suffer the exasperation of having a child in the classroom who disrupts other students, demands an excessive amount of teacher attention, roams about the room, blurts out, loses the necessary materials for class, does not do his homework, acts aggressively with other students, or pulls pranks when the teacher is out of the room or has his/her back turned. None of the usual teaching or discipline strategies seem to work with these students, or at least they don't work for very long. When traditional interventions fail, it is no wonder that teachers may throw up their hands and proclaim that "nothing works for this student." Even the best of teachers may feel ineffective with a student with **ADHD**.

Although many teachers and administrators understand the nature of **ADHD** and its effect on classroom functioning, there are also too many who fail to recognize this disorder and therefore resist implementing appropriate modifications and intervention strategies. In fact, many times throughout the years, teachers and school principals have said to my clients or to me that they don't believe in ADHD, that these students should be treated "normally," that they should be treated "fairly" like anyone else, and/or that teachers should not have to make modifications for them. These sentiments reflect a basic lack of understanding of the nature of ADHD and result in the problem getting worse, not better. Failure to make adaptations at the point when they are needed eventually requires *more* work for teachers as the student's functioning deteriorates further.

Consider the case of Ryan, a third-grade client of mine. His story illustrates what happened when school personnel did not understand ADHD and resisted appropriate interventions.

Ryan was very bright (he started reading and calculating math problems as a preschooler). He also had ADHD, severe degree. It was extremely difficult for Ryan to stay engaged in class discussions or to "hang in there" with the repetitive worksheets he had to do at his desk while his teacher worked with other students in the classroom. He was also very impulsive, and his emotions often overwhelmed him, causing him to blurt out his frustrations and inappropriately express his mounting anger. Ryan was often sent to time-out for leaving his desk (which was his way of breaking up the monotony, avoiding a boring task, and staying awake), blurting out comments such as, "I'm so bored," or "I hate this stuff," and for refusing to complete his worksheets. The more he was put in time-out or denied recess, the more disruptive he became.

It was clear that Ryan was indeed bored, and he was telling his teacher this. His teacher, however, interpreted his behavior as intentional disruption, willful noncompliance, and "downright laziness." She held these perceptions about Ryan despite the fact that Ryan was diagnosed with ADHD when he was in kindergarten, and she had been involved in meetings with Ryan's parents during which they explained Ryan's particular ADHD-related difficulties.

I finally called a meeting with the teacher, Ryan's parents, and the school principal. At the meeting I explained how Ryan's ADHD affected him academically, behaviorally, emotionally, and socially in the classroom. A number of appropriate modifications were offered that would help Ryan operate more successfully in the classroom: decreasing the number of worksheets; allowing him more computer time as an alternative; allowing sanctioned "stretch breaks" to increase his arousal; increasing teacher check-in and feedback; and employing a positive reinforcement program.

Ryan's teacher sat quietly throughout the meeting without offering comments, suggestions or criticisms. The school principal took notes throughout the meeting and thanked us for our observations and suggestions. She then announced that she could not allow such modifications because that would mean treating Ryan differently. She went on to say that she firmly believed in treating all children fairly, and to her that meant treating them equally.

When educators operate under the belief system that students with ADHD are "normal" and should be treated "fairly," just like any other student in the classroom, they ignore the disability. Students with ADHD *don't* function like "normal" children in the classroom because they *can't* function like other student. They can't maintain their attention as long as other students. They get bored sooner, and can't muster up the motivation to continue working like other students. They can't stay on task or ignore distractions like other students. And they can't stay organized and keep track of their assignments and papers like other students. They can't do these things without some degree of modification in expectations, curriculum and classroom management. As one individual aptly put it, "These students are not the *cause* of trouble, they are *in* trouble." [1]

Treating students with ADHD "fairly" means treating them *differently*: making appropriate modifications to set them up for success rather than treating them "just like any other student," which ignores their disability and sets them up for failure. If Ryan's teacher and principal had understood this and allowed themselves a more enlightened perspective, Ryan would not have had to endure the interminable time-outs, boredom, frustration, and ultimate failure which he experienced.

LAWS WHICH PROTECT STUDENTS WITH ADHD IN THE SCHOOL

This scenario with Ryan occurred in 1989, two years before the Department of Education recognized ADHD as an educational disorder deserving special interventions and accommodations.

For years educators have been confused and frustrated trying to determine whether children with ADHD qualify for special education or related services. Historically, it has been their belief that children with ADHD do not qualify for special education based on a diagnosis of ADHD alone. Rather, these children had to meet the eligibility criteria for either "specific learning disabilities" (SLD) or "emotional/behavior disorders" (EBD) in order to receive special education services.

Ryan was well on his way to qualifying for EBD services, in large part because his primary ADHD-related difficulties were not being addressed by the school, thereby creating high levels of frustration and anger. In fact, his behavior became so disruptive that he did qualify for EBD services by the end of that same school year. This "back door" way of servicing children with ADHD was a setup for failure, but unfortunately it was common across the country prior to 1991. The services put in place for these children often did not meet the specific educational/behavioral needs created by the student's ADHD. Furthermore, as in the case of Ryan, the interventions were initiated very late, after the primary ADHD-related problems developed into serious secondary academic, behavioral and emotional problems.

In 1990, Congress mandated that the Department of Education solicit comments from the public about how children with ADHD were educated in the public schools. After much investigation, on September 16, 1991, the Department issued a Policy Clarification Memorandum (referred to as the Mandate) recognizing that children with ADHD may qualify for special education and/or related services based solely on the diagnosis of ADHD **if it is deemed that the ADHD significantly impairs educational performance or learning.**[2]

These services are guaranteed under two existing federal laws: Public Law 94-142, Individuals with Disabilities Education Act or "IDEA" (under the section called Part B "Other Health Impaired" or "OHI")[3] and Section 504 of the federal Rehabilitation Act of 1973.[4] Children with ADHD no longer need to qualify for services under the "specific learning disabilities" or "serious emotional disorders" categories. These two laws apply to all public schools as well as to all private schools that receive federal funds.

KEY POINTS OF THE MANDATE:
IDEA, Part B

Students with ADHD may be eligible for services under Part B ("Other Health Impaired" or OHI) of the Individuals with Disabilities Education Act (IDEA) when it is found that the ADHD is a *"chronic or acute health problem resulting in limited alertness which adversely affects educational performance."* Thus a child with ADHD should be classified as eligible for services under the OHI category in instances where it is found that his ADHD significantly interferes with his educational performance. In such cases, that child may qualify for special education or related services based solely on his ADHD. It is not necessary to also document a learning disability or serious emotional problem in order to acquire services.

The Mandate further states that children with ADHD are also eligible for services under the "Specific Learning Disability" or the "Emotional Behavior Disordered" category of Part B if they meet the criteria. In other words, a student may qualify for services because of ADHD, and he may also qualify for services because of a learning disability or serious behavioral/emotional issues. Services for one disability do not exclude services for another disability.

The Mandate further stipulates an obligation on the part of state and local educational agencies to conduct a full and individual evaluation of a child who is suspected of having a disability and to determine the child's needs for special education and related services. This responsibility "is applicable to all children from birth through 21, regardless of the severity of their disability."

It is important to note that a parent's suspicion that his or her child may have ADHD does not automatically require that the school district conduct an evaluation. Furthermore, a medical diagnosis of ADHD alone is not sufficient to render a child eligible for services. There must be some evidence that the student's educational performance is significantly adversely affected. If an evaluation is to be conducted, schools are required to conduct the evaluation "without undue delay" and at no cost to the parent. If the school refuses to evaluate the student or if a parent disagrees with the outcome of the school's evaluation or decision about services, the parent may request a due process hearing (see section below on Due Process).

Section 504 of the Rehabilitation Act of 1973

If children with ADHD do not meet IDEA Part B criteria for special education services, they may still qualify for special accommodations and adaptations under the rights specified under Section 504 of the Rehabilitation Act of 1973. Section 504 stipulates that agencies that receive federal funds must meet the needs of individuals with handicaps as adequately as they meet the needs of individuals without handicaps. Within the classroom this means that schools must "level the playing field" by making changes (e.g., modified curriculum or homework, increased structure, more monitoring of progress, etc.) that help the student with ADHD to function as successfully as the student without ADHD. "Handicapped person" is defined as any person "who has a physical or mental impairment which substantially limits a major life activity" (e.g., learning). A child with ADHD may qualify as a "handicapped person" if his ADHD is found to adversely impact learning.

If parents believe that their child's ADHD renders their child handicapped, the school must evaluate the child to determine if he meets Section 504 requirements for "handicapped." If the child meets the criteria under Section 504, the school must evaluate the child's individual educational needs. The parent has the right to contest the evaluation if the school determines that the child is not handicapped.

The Mandate further states that "the child's education must be provided in the regular education classroom unless it is demonstrated that education in the regular environment with the use of supplementary aids and services cannot be achieved satisfactorily." Examples of adaptations for the regular education classroom were provided in the Mandate, including:

- providing a structured learning environment;

- repeating and simplifying instructions about in-class and homework assignments;

- supplementing verbal instructions with visual instructions;

- using behavioral management techniques;

- adjusting class schedules;

- modifying test delivery;

- using tape recorders, computer-aided instruction and other audio-visual equipment;

- selecting modified textbooks or workbooks; and

- tailoring homework assignments.

Other possible recommended provisions in the Mandate include:
- consultation to special resources;

- reduction in class size;

- use of one-on-one tutorials;

- classroom aides and notetakers;

- involvement of a "services coordinator" to oversee implementation of special programs and services; and

- modification of nonacademic times such as lunchroom, recess and physical education.

AMERICANS WITH DISABILITIES ACT

In 1990, the Americans with Disabilities Act was enacted, providing another means of legal protection for individuals with ADHD. Title II of the Act prohibits all public schools from denying educational services, programs or activities to students with disabilities. It also prohibits discrimination against these students once they are enrolled in such programs. Title III of the Act provides these same prohibitions for all non-religious private schools.

In response to the federal Mandate, each state was required to establish its own guidelines, procedures and timelines for implementing the laws. Parents should contact their state's Department of Education to secure a copy of that state's regulations. Parents can also contact their state's Department of Rights for the Disabled and the Protection and Advocacy Office for more information regarding state regulations and parent and child rights (the exact title of these agencies may vary across states).

REQUESTING A REFERRAL FOR SERVICES

Federal and state laws provide guidelines and procedures for requesting that a child be evaluated for services. Each state has its own guidelines and timelines for initiating a referral and conducting an evaluation. Many school districts have adopted the same evaluation processes and procedural safeguards for both IDEA and Section 504. You can obtain the regulations and procedures that apply to your school district from your State Department of Education.

The referral process can be initiated by a parent, a teacher, other school personnel, or even by the student. The referral is usually made to the school principal, school psychologist, guidance counselor, or special education director. The formal referral for services is made in writing by someone from the school, usually the classroom teacher. Important referral information includes teacher reports, test scores, classroom observations, classroom strategies that have been used with the student, and reports from parents.

The school's Child Study Team (a group of special education personnel; the name of this group varies across districts) receives this referral information, and must review the information within a designated number of days to determine if an evaluation is warranted. The team can recommend any of these primary options: the child be formally evaluated, the teacher try some additional strategies, or other professionals or specialists be consulted. The parents can request a written report of the team's recommendations.

If the Child Study Team recommends a formal evaluation, this recommendation is given to the district's Special Education Director within a designated number of days. The Child Study Team must make a written recommendation which includes the referral information. Parents must give their written permission before any evaluation can proceed and are entitled to receive a copy of this report.

A formal evaluation includes academic, medical, and psychological testing. In addition, background history information is collected, and an individual other than the classroom teacher must conduct a classroom observation.

The academic testing, conducted by a teacher certified in learning disabilities, may include assessment of reading, written language and math skills. Additional testing may be conducted to assess other processing areas such as visual-motor skills, memory, gross- and fine-motor skills, and auditory perception.

The medical evaluation is conducted by a school health person such as the school nurse. A complete developmental and medical history is taken, as well as vision and hearing screenings.

The psychological testing is conducted by the school psychologist. This testing includes an intelligence test and personality and behavioral assessments.

Background and social history is usually collected by the school social worker and may include interviews with the student and the parents. Parents may be asked to complete various behavioral questionnaires by the school psychologist and the school social worker.

If warranted, additional testing may be conducted by the school speech/language pathologist and occupational therapist.

All Child Study Team members must provide written reports of their evaluations. This comprehensive evaluation must be completed within a certain number of school days (usually 30) after the parents give their signed permission for the evaluation.

After all parts of the formal evaluation are completed, an Eligibility Committee meets to review the data and determine whether the student meets eligibility criteria for special education or related services. Parents may request any or all of the following: to attend the Eligibility Committee meeting; to have the evaluation results explained to them; and to receive written copies of the evaluation data and committee recommendations.

THE TWO LEVELS OF SERVICE

If the student is found to qualify for special education or related services, the Eligibility Committee meets within 30 calendar days to write one of two plans: a) an Individual Educational Plan (IEP) *if the student qualifies for special education instruction* under IDEA, Part B, or b) a section 504 Plan *if the student qualifies for classroom/curriculum adaptations and modifications* under Section 504. The IEP and Section 504 Plan are essentially written contracts in which the school outlines an educational program based on the student's individual needs. The IEP is more formal and detailed than the Section 504 Plan.

Remember, there are two levels of service depending on the severity of the disorder. Each has its own plan:

Law	Service	Plan
IDEA, Part B	Special Education	IEP
Rehabilitation Act of 1973	Non-special education (modifications and adaptations)	504 Plan

Parents meet with the Eligibility Committee to prepare the IEP or Section 504 Plan. Parents have input into the development of these two documents and have the right to ask another professional, such as the child's psychologist, a parent advocate or a friend, to attend the planning meeting. Parents can also take home a copy of the IEP or Section 504 Plan to review it with other professionals or parents who have gone through the process. No services can begin until the parents approve and sign the IEP or Section 504 Plan.

WRITING THE IEP FOR SPECIAL EDUCATION SERVICES

The actual form of the IEP varies across school districts. According to law, however, all IEPs must contain the following information:

1. **Documentation of the child's current levels of performance in basic academic areas.** Current test results in reading, math and written language, as well as vocational and/or social skills are included. The names of the tests administered, testing dates and results are listed. Any area that was determined to be a weakness must be identified.

2. **The educational services which the child is to receive.** The type of special education program for which the child qualified (SLD, EBD or OHI) is stated, as well as the level of service which the child will receive. There are nine levels of service, from least restrictive to most restrictive. The levels are:

I   Regular classroom placement with consultation to the regular education teacher from special education personnel

II   Regular classroom placement with supplementary teaching within the regular classroom provided by the special education teacher

III   Regular classroom placement with some instruction with the special education teacher in a resource room

IV   Full-time placement in a smaller special education self-contained classroom

V   Placement in a special school

VI   Homebound instruction

VII   Placement in a residential school

VIII Placement in a hospital school

IX   Placement in a hospital or treatment center

Additional components of the educational services that are detailed include:

- the number of hours per day the child will be in special education and regular education;
- any specific accommodations that will be made, including providing study carrels, reduced homework, oral testing, computer-aided instruction, etc.; and
- any related services that the child will receive, such as physical therapy, speech/language therapy, or counseling.

It is important for parents to realize that schools are mandated to provide a continuum of services. This means that if a school district cannot provide the needed services as outlined in the IEP, the school must find and provide these services outside of the district at the district's expense, including tuition and transportation.

3. **Projected dates for initiation of services and ending of services.**

4. **The annual goals and the short-term instructional objectives.** The annual goal statement specifies the outcome to be achieved, e.g., *Alec will increase his written language skills from first- to second-grade*

level. An annual goal is stated for every area that was documented as a weakness according to test scores and observations from the special education evaluation. The short-term instructional objectives are written for each goal. They detail the sequence of steps the student must achieve to meet his goal, e.g., *Using the classroom spelling list, Alec will spell the words with 80% accuracy by the end of the second quarter; Alec will write a sentence that makes sense to the reader two out of three times, by the end of the second quarter.*

For each annual goal and its related short-term instructional objective, the IEP stipulates what level the student must achieve to reach mastery, and how that level will be measured.

5. **The date for the annual review.** The IEP committee must review the IEP at least once a year to determine whether the student has made progress toward his goals and objectives and whether changes should be made.

The IEP is put into effect only after the parents sign it. Although a date for the annual review is stated in the IEP, parents can request a review before that date, if they have concerns or would like to discuss changes. Once a student enters special education, he must be re-evaluated by the special education team every three years. Parents can request an evaluation sooner if they feel the needs or condition of their child have changed.

WRITING THE SECTION 504 PLAN FOR NON-SPECIAL EDUCATION

If a student does not qualify for special education services, he may still qualify for "reasonable accommodations and adaptations" under Section 504 protection. Guidelines for Section 504 Plans are less formal than those for an IEP. A good plan will include the information described below:

- A detailed description of the problems the student has been experiencing.

- The results of any evaluations that were conducted to determine the student's disability. This could include a detailed developmental, psychological and medical history, and a review of the school history, records, academic performance, current functioning, etc.

- A description of how the disability affects a " major life activity." More than likely, the major life activity will be the student's ability to learn and perform well at school. Therefore, the consequences of the disability should be included, such as failure to achieve acceptable levels of achievement, failure to organize materials to complete academic work, lack of self confidence, poor self-esteem, excessive frustration, anxiety, peer rejection, etc.

- Supplementary aids, services, and accommodations. These may include:

  - the designation of a morning check-in person to help the student with organization;

  - an assignment book monitored by teachers;

  - special instruction in study skills and test taking;

  - seating near the front of the classroom;

  - reduced homework load;

  - teacher classroom notes;

  - oral testing;

  - a second set of books for the home;

  - extra sessions with a particular teacher to supplement classroom instruction;

  - additional teacher monitoring of the student's academic progress; and

  - word processing to aid written language, etc.

- The dates for review of the Section 504 Plan and reassessment of the student.

- The designation of a case manager, who will be in charge of overseeing the execution and monitoring of the program and who will be responsible for regular communication with the parents.

The planning meeting should include all the teachers who work with the student, the parents, and perhaps the student himself (depending upon the student's age). The parents approve and sign the Plan before it can go into effect. Each teacher should have a copy of the final Plan. Although the Plan is to be reviewed yearly, parents or teachers may request changes or revisions at any time.

ADDITIONAL RIGHTS

The Individuals with Disabilities Education Act also gives parents certain rights regarding their child's school records. If parents request it, they can obtain a list of all records kept on their child; and they can inspect, review and copy any of their child's records without undue delay. An individual at the school must be available to explain the records to the parents, if they request, or parents may select an individual of their choosing to review the records.

If parents feel that any information in the records is inaccurate or misleading, they can request that the school delete it. If the school refuses, the school must inform the parents and tell them of their right to a hearing, which is conducted by an impartial school official. If the hearing renders a decision in the parents' favor, the school must make the requested changes in the record and inform the parents in writing that it has done so. If the hearing renders a decision in the school's favor, the parents have the right to add a statement to their child's records.

DESPITE THE LAWS, PROBLEMS PERSIST

Although the Department of Education has come a long way in recognizing the fact that students with ADHD are at risk and deserve special help or appropriate accommodations when their ADHD is serious enough, many school districts are not yet in compliance. They are still working to determine which students actually qualify for special education or related services based on ADHD and how to implement the necessary services. Parents often find that although their child is struggling in the classroom or on the playground, his difficulties do not meet eligibility criteria for services. That is, the child's difficulties are not yet considered serious enough by the school district to warrant special help.

Failure to qualify for services is particularly a problem when it comes to seeking special education services under "Other Health Impaired" (OHI). Most school districts adopt stringent criteria for eligibility for services under this category, requiring that a student with ADHD fall at least 1.5 to 1.75 standard deviations below his ability level (I.Q. score) in at least one academic area before the student qualifies for services. Translated, this means that a student must be underachieving by at least two grade levels below his ability before he can receive special education services. Unfortunately, this often proves to be a setup for failure. A student with ADHD cannot get much-needed help until he has nearly failed in at least one academic area. By then he is probably very demoralized and has developed a negative attitude toward school.

Theoretically, a Section 504 Plan is designed to help a student with ADHD so that he does not fall so far behind. However, a common problem with a Section 504 Plan is that no one in the school takes responsibility for overseeing the plan to make sure it gets implemented. Many times I have contacted teachers, particularly at the junior or senior high school level, who were not even aware that a particular student had a Section 504 Plan or that they were supposed to be implementing certain modifications.

These points are raised to caution you that although your child may be recognized by the school as having ADHD, and your child may even have a formal intervention plan, you must continue to advocate for your child at school and oversee his programming. As long as your child is in school, do not abdicate your role as primary advocate.

IF YOU DISAGREE WITH THE SCHOOL: DUE PROCESS

The Education for All Handicapped Children Act provides a legal means for parents to resolve a conflict with the school regarding their child's educational program. This is called "due process." Due process can be time-consuming, costly and emotionally draining. Therefore, all attempts should be made to resolve problems before resorting to this formal hearing. Be assertive and exert your parental rights. Meet with your child's teachers and school principal to come to some sort of compromise or resolution. Parents must understand, however, that by law school districts are not required to provide the *best* program for their child. Schools are required to provide an *appropriate* program.

If no resolution is achieved with school personnel, parents may file a complaint with their state's Department of Education. This step is appropriate when parents feel that the school district is not properly following procedures (e.g., mishandling records) or not following-through with services stipulated in the IEP. If parents have a complaint related to substance, they can ask for mediation or initiate due process by contacting the district's special education director. Matters relating to substance include such concerns as whether the child's educational program is appropriate, whether he is in the right setting, etc.

Mediation involves a review of the parents' complaints and concerns by a high-level administrator in the school district. If mediation fails, and parents choose to initiate due process, they must send a written copy of their dispute and a summary of the action taken to the school superintendent and the state's Department of Education, requesting a due process hearing. School districts typically retain an attorney who specializes in these matters to represent their interests. It is advisable that parents at least contact a parent advocacy group for direction and support, and you may want to hire a lawyer as well.

During the due process hearing, involved school personnel and parents will address a hearing officer. The hearing is conducted like a judicial process, with the facts of the case heard from both sides, including documents, testimony, and any other evidence. A decision is based on presented facts as well as statutes, regulations and case law. If parents disagree with the decision rendered, they may request a review of the decision. A review hearing is then conducted by an appointed reviewing officer. If either party disagrees with the decision, they may appeal by filing a civil suit in their state or with the U.S. District Court. Parents may be reimbursed by the school district for legal fees and related costs if the decision is in their favor.

SUMMARY

- Students with ADHD may qualify for special education and/ or related services if it is deemed that the disorder significantly impairs educational performance or learning.

- There are two federal laws which provide services for students with ADHD: The Individuals with Disabilities Education Act (IDEA) and the 1973 Rehabilitation Act.

- To receive services under either of these laws, a process is initiated that culminates with a formal plan, called an Individual Educational Plan (IEP) for special education services or a 504 Plan for non-special education classroom modifications and adaptations.

- Developing the plans is a collaborative effort among parents, teachers and other school personnel.

- Despite the federal laws, roadblocks can appear, especially for the 504 Plan: some districts or schools may not be current in their awareness or processes; the plan is written but not fully implemented; there may be honest disagreement about the diagnosis. As always, the parent is the ultimate advocate for his/her child.

CHAPTER

25 Keeping Records of Your Child

To be an effective advocate, you must collect and organize important data and facts about your child, and you must have this information readily available. Therefore, build a file of important records on your child. Start with the documents you have accumulated over the years:

- Birth and developmental history records
- Medical records
- School report cards
- Copies of standardized achievement test results
- Notes from teachers
- Samples of your child's schoolwork and tests
- Notes from school meetings
- Evaluation reports from psychologists, speech/language pathologists, neurologists and other professionals
- Notes from telephone calls
- Photos of your child

Organize this information and file it in categories for easy access. The National Center for Learning Disabilities has offered some excellent suggestions for organizing your file. Their suggestions are listed below, taken from *Understanding Learning Disabilities: A Parent Guide and Workbook.*[1]

- Date each item in the lower, right-hand corner in pencil. Do this even if the date appears elsewhere on the document. This date will be used to keep and to locate documents in chronological order. For documents which span a period of time, such as report cards and telephone logs, use the date of the last entry.

- Maintain your records in an oversized, three-ring looseleaf notebook whenever possible. Arrange the records in chronological order, oldest document last, most recent first. Use this notebook to keep all records pertaining to your child's disability and educational progress. You will want to include the following:

  - Report Cards: Official school and interim report cards, as well as written comments from teachers, camp counselors, Sunday School teachers, tutors, etc.

  - Correspondence: All correspondence received as well as copies of letters which you have written about your child.

  - Medical Test Reports: Significant birth and developmental history, visual exams, auditory evaluations, etc.

  - Psychological and Educational Test Reports: Formal results plus any notes you made during interpretive conferences following these evaluations.

  - Telephone Log: A record of significant telephone conversations with teachers and other professionals. Be sure to include date, time, name of person with whom you spoke, the subject and substance of the conversation, and any follow-up steps to be taken.

  - Special Education Documentation: Referrals, child study eligibility, IEP, Section 504, and all other official documents pertaining to your child's special education process and program.

- Never highlight or write on the documents (except the date in the lower right corner). If you wish to call attention to particular passages, affix "Post-It" notes with your comments.

- Keep a log of your telephone communications (see above).

- Keep a written and dated summary of each meeting you have with teachers and other professionals.

- Secure a complete copy of your child's cumulative and confidential file from the school system and from all agencies that have ever evaluated or worked with your child. Familiarize yourself with these records and place them in the notebook in chronological order.

- Maintain a table of contents or chronological list of the documents. Each document is entered according to date and should include the author, description of the type of document, and brief summary explanation. If the author is unknown or not available, use the name of the agency or school system. It is helpful to store this chronological list of documents on a computer for case in making insertions and changes.

- Keep dated samples of your child's school papers in a separate notebook.

- Never leave your notebook with a professional or school system for more than a day or two. Have extra copies of your chronological list of documents available for them so they can indicate which reports they want you to copy and provide to them.

From A Parent Guide and Workbook published by the Learning Disabilities Council Inc. copyright © 1989 and 1991. Reprinted by permission of the publisher.

SUMMARY

- A record of important data about your child is an important resource to maintain. Your written notes (e.g., summaries of meetings and telephone calls) are just as valuable as formal documents (e.g., school reports).

- A looseleaf notebook is the recommended format. Remember to keep a table of contents or chronological log for easy retrieval.

CHAPTER

26 Preparing for the IEP or Section 504 Meeting

The IEP or Section 504 meeting gives you the opportunity to officially advocate for your child. It is important that you are well prepared. Remember that no one at that meeting knows your child better than you. You can provide the team members with valuable information and insight. Therefore, before the meeting spend some time making a list of your concerns and issues. Refer to your file to gather information and formulate your thoughts. Detail your child's various difficulties.

You may want to share with the school all of the extra support that you provide to your child on a daily basis just to keep him afloat (the school may see the fruits of your labor, but not appreciate how much labor it takes!). If you are spending hours each night helping your child organize and complete his homework, the school needs to know this. The school should also be aware if your child becomes very frustrated with the amount of his homework, if he tends to forget his assignments or if he regularly forgets his materials at school. Make a list of other problems: difficulties with transitions, lethargy, boredom, peer rejection, school refusal, conflict with a teacher, etc. Also share with the school your child's strengths and assets, such as his talents in drawing, music, fishing, dancing, his good sense of humor, his sensitivity, etc.

You may want to consult with another parent who has already gone through this process to gather more suggestions and gain a clearer image of what it will be like. If you and your child are working with a psychologist who is knowledgeable about special education, ask this professional for further guidance and suggestions. It is also important to review the information about IDEA and Section 504 in this book so that you understand the process and your rights.

The IEP or Section 504 meeting is attended by teachers and other professionals from the school. For some parents, it is intimidating to meet with such a group. Try not to be intimidated. **You are the expert**

on your child. Approach the meeting with a positive attitude and with the expectation that all the individuals involved have your child's best interests in mind. Remember, if you feel the need for extra support, you have the right to bring another person, including a parent, spouse, friend or professional.

During the meeting, the individuals from the Child Study Team may share their evaluation results with you and offer their suggestions for intervention. If you do not understand, or if they are using confusing, professional jargon, be assertive and ask them to explain the information in a more understandable way. Don't be afraid to disagree with their conclusions or recommendations, but do not voice your disagreements in a hostile or accusing tone. Try to work as part of the team.

Although it is not your responsibility to determine what services and modifications are appropriate for your child, it is your right to provide input. Understanding the various modifications that are appropriate and knowing which ones to consider can be overwhelming to parents. However, you will feel more confident going into the meeting if you are aware of the different options to consider. To help organize your thoughts and acquaint you with different service options, the Educational Planning Guide is provided on the following pages. I devised this form to help parents and school personnel consider service options when writing the IEP or Section 504 Plan.

EDUCATIONAL PLANNING GUIDE FOR STUDENTS WITH ADHD

Student _____ Date _____

School _____ Grade _____

Person(s) completing this form_____

    The following school-based modifications are those which are recommended for students with ADHD. They can be used as a guideline when writing the student's Individual Educational Plan or Section 504 Plan; or they can be used by the student's regular education teacher(s) as a guide for helping the student become more successful.

    Any recommendations which are checked (√) are those which are considered especially pertinent for this student.

CLASSROOM MODIFICATIONS

_____   Seat student near teacher

_____   Seat student away from distractions (doorways, windows, other disruptive students, etc.)

_____   Seat student next to positive peer role model

_____   Eliminate excessive classroom clutter

_____   Reduce extraneous noise during teaching/study times

_____   Assign to an enclosed classroom with four walls

_____   Provide study carrels (so this student and others can go to a quiet place to work)

_____   Provide individual and separate desks (avoid grouped desks or long tables)

_____   List classroom rules on wall

    Other: _____

CURRICULUM MODIFICATIONS

_____   Shorten seatwork to fit student's attentional capacity (e.g., if student can effectively pay attention for only 15 minutes, don't give a 30-minute task)

_____   Break seatwork into shorter segments

_____   Give short directions

_____   Repeat directions

_____   Provide written instructions for homework

_____   Limit amount of lecturing

_____   Limit amount of note-taking

_____   Designate another student as note-taker, using carbon paper or photocopying

_____   Allow student to tape-record lessons

_____   Use visual aids, overhead projectors, filmstrips, videos, etc.

_____   Allow student participation (writing on board, pointing on charts, etc.)

_____   Limit the amount of worksheet teaching

_____   Hand out one worksheet at a time

_____   Provide hands-on learning experiences (projects, experiments, models, field trips, etc.)

_____   Vary teaching format and task materials (intersperse low-interest, student-listening tasks with more stimulating, hands-on, student-involvement tasks)

_____   Allow high-interest reading material in place of/in addition to curriculum reading

_____   Reduce amount of required reading

_____   Allow frequent breaks to increase student's arousal

_____   Allow student to stand or take "movement breaks" to increase arousal

_____   Schedule academics predominantly in the morning hours

_____   Decrease time pressures and competition

_____   Call on student more frequently and randomly

_____   Provide reinforcement for accuracy as well as for work completion

_____   Offer small-group instruction

_____   Provide computer-aided instruction

_____   Provide weekly class/subject written outlines

_____ Reduce amount of homework only to that which is necessary to learn the concept(s)

_____ Allow extra time to complete homework

_____ Provide immediate feedback for correctness of responses

_____ Allow alternatives for written assignments (oral presentations, tape-recorded presentations, word-processed documents, etc.)

_____ Decrease quantity of required written work

Other: _____

ORGANIZATION

_____ Assign case manager to oversee student's program and progress

_____ Arrange a beginning-of-day check-in to prepare for day

_____ Arrange noon check-in to review progress and prepare for afternoon

_____ Arrange end-of-day check-out to review day and organize for homework

_____ Schedule regular desk clean-outs

_____ Use folders for finished and unfinished work

_____ Use color-coded notebooks, folders, and textbooks

_____ Provide daily assignment sheets with teacher check-off

_____ Allow extra time to gather materials for next class

_____ Write daily schedule on board

_____ Establish regular class routines

_____ Plan long-term projects on calendar

_____ Assist student in setting short-term academic goals

_____ Limit classroom and teacher transitions throughout the day

_____ Inform all teachers of the student's behavior/curriculum modifications

_____ Provide an extra set of textbooks for home

Other: _____

BEHAVIOR MANAGEMENT

_____	Involve student in developing behavior plan, goals, rewards
_____	Use daily rating card for behavior/academics
_____	Use secret signal to cue inappropriate behavior
_____	Write private contract between student and teacher
_____	Provide opportunities for student to engage in leadership roles
_____	Designate staff person to whom student can go to calm down
_____	Identify a limited number of behavioral goals
_____	Keep goals short-term (daily and weekly goals)
_____	Start goals at a level where student can achieve success relatively soon
_____	Increase positive attention for appropriate behavior
_____	Give specific verbal praise ("I see that you started your work right away.")
_____	Decrease negative attention for relatively minor inappropriate behavior
_____	Provide _immediate_ and ongoing positive feedback for appropriate behavior
_____	Develop a classroom token system
_____	Use response cost system for inappropriate behavior (loss of some tokens previously earned when engages in inappropriate behavior)
_____	Use modified response cost (start day with full number of tokens but student loses tokens for negative behavior)
_____	Give bonus points for exceptional behavior or performance beyond goals
_____	Devise behavior management system for unstructured times (hallways, lunchroom, playground, bus, bathrooms, etc.)
_____	Get student's input when selecting appropriate rewards for attainment of goals

_____ Change rewards periodically to maintain motivation
_____ Allow student to work toward a class reward (popcorn party, movie, etc.)
_____ Use daily and end-of-week rewards to maintain motivation
_____ Use daily notebook system for communication between school and home
_____ Use kitchen timer to set time limits
_____ Use attention tape for reminding on-task behavior and teaching student self-monitoring
_____ Use card system for limiting demands for teacher attention
_____ Develop time-out plan
_____ Modify school rules which discriminate against ADHD (e.g., assertive discipline)
         Other: _____

GRADING MODIFICATIONS

_____ Give daily grades and average into quarter grades
_____ Change amount of work required for passing grade
_____ Provide clear guidelines for amount of work required for each letter grade
_____ Provide a separate grade for persistence
_____ Give more weight to daily work rather than tests
         Other: _____

TESTING MODIFICATIONS

_____ Avoid timed tests
_____ Allow more time to take tests
_____ Allow student to take tests in resource room or other room with limited distractions and less pressure
_____ Teach student how to study for tests (select important from less important information, outline, highlight, learn mnemonics, etc.)

_____ Substitute oral tests for written tests

_____ Allow independent projects in place of tests

_____ Allow student to retake tests

_____ Use multiple choice, true-false, or matching format instead of essays

_____ Allow take-home and open book tests

_____ Divide tests into sections to fit student's attention/work capacity

Other: _____

SUPPLEMENTAL SUPPORTS

_____ Paraprofessional in classroom

_____ Classroom consultation by school psychologist, social worker, counselor, speech pathologist, or EBD teacher

_____ Peer tutoring

_____ Older-student tutoring

_____ Learning partner

_____ After- or before-school tutoring

Other: _____

SUPPLEMENTAL SKILLS TRAINING

_____ Study skills

_____ Test-taking skills

_____ Work review strategies

_____ Behavioral self-monitoring strategies

_____ Impulse control

_____ Anger control

_____ Social skills

_____ Word processor/computer skills

Other: _____

ADDITIONAL INTERVENTIONS

_____	Parent training
_____	Family therapy
_____	Individual therapy with student
_____	Medication
_____	School inservice on ADHD
_____	Teacher workshop on ADHD
_____	Books, videos, and handouts on ADHD
_____	Friendship group
_____	Family change group
_____	Join CH.A.D.D.
_____	Attend CH.A.D.D. parent support group
_____	Attend CH.A.D.D. quarterly informational meetings
	Other: _____

MEDICATION MANAGEMENT

_____	Devise system for monitoring medication effectiveness within the classroom (Conners, Academic Performance Rating Scale, etc.)
_____	Devise system for monitoring side effects (Side Effects Questionnaire)
_____	Give teacher permission to consult with pediatrician or psychologist overseeing medication management
_____	Develop system for dispensing medication during school day (do not expect student to take this responsibility alone)
_____	Be aware of indications that medication is wearing off and adjust expectations
_____	Be aware of medication transitions (behavior change near end of medication period, before noon and at end of school day)
_____	Avoid announcing to student to take medication over school loudspeaker or in front of class
	Other: _____

ADDITIONAL CONSIDERATIONS

_____   Establish regular communication system between school and home

_____   Agree on special instructions for totally inappropriate/ aggressive behavior

_____   Schedule planning meeting with parent(s) and teacher(s) at beginning of school year to review student's special needs and develop appropriate modifications

_____   Schedule meeting with parent(s) and school staff at end of school year to select teacher for following year

Other: _____

SUMMARY

- Preparing thoroughly for the IEP or Section 504 meeting ensures that you as a parent can participate as an equal partner with school personnel.

- Reviewing a checklist for possible adaptations or service options to discuss will make the meeting more effective and efficient plus promote an atmosphere of true collaboration.

Providing Input Into the Selection of Your Child's Teacher

Perhaps the most critical factor in the success that your child enjoys in the classroom is the "goodness of fit" between your child and his/her teacher. Undoubtedly, students with ADHD are a challenge to teach. They require more work than other students and often disrupt the flow of the classroom. They can bring out the worst in the best of teachers, leaving them frustrated and defensive. It takes a teacher with special qualities and expertise to effectively teach a student with ADHD.

The challenge of having a student with ADHD in the classroom creates a unique and often troublesome dynamic. Studies of classrooms with disruptive children indicate that teachers engage in negative, controlling behaviors with these children approximately 77 percent of their time. In contrast, only 23 percent of teacher interactions with these students are positive or neutral. Observational studies have found that teachers are more likely to respond to students with ADHD with commands, reprimands, punishment, and generally negative interactions. They are less likely to praise or interact positively with these students.[1]

These dynamics are especially distressing because a child's relationship with his teacher is one of the most significant he will have as a child. The school-age child shapes his self-esteem largely by the success he feels in the classroom. This is where he spends the majority of his waking day.

The critical influence of teachers is underscored by follow-up studies. Students with ADHD report that the main factor that helped them get through school was the caring and understanding of a particular teacher. Conversely, they report that a significant factor that made school a negative experience was a particular teacher who did not understand their difficulties and was not willing to make modifications.[2] Indeed, the student's relationship with his teacher is critical to his level of success *and* his level of motivation. A child who feels he is not well-liked or is misunderstood by his teachers will not be motivated to do well for that teacher.

When a teacher sees the child with ADHD in a negative light, it may create a negative spillover that permeates the entire classroom. Negative spillover can lead to the following scenarios:

- The teacher becomes hypersensitive to the behaviors of the student with ADHD and begins to monitor milder forms of these same behaviors in the rest of the students, creating a "boot camp" climate

- Other students begin to identify the student with ADHD as the "bad kid" in the classroom and avoid or actively reject him

- Other students become disruptive as they realize that disruptive behavior gains teacher and peer attention

A key factor in preventing negative spillover is recognizing and responding to a poor "goodness of fit" between a teacher and your child.

MATTHEW'S STORY: A CASE OF POOR "GOODNESS OF FIT"

The importance of the "goodness of fit" between teacher and student was never so clear as in the case of Matthew.

> I first met Matthew when he was in fourth grade, soon after his family moved to Minnesota from an eastern state. Matthew had been diagnosed with ADHD when he was in first grade. Each year his parents had provided input into the selection of his teacher and successfully formed a working alliance with each one, developing appropriate classroom modifications and behavior interventions. Consequently, despite Matthew's prominent ADHD-related difficulties, school had been a successful experience for him, and he was a happy and outgoing child.

> Based upon the cooperation and support they found with each teacher, Matthew's parents assumed that they would have no difficulty working with Matthew's new teacher when they moved to their new state. They had heard that Minnesota was known for its excellent school systems and that schools and mental health professionals were on the "cutting edge" of the field of ADHD.

> When this family came to me after the first two months of school, things had already gone terribly wrong. Matthew's

parents had met with his new teacher the first week of school to introduce themselves, to share Matthew's special needs, and to suggest that they work together to make this another successful year for Matthew.

Unfortunately, these parents were immediately met with defensiveness. The teacher informed them that she was well aware of ADHD and what to do. After all, her school district was engaged in a longitudinal treatment-outcome study with a local university. She wanted these parents to know that she was knowledgeable about ADHD, and that she could handle Matthew without their "help."

Within the first two weeks of school, Matthew was coming home with behavior slips and discipline reports from his teacher for leaving his seat, not listening, blurting out, not completing desk work, and for "wiggling too much in his seat." Repeatedly, Matthew's mother attempted to explain to his teacher that much of what she was punishing Matthew for was not completely within his control, especially the "wiggling in his seat." She offered various suggestions, based on what other teachers had done successfully in the past. She also asked the teacher if she had any ideas based on her experience with kids with ADHD. This teacher's general response was that Matthew was now old enough to control this behavior, that she did not have time to do all of these "special things," and that it would not be fair to the other students in the classroom if she made exceptions for Matthew.

As the days progressed, Matthew's behavior deteriorated at school and at home. For the first time he was shunned by classmates as that "new boy who is always in trouble." Whereas Matthew had always been eager to go to school, he now was resisting; there was a daily battle between his mother and him to get him on the bus. He was withdrawing from peers and family members, and his mother was concerned that Matthew was depressed.

We decided that it was time for Matthew's parents to meet with this teacher and the school principal. At the meeting, the principal agreed that the situation was serious and that the modifications which the parents and I were requesting were indeed reasonable. A plan was devised with input from the classroom teacher, and it was agreed that it would be implemented the following Monday.

It took less than one week for Matthew's parents to realize that the plan had fallen on deaf ears.

A few days after our "successful school meeting," I received a distressing phone call from Matthew's mother. She was extremely upset and crying, and it was difficult to understand her. I told her to take a few deep breaths and try to collect her thoughts; I would wait until she was able to talk.

As Matthew's mother regained her composure, she began to tell me something that still shocks me to this day. She had just received a call from another mother in Matthew's class who wanted to know if Matthew had reported what happened in class that day. Matthew had not said anything, although his mother was concerned that he was unusually quiet and had gone directly to his room after school, not even stopping for his after-school snack. Her heart started to pound and she could feel an overwhelming rush of anxiety as this other mother proceeded to tell her what had happened to Matthew. Apparently Matthew was "wiggling in his seat" too much for his teacher to tolerate. To teach him a lesson about the importance of sitting still, Matthew's teacher taped him to his chair with a roll of duct tape and demanded that he sit that way for an entire class period.

Needless to say, Matthew was humiliated and shamed beyond comprehension. Even Matthew's classmates were shocked and frightened by this teacher's solution to this "problem." After an emergency meeting with the principal (who responded with lackluster concern and no action), a letter to the school board and the school superintendent, and a meeting with a lawyer (who assured them they clearly had grounds for a lawsuit), Matthew's parents decided to pull him out of the school and out of the district. They made the personal decision to channel their anger and frustration in a positive direction. Instead of filing a lawsuit, for which they were certainly justified, they focused on finding the best possible school placement for their son.

The next week Matthew was enrolled in a new school, where the teacher and principal readily met with us for a planning meeting. The teacher eagerly implemented those strategies which had worked for Matthew in the past. She stayed in regular contact with Matthew's parents by way of a notebook system and often offered many of her own suggestions to further help Matthew. It was evident that this teacher cared about Matthew, and he could tell. He was motivated to work hard in school because he knew his teacher supported him. The remainder of fourth grade was very successful. Matthew regained his sense of competency and self-esteem, thanks to the perseverance of his parents and the "goodness of fit" between his enlightened teacher and him.

Most school districts have a policy prohibiting parents from re-questing a specific teacher for their child. However, schools usually do have a process by which parents can inform a principal of any special considerations or particular concerns about their child that they would like considered when classes are determined. Although it may not be appropriate for parents to request a specific teacher, it is appropriate for them to list specific teacher and classroom characteristics that they feel would provide the "best fit" for their child, given his ADHD.

TEACHER CHARACTERISTICS FOR THE STUDENT WITH ADHD

There are a number of teacher characteristics you should consider when advocating for your child. It is important that your child's teacher:

- believes in and understands ADHD and its effects on behavior and academic performance;
- has current knowledge about ADHD (e.g., has attended workshops in the last five years and has read recently-published books);
- is willing to learn about ADHD if he/she does not understand it;
- understands that even though a student may be medicated, he still needs classroom interventions to foster appropriate behavioral and academic skills;
- is open to suggestions by you or outside professionals;
- is willing to meet with you and any appropriate professionals at the beginning of the school year to devise behavioral and academic strategies; then to meet throughout the school year to monitor progress, consider modifications, etc.
- runs an organized and structured classroom;
- is knowledgeable in behavior modification strategies and interventions, including schedules of reinforcement, points, charting, token or other reward systems, response cost, etc.;

- is flexible, calm, warm, and friendly (i.e., does not operate like a drill sergeant);
- relies predominantly on positive attention and minimizes negative attention; and
- makes herself easily accessible to you, either by phone or some written communication system.

CLASSROOM CHARACTERISTICS FOR THE STUDENT WITH ADHD

Also be aware of the classroom characteristics that provide the best fit for your child with ADHD:

- There is the smallest student-to-teacher ratio possible.
- The classroom is physically enclosed with four walls.
- The student with ADHD has an individual desk that is not touching other students' desks.
- The student's desk is away from other disruptive or distractible children and close to the teacher at the front of the room.
- The classroom structure is well-organized and predictable.
- Classroom clutter is minimal.
- Classroom rules are posted.
- A daily schedule is written on the board and reviewed with the class and changes are noted.
- The student with ADHD is helped to get through classroom transitions by allowing him more advanced preparation if needed, by providing supervision during transitions, and by giving the student readjustment time following the transition.
- Positive attention is used, and minor daydreaming/off-task behavior is ignored.
- The presentation format and task materials are varied, with low-interest or passive tasks interspersed with high-interest or active tasks to maintain interest/ motivation.
- Seatwork is brief and/or broken down into segments to fit the student's attentional capacity.
- Feedback about the accuracy of seatwork is given often and as immediately as possible.

- Classroom lectures or academic periods are interspersed with brief moments of physical exercise/movement, diminishing the fatigue and monotony of extensive academic work periods.

- Academic subjects are scheduled predominantly in the morning hours, leaving more active, nonacademic subjects for the afternoon hours because the student's activity level progressively increases and attentiveness progressively decreases throughout the day.

- Classroom instruction is supplemented with individualized instruction or computer-assisted instruction.

- A behavior management system, using token reinforcements and a daily reporting system, is used to manage classroom behavior, seat work, and homework.

- Daily and/or weekly assignment sheets are used, and student follow-through of homework is monitored.

- Behavior and academic progress charts are maintained and reviewed with the student regularly.

- Older students (third grade and above) are taught a self-monitoring system for behavior and academics.

- The amount of homework is modified to fit the student's processing speed and attentional capacity.

- There is a formal and consistent system of communication between teachers and parents.

These lists are comprehensive and define an ideal fit for your child at school. Realistically, you can't expect a perfect world. However, you can expect that your child has a positive experience at school.

If you find that the fit between your child and his teacher or his classroom is not a good one, be a courageous advocate for him. Your child's self-esteem and education are much too precious to be timid about speaking up. Talk to the school principal about your concerns. If appropriate changes are not made in the classroom, request a transfer to a different classroom. There are many excellent teachers who understand ADHD or who are open to learning. Do everything you can to bring them into your child's school experience.

SUMMARY

- The "goodness of fit" between a teacher and a student is a key factor in doing well in school. For the child with ADHD, it is even more important, not only for that student but also for the rest of the classroom because of possible negative spillover.

- Parents typically cannot select a teacher for their child. However, they can provide input for the school about characteristics of both the teacher and the classroom that will help ensure a good fit for their child.

CHAPTER

28 Communicating With the School

STRATEGY MEETINGS AT THE BEGINNING AND END OF THE SCHOOL YEAR

Parents often report that with the start of a new school year or transfer to a new school, they are reluctant to tell the new teacher that their child has an attention deficit disorder. They fear that this information may cause the teacher to develop a negative mindset about their child, resulting in the teacher treating him unfairly and automatically blaming him for problems in the classroom. Parents don't want to create a self-fulfilling prophecy. Consequently, they adopt a "wait and see" approach: they don't tell the teacher that their child has difficulties or has been diagnosed with ADHD in the hopes that the teacher will deal with the child more positively, thereby increasing his chances for success.

As rational as this "wait and see" approach may sound, it usually backfires. It is akin to sending the child outside without a raincoat or umbrella when there is a 90 percent chance of rain. More than likely he is going to get wet. There is no doubt that a teacher's positive attitude is essential with ADHD, but a positive attitude is not enough to help the student overcome his inherent ADHD-related difficulties. Valuable ground can be lost with a "wait and see" approach. In the process, the relationships between the student and his teacher and peers can be damaged.

It is better that parents begin an honest partnership with their child's teacher at the beginning of the year. You should document your child's needs as well as what classroom strategies have and have not worked in the past. This information should be shared at a planning meeting with all regular and special education teachers who work with your child. It is also helpful to invite your child's teacher from the previous school year so that she can share her special insight and offer suggestions.

Schedule this meeting shortly before or soon after the school year begins. Important points to cover at this meeting include:

- the need for any specialized behavior program;
- a method of monitoring your child's behavior and academics on a daily/weekly basis;
- the reinforcement system to be used;
- any modifications necessary for test delivery or homework load;
- seating arrangements;
- a method for consistent and frequent communication between school and home;
- special concerns such as social issues, conflict with a particular peer, and emotional problems;
- notification if your child is on medication; and
- medication management procedures.

If a child has a Section 504 Plan or IEP, it should be reviewed with all the teachers, and the need for any changes or additions should be discussed. Any meeting should end with the questions, "What is our next step?" and "What date and time should we meet again to discuss progress?"

Near the end of the school year, schedule a meeting with your child's teacher(s) to review how the year went and to determine what modifications and strategies worked for your child and which ones did not. Find out if the teacher(s) has any special concerns for your child for next school year. Inquire about his/her recommendations for teacher and classroom selection for next year. Also, request that your child's teacher(s) communicate with next year's teachers about his special learning and behavior styles and appropriate strategies and adaptations.

CONSISTENT COMMUNICATION BETWEEN SCHOOL AND HOME

A common complaint voiced by parents is that they don't find out that assignments are missing and/or that their child is failing a class until school conference time (often midway through the semester or quarter), or when report cards are issued. Parents can actively work to prevent these late notices. Regular communication between you and your child's teacher(s) is critical for your child's academic and behavioral success. Therefore, work together to establish a format of regular communication. It is important to be aware of the teachers' expectations, daily assignments, long-term assignments, reports about your child's behavior, peer relationships in the school, etc.

Likewise, it is important for teacher(s) to be aware of any special circumstances, concerns or questions that arise at home, such as your child's confusion about a particular homework assignment, your concern that he is bringing home too much homework because he can't finish his classwork at school, family stressors or illness; etc.

When you meet with the teacher(s) at the beginning of the school year, develop a consistent format of communication. There are many possibilities. You can use a system in which you and the teachers make comments in a daily notebook that is transported by your child between home and school. Or you can design a weekly progress report that contains information about work habits, social behavior and assignments. This progress report is sent home by the teacher at the end of each week (see Appendix C for a sample). Some teachers write weekly newsletters informing parents about topics studied in class as well as daily and long-range assignments. Other teachers send home notices whenever an assignment was not turned in. Parents are required to sign this form, and the student returns it the following day. Other teachers schedule a weekly telephone conference with a parent to inform them of the child's progress. Some parents and teachers communicate regularly by e-mail.

SUMMARY

- Communication with the school has many benefits: clarifying expectations, reviewing progress, facilitating changes, and evaluating results.

- Meetings at the beginning and the end of the school year set the tone of partnership between the parents and the teacher. They also ensure a common understanding about goals, strategies, etc., thereby building trust.

Concluding Remarks for Parents

I hope you now have a better understanding of ADHD and your child. You now know that you did not cause your child's behavior, and that his behavioral difficulties are inherent in his biological make-up. You also know how important it is to form realistic expectations about what your child can and cannot do. And now you know that before you can change your child, you have to change yourself by looking at your own temperament, parenting proactively, avoiding over-punishing, giving lots of positive feedback and attention, actively listening to your child, avoiding the cycle of arguing and threatening, and providing much-needed structure.

But knowing and doing are two very different things. Just like your child with ADHD, you may now know what to do, but can you do it? The answer is yes — if you have support, a healthy attitude, and a commitment to be your child's staunchest advocate. If you still have nagging feelings of guilt or embarrassment, work on getting rid of them. Focus on your control zone and redirect your valuable energy in a more positive direction, toward that which you can change. Guilt, shame, embarrassment, and your own stubborn pride don't help your child. Proactivity does. Proactivity must be your way of life. Being proactive is ongoing hard work, not something that you do only once in a while or in reaction to the problem at the moment. You must be an advocate for your child, and your advocacy must be a long-term commitment. This is an investment in your child that will pay rich dividends for him or her, for you, and for society.

To be an effective advocate, you must also be an informed consumer. Knowledge is power. Reading this book is a start. Other excellent books are listed in Appendix A. You can also attend seminars about ADHD sponsored by local professional organizations and schools. There are many informative videos and newsletters available. The National CH.A.D.D. (Children and Adults with Attention Deficit Disorders) organization has an excellent newsletter, *Inside CH.A.D.D.*, as well as a wonderful magazine, *Attention!* Both are included as part of your membership. Videos, newsletters and organizations are also listed in Appendix A.

An effective advocate gains knowledge and strength through support. Don't be a lone ranger in your struggle to help your child. Find support inside and outside of your home. If you are married, talk to your spouse and form a joint commitment to share in the extra responsibilities of parenting your child. Too often the burden falls to one parent, usually the mother. Find a confidant — someone with whom you can talk to gain support, comfort and maybe ideas. A confidant can be anyone who has an interest in your child: a spouse or significant other, a relative or a friend.

You can also seek the help of a licensed professional who specializes in ADHD, such as an educational or clinical psychologist, a behavioral pediatrician, an educational consultant, or a clinical social worker. Be sure this individual is well-trained and has significant experience with children with ADHD. He or she should have a broad understanding of ADHD, behavior management methods, and the federal and educational laws that relate to ADHD. An outside professional should also be able to guide you as advocate for your child at school, especially if your child needs special or related services. Ask your pediatrician, a respected friend, or other parents of children with ADHD for recommendations of such a professional.

You can also find comfort and support at local parent support groups or at meetings of local organizations such as CH.A.D.D. or LDA (Learning Disabilities Association). You can call the national headquarters of these organizations (listed in Appendix A) to find out about chapters and support groups in your area. You may find other resources in your area by contacting your child's teacher; your school's psychologist, nurse, social worker or counselor; your school district's special education department; local mental health centers; area colleges or universities; and pediatric departments in local hospitals or clinics.

Being an effective advocate for your child also means doing, but not over-doing. It's a fine line between advocating for your child and teaching him "learned helplessness." Therefore, it's important that you teach your child how to be his own advocate. Help him understand his needs and how to ask for help. Teach him to speak up when he needs assignments written down, more time on tests, seating away from distractions, shorter assignments, and help in taking notes. The more your child learns to advocate for himself, the sooner he will move toward successful independence.

Reading books, attending seminars, and finding support are essential ingredients for effective advocacy. But there is one element that is ultimately more important than all the information you could gather over a lifetime. **Your most powerful tool is your attitude.** Having ADHD does not mean that your child is destined for a maladjusted life. Remember Thomas Edison and other notable people such as Benjamin Franklin, Winston Churchill, Mozart, Albert Einstein, and Dustin Hoffman, who overcame the "disability" of ADHD by virtue of their attitudes. The attitude which you adopt about ADHD will be the attitude that you convey to your child. Your attitude can be your child's most effective medicine and your most comforting companion.

> The longer I live, the more I realize the impact of attitude on life. Attitude, to me, is more important than the past, than education, than money, than circumstances, than failures, than success, than what other people think or say or do. It is more important than appearances, giftedness, or skill. It will make or break a company ... a church ... a home. The remarkable thing is we have a choice every day regarding the attitude we will embrace for that day. We cannot change our past ... we cannot change the fact that people will act in a certain way. We cannot change the inevitable. The only thing we can do is play on the one string we have, and that is our attitude ... I am convinced that life is 10% what happens to me and 90% how I react to it. And so it is with you ... we are in charge of our Attitudes.
>
> Charles Swindoll

Where to Get Information

SUPPORT ORGANIZATIONS

ADDA (Attention Deficit Disorder Association)
P.O. Box 972
Mentor, OH 44061
800-487-2282

ADD Advocacy Group
8091 South Ireland Way
Aurora, CO 80016
(303) 690-7548

Adult Attention Deficit Foundation
132 North Woodward Avenue
Birmingham, MI 48009
800-540-6335

Adult ADD Association
1225 East Sunset Drive, No. 640
Bellingham, WA 98226

ADDult Support Network
2620 Ivy Place
Toledo, OH 43613

Attention Deficit Information Network
475 Hillside Avenue
Needham, MA 02194

CH.A.D.D. (Children and Adults with Attention Deficit Disorders)
A parent support group with local chapters nationwide
499 N.W. 70th Ave., Suite 308
Plantation, FL 33317
(954) 587-3700   800-233-4050

Pacer Center
4826 Chicago Avenue South
Minneapolis, MN 55417-1098
(612) 827-2966

Learning Disability Association
National Headquarters
4156 Library Road
Pittsburgh, PA 15234
(412) 341-1515

National Information Center for
Children and Youth with Disabilities
P.O. Box 1492
Washington, DC 20013-1492

National Institute for Attention Deficit Disorder
407 Resor Avenue
Cincinnati, OH 45220

NEWSLETTERS

ADDA (publishes a newsletter, see above)

ADDendum (for adults with ADD)
c/o C.P.S.
5041-A Backlick Road
Annandale, VA 22003
(703) 986-1953

The ADHD Report
R. Barkley & Associates, Editors
Guilford Publications
72 Spring St.
New York, NY 10012
800-365-7006

ADDult News
c/o Mary Jane Johnson
ADDult Support Network
2620 Ivy Place
Toledo, OH 43613
(419) 866-9183

ATTENTION Please!
Bimonthly Newsletter for Children with ADD
2106 3rd Avenue North
Seattle, WA 98109-2304

Brakes: The Interactive Newsletter for Kids with ADD
J. Stern & P. Quinn, Editors
A.D.D WareHouse
300 N.W. 70th Ave., Suite 102
Plantation, FL 33317
800-233-9273

Inside CH.A.D.D.
CH.A.D.D. National Headquarters
499 NW 70th Ave., Suite 308
Plantation, FL 33317
(954) 587-3700   800-233-4050
Fax: (305) 587-4599

Challenge: A Newsletter on
Attention Deficit Hyperactivity Disorder
P.O. Box 2001
West Newbury, MA 01985
(508) 462-0495

WEBSITES

www.alt.support.attn-deficit
www.chadd.org

BOOKS FOR PARENTS

Bain, L. (1991). *A Parent's Guide to Attention Deficit Disorders*. New York: Delta/Dell.

Balter, L. (1988). *Who's in Control?* New York: Poseidon Press.

Barkley, R. (1995). *Taking Charge of ADHD*. New York: Guilford Press.

Bloomquist, M.L. (1996). *Skills Training for Children*. New York: Guilford Press.

Budd, L. (1993). *Living With the Active Alert Child*. New York: Parenting Press.

Crary, E. (1990). *Pick Up Your Socks*. Seattle, Washington: Parenting Press, Inc.

Dendy, C.A. (1995). *Teenagers with ADD: A Parent's Guide*. Rockville, Maryland: Woodbine House.

Dinkmeyer, D. and McKay, G. (1973). *Raising A Responsible Child*. New York: Simon and Schuster.

Erickson, Erik. (1950). *Childhood and Society*. New York: W.W. Norton & Co.

Faber, A. and Mazlish, E. (1982). *How to Talk So Kids Will Listen & Listen So Kids Will Talk*. New York: Avon Books.

Faber, A. and Mazlish, E. (1987). *Siblings Without Rivalry*. New York: Avon Books.

Flick, G. L. (1996). *Power Parenting for Children with ADD/ADHD: A Practical Parent's Guide for Managing Difficult Behaviors*. New York: Center for Applied Research in Education.

Fowler, M. (1992). *CH.A.D.D. Educators Manual*. Plantation, Florida: CASET Associates.

Fowler, M. (1990). *Maybe You Know My Kid: A Parent's Guide to Identifying, Understanding and Helping Your Child with ADHD*. New York: Birchlane Press.

Friedman, R.J. and Doyal, G.T. (1987) *Attention Deficit Disorder and Hyperactivity* (2nd ed.). Danville, Illinois: Interstate Printers and Publishers, Inc.

Goldstein, S. and Goldstein, M. (1992) *Hyperactivity: Why Won't My Child Pay Attention?* New York: John Wiley & Sons, Inc.

Goldstein, S. and Ingersoll, B. (1995). *Lonely, Sad and Angry: A Parent's Guide to Depression in Children and Adolescents*. New York: Doubleday.

Gordon, M. (1990). *ADHD/Hyperactivity: A Consumer's Guide*. DeWitt, New York: GSI Publications.

Gordon, T. (1975). *Parent Effectiveness Training*. New York: Penguin Books.

Hallowell, E. and Ratey, J. (1994). *Driven to Distraction*. New York: Pantheon Books.

Hallowell, E. and Ratey, J. (1994). *Answers to Distraction*. New York: Pantheon Books.

Ingersol, B. (1988). *Your Hyperactive Child: A Parent's Guide to Coping with Attention Deficit Disorder*. New York: Doubleday Books.

Ingersoll, B. and Goldstein, M. (1993). *Attention Deficit Disorder and Learning Disabilities: Realities, Myths, and Controversial Treatments*. New York: Doubleday.

Johnson, D.D. (1992) *I Can't Sit Still*. Santa Cruz, California: ETR Associates.

Kennedy, P. ,Terdal, L., and Fusetti, L. (1993). *The Hyperactive Child Book*. New York: St. Martin's Press.

Kurcinka, M. (1991). *Raising Your Spirited Child*. New York: Harper Collins.

Latham, P. and Latham, P. (1993). *ADD and the Law*. Washington, DC: JKL.

Levine, M. (1990). *Keeping A Head In School*. Cambridge, Massachusetts: Educators Publishing Services, Inc.

McKay, M., Fanning, P., Paleg, K., and Landis, D. (1996). *When Anger Hurts Your Kids*. Oakland, California: New Harbinger Publications, Inc.

Parker, H. (1988). *The Hyperactivity Workbook for Parents, Teachers and Kids*. Plantation, Florida: Impact Publications.

Patterson, G. R. (1982). *Coercive Family Process*. Eugene, Oregon: Castalia.

Phelan, T. (1985). *1-2-3: Magic: Training Your Preschoolers and Preteens to do What You Want*. Glen Ellyn, Illinois: Child Management Press.

Phelan, T. (1990) *Hyperactivity and Attention Deficit Disorders*. Glen Ellyn, Illinois: Child Management Press.

Phelan, T. (1991). *Surviving Your Adolescents*. Glen Ellyn, Illinois: Child Management Press.

Robin, A. L. and Foster, S.L. (1989). *Negotiating Parent-Child Adolescent Conflict*. New York: Guilford Press.

Silver, L.B. (1992). *Attention-Deficit Hyperactivity Disorder: A Clinical Guide to Diagnosis and Treatment*. Washington, DC: American Psychiatric Press.

Silver, L. B. (1993). *Dr. Silver's Advice to Parents on Attention-Deficit Hyperactivity Disorder.* Washington, DC: American Psychiatric Press.

Taylor, J.F. (1990). *Helping Your Hyperactive Child.* Rocklin, California: Prima Publishing.

Turecki, S. (1985). *The Difficult Child.* New York: Bantam Books.

Wender, P.H. (1987). *The Hyperactive Child, Adolescent, and Adult: Attention Disorder Through the Life Span.* New York: Oxford University Press.

Woodrich, D. (1994). *What Every Parent Wants to Know: Attention Deficit Hyperactivity Disorder.* Baltimore: Brookes.

VIDEOTAPES FOR PARENTS

Barkley, R.A. (1992). *ADHD: What Do We Do?* A.D.D. WareHouse: 800-233-0273.

Barkley, R.A. (1992). *ADHD: What Do We Know?* A.D.D. WareHouse: 800-233-0273.

Goldstein, S. (1989). *Why Won't My Child Pay Attention?* The Neurology, Learning and Behavior Center, 230 South 500 East, Suite 100, Salt Lake City, Utah 94102.

Goldstein, S. and Goldstein, M. (1991). *It's Just Attention Disorder.* The Neurology, Learning and Behavior Center, 230 South 500 East, Suite 100, Salt Lake City, Utah 94102.

Gordon, M. (1993). *Jumpin' Johnny Get Back to Work!: The Video.* A.D.D. WareHouse 800-233-0273.

Lavoie, R. (1974). *Understanding LD: How Difficult Can This Be?* The FAT City Workshop, 508-888-0489.

Phelan, T. (1990). *All About Attention Deficit: Parts 1 and 2.* A.D.D. WareHouse: 800-233-0273

Phelan, T. (1990). *1-2-3: Magic.* A.D.D. WareHouse: 800-233-0273.

Phelan, T. (1994). *Medication for ADD.* A.D.D. WareHouse: 800-233-0273

BOOKS FOR CHILDREN AND ADOLESCENTS

Corman, C. and Trevino, E. (1995). *Euclee the Jumpy Jumpy Elephant.* Plantation, Florida: Specialty Press; A.D.D. WareHouse: 800-233-9273.

Galvin, M. (1988). *Otto Learns About his Medicine*. New York: Magination Press.

Goldstein, S. (1991). *It's Just Attention Disorder: A Video Guide for Kids*. Salt Lake City, Utah: Neurology, Learning and Behavior Center.

Gordon, M. (1991) *Jumpin' Johnny Get Back to Work: A Child's Guide to ADHD/Hyperactivity*. DeWitt, New York: GSI Publications.

Gordon, M. (1992). *I Would if I Could*. DeWitt, New York: GSI Publications.

Gordon, M. (1992). *My Brother's a World Class Pain: A Sibling's Guide to ADHD/Hyperactivity*. DeWitt, New York: GSI Publications.

Moss, D.M. (1989). *Shelly the Hyperactive Turtle*. Kensington, Maryland: Woodbine House Publishers.

Nadeau, K. (1994). *Survival Guide for College Students with ADD or LD*. New York: Brunner/Mazel.

Nadeau, K. and Dixon, E. (1991). *Learning to Slow Down and Pay Attention*. Plantation, Florida: Impact Publications.

Parker, R.N. (1992). *Making the Grade: An Adolescent's Struggle with ADD*. Plantation, Florida: Impact Publications.

Quinn, P.O. (1994). *ADD and the College Student*. New York: Magination Press.

Quinn, P.O., and Stern, J.M. (1991). *Putting on the Brakes: Young People's Guide to Understanding Attention Deficit Hyperactivity Disorder*. New York: Magination Press.

BOOKS FOR ADULTS WITH ADHD

Hallowell, E. and Ratey, J. (1994). *Driven to Distraction*. New York: Pantheon.

Gordon, M. and McClure, F.D. (1995). *The Down and Dirty Guide to Adult Attention Deficit Disorder*. DeWitt, New York: GSI Publications.

Kelly K. and Ramundo, P. (1993). *You Mean I'm Not Lazy, Stupid, or Crazy!* Cincinnati, Ohio: Tyrell & Jerem Press.

Murphy, K. and Levert, S. (1995). *Out of the Fog*. New York: Hyperion.

Nadeau, K. (1995). *ADD in Adults: Research, Diagnosis and Treatment*. New York: Brunner/Mazel.

Nadeau, K. (1996). *A User-Friendly Guide to Understanding Adult ADD*. New York: Brunner/Mazel.

Solder, S. (1995). *Women with Attention Deficit Disorder: Embracing Disorganization at Home and in the Workplace*. Grass Valley, California: Underwood Books.

Weiss, L. (1992). *ADD in Adults*. Dallas, Texas: Taylor.

Wender, P.H. (1987) *The Hyperactive Child, Adolescent, and Adult*. New York: Oxford University Press.

Wender, L. (1995). *Attention-Deficit Hyperactivity Disorder in Adults*. New York: Oxford University Press.

VIDEOTAPES FOR ADULTS

Barkley, R.A. (1993). *ADHD in adults*. A.D.D. WareHouse: 800-233-0273.

Phelan, T. (1995). *Adults with Attention Deficit Disorder: Essential Information for ADD Adults*. A.D.D. WareHouse: 800-233-0273.

BOOKS FOR EDUCATORS

Barkley, R.A. (1997). *ADHD and the Nature of Self-Control*. New York: Guilford Press.

Barkley, R.A. (1990). *Attention-Deficit Hyperactivity Disorder: A Handbook for Diagnosis and Treatment*. New York: Guilford Press.

Braswell, L., Bloomquist, M. and Pederson, S. (1991). *A Guide to Understanding and Helping Children with ADHD in School Settings*. Minneapolis, Minnesota: University of Minnesota Press.

Copeland, E.D., and Love, V.L. (1990). *Attention Without Tension: A Teacher's Handbook on Attention Disorders (ADHD and ADD)*. Atlanta, Georgia: 3 C's of Childhood, Inc.

DuPaul, G., and Stoner, G. (1994). *ADHD in the Schools: Assessment and Intervention Strategies*. New York: The Guilford School Practitioner Series.

Fowler, M.C. (1992). *CH.A.D.D. Educators Manual*. Plantation, Florida: CASET Associates: 800-545-5583.

Goldstein, S. (1994). *Understanding and Managing Children's Classroom Behavior*. New York: John Wiley & Sons, Inc.

Johnson, D. (1992). *I Can't Sit Still: Educating and Affirming Inattentive and Hyperactive Children*. Santa Cruz, California: ETR Associates.

McCarney, S.B. (1989). *The Attention Deficit Disorders Intervention Manual* Columbia, Missouri: Hawthorne Educational Services.

Parker, H. (1992). *The ADD-Hyperactivity Handbook for Schools.* Plantation, Florida: Impact Publications.

Parker, H. (1992). *ADAPT: Attention Deficit Accommodation Plan for Teaching.* Plantation, Florida: Specialty Press: A.D.D. WareHouse: 800-233-9273.

VIDEOTAPES FOR EDUCATORS

Barkley, R. (1994). *ADHD in the Classroom: Strategies for Teachers.* New York: Guilford Press.

Copeland, E.D. (1990). *ADHD/ADD Video Resource for Schools.* Atlanta, Georgia: 3 C's of Childhood, Inc.

Goldstein, S. and Goldstein, M. (1990). *Educating Inattentive Children.* Available from the Neurology, Learning and Behavior Center, 230 South 500 East, Suite 100, Salt Lake City, Utah 84102.

Reiff, S. (1996). *ADHD: Inclusive Instruction & Collaborative Practices.* A.D.D. WareHouse: 800-9273.

LEARNING DISABILITIES ORGANIZATIONS

LDAA
(Learning Disabilities Association of America)
4156 Library Road
Pittsburgh, PA 15234
(412) 341-1515

Learning Disabilities Council
Post Office Box 8451
Richmond, VA 23226
(804) 748-5012

NCLD
(National Center for Learning Disabilities)
99 Park Ave.
New York, NY 10016
(212) 687-7211
Orton Dyslexia Society

8600 LaSalle Road
Baltimore, MD 21204
(301) 296-0232

ADHD/EDUCATIONAL VENDORS

A.D.D. WareHouse
300 NW 70th Ave., Suite 102
Plantation, FL 33317
1-800-233-9273

The Attention Deficit Resource Center
1344 Johnson Ferry Road, Suite 14
Marietta, GA 30068

Professional Advancement Seminars
P.O. Box 746
Worcester, MA 0160

APPENDIX

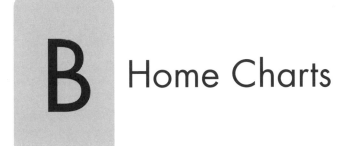

B Home Charts

Let's Get Ready

You will get a star every time you _____

_____.

However, if you _____,

then you _____.

When you get_____stars on your chart, you can

_____.

Home Behavior Chart

Color in a leaf each time you _____

When you reach the flower, you get _____

Home Behavior Chart

0	1	2	3
Needs Improvement	Satisfactory	Good	Excellent

BEHAVIORS	S	M	T	W	TH	F	SA
1.							
2.							
3.							
4.							
TOTAL DAILY SCORE							

Excellent Day = 9-12   Good Day = 5-8   Try Again = 0-4   **WEEK TOTAL**

MY GOAL IS TO GET _____**POINTS A DAY.**

IF I DO I WILL GET _____.

IF I EARN _____ **POINTS AT THE END OF A WEEK, I CAN** _____ _____.

Self-Control Contract

I, _____, agree to do the following:

If I do these things as agreed upon, I will receive:

If I do not do these things, I will lose:

I agree to fulfill this contract to the best of my ability.

_____   _____   _____   _____
Child   Date   Parent   Date

This contract will be reviewed by _____
                                            Date

Reward Menu

	Points
BASEBALL CARD	5
STICKER	5
SPECIAL DESSERT	10
SPECIAL SNACK	10
STAY UP 30 MINUTES LATER	20
CHOOSE FAMILY MEAL	20
$2 TOY	30
PLAY GAME WITH MOM/DAD	30
RENT VIDEO	50
EAT AT RESTAURANT	50
SLEEPOVER	80
MOVIE AT THEATER	80

Reward Menu

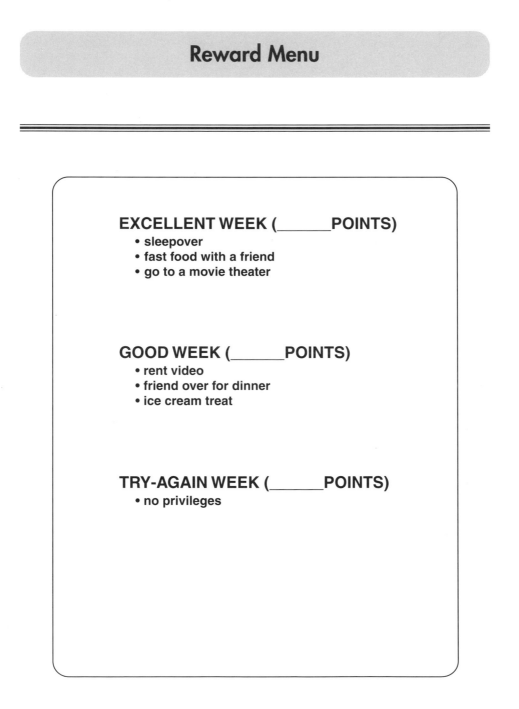

EXCELLENT WEEK (_____POINTS)
- sleepover
- fast food with a friend
- go to a movie theater

GOOD WEEK (_____POINTS)
- rent video
- friend over for dinner
- ice cream treat

TRY-AGAIN WEEK (_____POINTS)
- no privileges

Reward Menu for
Adolescents With ADHD

Item/Activity	Points
Special Snack	_____
Telephone Time: _____ Minutes	_____
Use of Family Car	_____
Compact Disc	_____
Extra Money $_____	_____
Activity with Friends	_____
Clothes	_____

APPENDIX

C School Charts

Daily Report

Name _____

Week _____

CODE:

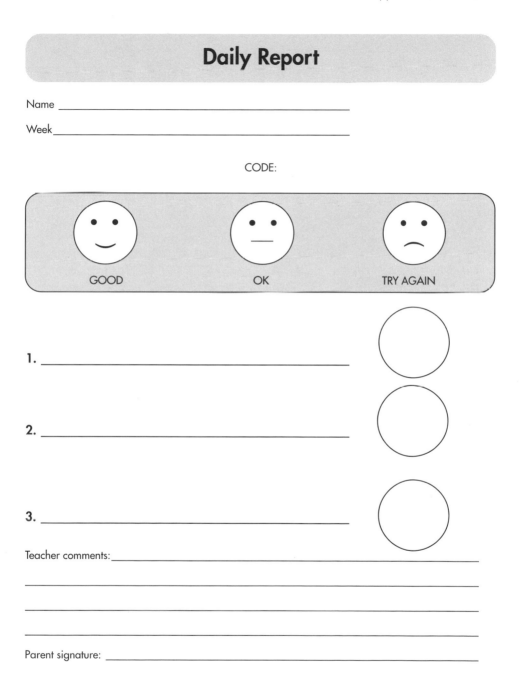

GOOD   OK   TRY AGAIN

1. _____   ◯

2. _____   ◯

3. _____   ◯

Teacher comments: _____

_____

_____

_____

Parent signature: _____

Daily Report

NAME _____   DATE _____

Please rate this student in each of the following:

Completed classwork

Followed class rules

Got along well with others

Used class time wisely

Comments: _____

_____

_____

_____

Teacher Initials _____

Daily Rating Card

NAME _____   DATE _____

Please rate this student in each of the following:

	Poor		Good		Excellent
Handed in homework	1	2	3	4	5
Completed classwork	1	2	3	4	5
Followed directions	1	2	3	4	5
Participated	1	2	3	4	5

Homework _____

Comments_____

_____

_____

Overall today was a ☐ great day
                     ☐ good day
                     ☐ average day
                     ☐ mediocre day
                     ☐ very poor day

Teacher's initials _____

Daily Rating Card

STUDENT_____   DATE_____

GOAL:_____

0 = Needs Improvement	1 = Satisfactory	2 = Good	3 = Excellent

List each subject for this student, then circle a rating for work completion and for class behavior.

SUBJECT	WORK COMPLETION	CLASS BEHAVIOR
1._____	0 1 2 3	0 1 2 3
2._____	0 1 2 3	0 1 2 3
3._____	0 1 2 3	0 1 2 3
4._____	0 1 2 3	0 1 2 3
5._____	0 1 2 3	0 1 2 3
	TOTAL =	TOTAL =

ASSIGNMENTS (Teacher, please initial each assignment)

SUBJECT

1._____: _____

_____

2._____: _____

_____

3._____: _____

_____

4._____: _____

_____

5._____: _____

_____

OVERDUE ASSIGNMENTS

_____

504 Plan: Student Progress Report

Student: _____Grade: _____Date: _____

Teacher: _____Subject: _____Period: _____

Requested by: ❑ Parent   ❑ Counselor   ❑ Other: _____

- Level of Work: (circle)   A   B   C   D   F
- Attitude: (circle)   +2   +1   0   -1   -2
- Conduct: (circle)   +2   +1   0   -1   -2

Missing Work:_____

_____

Should be preparing for:_____

_____

Remarks: _____

_____

Each Friday, please return to: _____.

Thank You!

Behavior Scales
for Medication
Monitoring

ACADEMIC PERFORMANCE RATING SCALE

Student _____ Date _____

Age _____ Grade _____ Teacher _____

For each of the below items, please estimate the above student's performance over the *past week*. For each item, please circle **one** choice only.

1.	Estimate the percentage of written math work *completed* (regardless of accuracy) relative to classmates.	0-49% 1	50-69% 2	70-79% 3	80-89% 4	90-100% 5
2.	Estimate the percentage of written language arts work *completed* (regardless of accuracy) relative to classmates.	0-49% 1	50-69% 2	70-79% 3	80-89% 4	90-100% 5
3.	Estimate the *accuracy* of completed written math work (i.e., percent correct of work done).	0-64% 1	65-69% 2	70-79% 3	80-89% 4	90-100% 5
4.	Estimate the *accuracy* of completed written language arts work (i.e., percent correct of work done).	0-64% 1	65-69% 2	70-79% 3	80-89% 4	90-100% 5
5.	How consistent has the quality of this child's academic work been over the past week?	Consistently Poor 1	More Poor Than Successful 2	Variable 3	More Successful Than Poor 4	Consistently Successful 5
6.	How frequently does the student accurately follow teacher instructions and/or class discussion during *large-group* (e.g., whole class) instruction?	Never 1	Rarely 2	Sometimes 3	Often 4	Very Often 5
7.	How frequently does the student accurately follow teacher instructions and/or class discussion during the *small-group* (e.g., reading group) instruction?	Never 1	Rarely 2	Sometimes 3	Often 4	Very Often 5
8.	How quickly does this child learn new material (i.e., pick up novel concepts)?	Very Slow 1	Slow 2	Average 3	Above Average 4	Excellent 5

9.	What is the quality or neatness of this child's hand-writing?	Poor	Fair	Average	Above Average	Excellent
		1	2	3	4	5

10.	What is the quality of this child's reading skills?	Poor	Fair	Average	Above Average	Excellent
		1	2	3	4	5

11.	What is the quality of this child's speaking skills?	Poor	Fair	Average	Above Average	Excellent
		1	2	3	4	5

12.	How often does the child complete written work in a careless, hasty fashion?	Never	Rarely	Sometimes	Often	Very Often
		1	2	3	4	5

13.	How frequently does this child take more time to complete work than his/her classmates?	Never	Rarely	Sometimes	Often	Very Often
		1	2	3	4	5

14.	How often is the child able to pay attention without you prompting him/her?	Never	Rarely	Sometimes	Often	Very Often
		1	2	3	4	5

15.	How frequently does this child require your assistance to accurately complete his/her academic work?	Never	Rarely	Sometimes	Often	Very Often
		1	2	3	4	5

16.	How often does the child begin written work prior to understanding the directions?	Never	Rarely	Sometimes	Often	Very Often
		1	2	3	4	5

17.	How frequently does this child have difficulty recalling material from a previous day's lessons?	Never	Rarely	Sometimes	Often	Very Often
		1	2	3	4	5

18.	How often does the child appear to be staring excessively or "spaced out"?	Never	Rarely	Sometimes	Often	Very Often
		1	2	3	4	5

19.	How often does the child appear withdrawn or tend to lack an emotional response in a social situation?	Never	Rarely	Sometimes	Often	Very Often
		1	2	3	4	5

Page 2 of 2

From *Teacher Ratings of Academic Performance: The Development of the Academic Performance Rating Scale* by G. J. DuPaul, M. Rapport, and L. M. Perrielo, 1990, unpublished manuscript, University of Massachusetts Medical Center, Worcester.

ADHD RATING SCALE

Name of student _____ Age _____ Grade _____ Completed by _____

		Not at All	Just a Little	Pretty Much	Very Much
Inattention					
(a)	often fails to give close attention to details or makes careless mistakes in schoolwork, work, or other activities	0	1	2	3
(b)	often has difficulty sustaining attention in tasks or play activities	0	1	2	3
(c)	often does not seem to listen when spoken to directly	0	1	2	3
(d)	often does not follow through on instructions and fails to finish schoolwork, chores, or duties in the workplace (not due to oppositional behavior or failure to understand instructions)	0	1	2	3
(e)	often has difficulty organizing tasks and activities	0	1	2	3
(f)	often avoids, dislikes, or is reluctant to engage in tasks that require sustained mental effort (such as schoolwork or homework)	0	1	2	3
(g)	often loses things necessary for tasks or activities (e.g., toys, school assignments, pencils, books, or tools)	0	1	2	3
(h)	is often easily distracted by extraneous stimuli	0	1	2	3
(i)	is often forgetful in daily activities	0	1	2	3
Hyperactivity					
(a)	often fidgets with hands or feet or squirms in seat	0	1	2	3
(b)	often leaves seat in classroom or in other situations in which remaining seated is expected	0	1	2	3
(c)	often runs about or climbs excessively in situations in which it is inappropriate (in adolescents or adults, may be limited to subjective feelings of restlessness)	0	1	2	3
(d)	often has difficulty playing or engaging in leisure activities quietly	0	1	2	3
(e)	is often "on the go" or acts as if "driven by a motor"	0	1	2	3
(f)	often talks excessively	0	1	2	3
Impulsivity					
(g)	often blurts out answers before questions have been completed	0	1	2	3
(h)	often has difficulty awaiting turn	0	1	2	3
(i)	often interrupts or intrudes on others (e.g., butts into conversations or games)	0	1	2	3

Conners' Teacher Rating Scale - Revised (S)

by C. Keith Conners, Ph. D.

Child's Name_____Gender: M   F

Birthdate: ____/ ____/ _____   Age: _____   School Grade: _____
       Month Day Year

Teacher's Name:_____   Today's Date: ____/ ____/ ____
                                            Month Day Year

Instructions: Below are a number of common problems that children have. Please rate each item according to your child's behavior in the last month. For each item, ask yourself, "How much of a problem has this been in the last month?", and circle the best answer for each one. If none, not at all, seldom, or very infrequently, you would circle a 0. If very much true, or it occurs very often or frequently, you would circle 3. You would circle 1 or 2 for ratings in between. Please respond to each item.

	NOT TRUE AT ALL (Never, Seldom)	JUST A LITTLE TRUE (Occasionally)	PRETTY MUCH TRUE (Often, Quite a Bit)	VERY MUCH TRUE (Very Often, Very Frequent)
1. Inattentive, easily distracted...	0	1	2	3
2. Defiant..	0	1	2	3

Conners' Parent Rating Scale - Revised (S)

by C. Keith Conners, Ph. D.

Child's Name_____Gender: M   F

Birthdate: ____/ ____/ _____   Age: _____   School Grade: _____
       Month Day Year

Parent's Name:_____   Today's Date: ____/ ____/ ____
                                         Month Day Year

Instructions: Below are a number of common problems that children have. Please rate each item according to your child's behavior in the last month. For each item, ask yourself, "How much of a problem has this been in the last month?", and circle the best answer for each one. If none, not at all, seldom, or very infrequently, you would circle a 0. If very much true, or it occurs very often or frequently, you would circle 3. You would circle 1 or 2 for ratings in between. Please respond to each item.

	NOT TRUE AT ALL (Never, Seldom)	JUST A LITTLE TRUE (Occasionally)	PRETTY MUCH TRUE (Often, Quite a Bit)	VERY MUCH TRUE (Very Often, Very Frequent)
1. Inattentive, easily distracted...	0	1	2	3
2. Angry and resentful...	0	1	2	3

References

CHAPTER 1: The Evolution of ADHD

1. American Psychiatric Association (1994). *Diagnostic and Statistical Manual of Mental Disorders* (4th ed.). Washington, DC: American Psychiatric Association.

2. Barkley, R. (1997). *ADHD and the Nature of Self-Control.* New York: Guilford Press.

3. Fowler, M. (1992). *CH.A.D.D. Educators Manual.* Fairfax, Virginia: CASET Associates, Ltd.

CHAPTER 2: ADHD Through the Lifespan

1. Barkley, R., Fischer, M., Newby, R. and Breen, M. (1988). Development of a Multi-Method Clinical Protocol for Assessing Stimulant Drug Responses in ADHD Children. *Journal of Clinical Child Psychology*, 17, 14-24.

2. Hartsough, C.S. and Lambert, N.M. (1985). Medical Factors in Hyperactive and Normal Children: Prenatal, Developmental, and Health History Findings. *American Journal of Orthopsychiatry*, 55, 190-210.

3. Barkley, R. (1990). *Attention Deficit Hyperactivity Disorder: A Handbook for Diagnosis and Treatment.* New York: Guilford Press.

4. Ibid.

5. Barkley, R., Fischer, M., Edelbrock, C.S. and Smallish, L. (1990). The Adolescent Outcome of Hyperactive Children Diagnosed by Research Criteria: I. An 8 Year Prospective Follow-Up Study. *Journal of the American Academy of Child and Adolescent Psychiatry.* 29, 546-557.

6. Ibid.

7. Barkley, R., op. cit.

8. Brown, R.T. and Borden, K.A. (1986). Hyperactivity at Adolescence: Some Misconceptions and New Directions. *Journal of Clinical Child Psychology*, 15, 194-209.

9. Weiss, G. and Hechtman, L. (1986). *Hyperactive Children Grown Up*. New York: Guilford Press.

10. Blouin, A.G., Bornstein, M.A. and Trites, R.L. (1978). Teenage Alcohol Abuse Among Hyperactive Children: A Five Year Follow-Up Study. *Journal of Pediatric Psychology*, 3, 188-194.

11. Loney, J., Kramer, J. and Milich, R. (1981). The Hyperkinetic Child Grows Up: Predictors of Symptoms, Delinquency, and Achievement at Follow-Up. In K.D. Gadow & J. Loney (Eds.), *Psychosocial Aspects of Drug Treatment for Hyperactivity*. Boulder, Colorado: Westview Press.

12. Weiss, G. and Hechtman, L., op. cit.

13. Barkley, R., op. cit.

14. Hallowell, E.M. and Ratey, J.J. (1994). *Driven to Distraction*. New York: Pantheon Books.

15. Weiss, G. and Hechtman, L., op. cit.

16. Barkley, R., op. cit.

17. Paternite, C. and Loney, J. (1980). Childhood Hyperkinesis: Relationship Between Symptomatology and Home Environment. In C.K. Whalen & B. Henker (Eds.), *Hyperactive Children: The Social Ecology of Identification and Treatment* (pp. 105-141). New York: Academic Press.

18. Weiss, G. and Hechtman, L., op. cit.

19. Whalen, C.K. and Henker, B. (Eds.). (1980). *Hyperactive Children: The Social Ecology of Identification and Treatment*. New York: Academic Press.

CHAPTER 3: Causes: Fiction and Fact

1. Barkley, R. and Cunningham, C. (1980). *The Parent-Child Interactions of Hyperactive Children and Their Modification by Stimulant Drugs in Treatment of Hyperactive & Learning Disabled Children*, edited by R. Knight & D. Baker. Baltimore: University Park Press.

2. Cantwell, D. P. (1981). Foreward. In R.A. Barkley, *Hyperactive Children: A Handbook for Diagnosis and Treatment* (pp. vii-x). New York: Guilford Press.

3. Werner, H. and Strauss, A.A. (1941). Pathology of Figure-Background Relation in the Child. *Journal of Abnormal and Social Psychology*, 36, 236-248.

4. Reeves, J.C. and Werry, J.S. (1987). Soft Signs in Hyperactivity. In D.E. Tupper (Ed.), *Soft Neurological Signs*. New York: Grune & Stratton.

5. Feingold, B. (1974). *Why Your Child is Hyperactive*. New York: Random House.

6. Milich, R., Wolraich, M. and Lindgren, S. (1986). Sugar and Hyperactivity: A Critical Review of Empirical Findings. *Clinical Psychology Review*, 6, 493-513.

7. Conners, C.K. (1989). *Feeding the Brain: How Foods Affect Children*. New York: Plenum Press.

8. Barkley, R. DuPaul, G.J. and McMurray, M.B. (1990). A Comprehensive Evaluation of Attention Deficit Disorder With and Without Hyperactivity Defined by Research Criteria. *Journal of Consulting and Clinical Psychology*, 58, 775-789.

9. Hartsough, C.S. and Lambert, N.M. (1985). Medical Factors in Hyperactive and Normal Children: Prenatal, Developmental, and Health History Findings. *American Journal of Orthopsychiatry*, 55, 190-210.

10. Goodman, R. and Stevenson, J. (1989). A Twin Study of Hyperactivity: II. The Aetiological Role of Genes, Family Relationships, and Perinatal Adversity. *Journal of Child Psychology and Psychiatry*, 30, 691-709.

11. Zametkin, A.J. and Rapoport, J.L. (1986). The Pathophysiology of Attention Deficit Disorder with Hyperactivity: A Review. In B. Lahey & A. Kazdin (Eds.), *Advances in Clinical Child Psychology* (Vol. 9, pp. 177-216). New York: Plenum.

12. Hastings, J. and Barkley, R.A. (1978). A Review of Psychophysiological Research with Hyperactive Children. *Journal of Abnormal Child Psychology*, 7, 413-337.

13. Ibid.

14. Lou, H.C., Henriksen, L. and Bruhn, P. (1984). Focal Cerebral Hypoperfusion in Children with Dysphasia and/or Attention Deficit Disorder. *Archives of Neurology*, 41; 825-29.

15. Hastings, J. and Barkley, R.A., op. cit.

16. Zametkin, A. J. et al. (1990). Cerebral Glucose Metabolism in Adults with Hyperactivity of Childhood Onset. *New England Journal of Medicine,* 323; 1361-66.

17. Ibid.

18. Ibid.

CHAPTER 5: ADHD Affects the Ability to Follow Rules

1. Fowler, M. (1992). *CH.A.D.D. Educators Manual.* Fairfax, Virginia: CASET Associates, Ltd.

2. I attribute this great mantra to my colleague and friend Gayl Staver, M.A., LP.

CHAPTER 6: Twelve Common Behavioral Patterns

1. Phelan, T. (1990). *All About Attention Deficit: Parts 1 and 2.* A.D.D. WareHouse 800-233-0273

2. Levine, M. D. (1993). *Keeping a Head in School.* Cambridge: Educators Publishing Service, Inc.

3. Barkley, R. (1997). *ADHD and the Nature of Self-Control.* New York: Guilford Press.

4. Zentall, S. S. (1986). Effects of Color Stimulation on Performance and Activity of Hyperactive and Nonhyperactive Children. *Journal of Abnormal Child Psychology*, 78, 159-165.

5. Barkley, R. (1990). *Attention Deficit Hyperactivity Disorder: A Handbook for Diagnosis and Treatment.* New York: Guilford Press.

6. Loney, J. and Milich, R. (1982). Hyperactivity, Inattention, and Aggression in Clinical Practice. In D. Routh & M. Wolraich (Eds.), *Advances in Developmental and Behavioral Pediatrics* (Vol. 3, pp. 113-147). Greenwich, Connecticut: JAI Press.

CHAPTER 7: Form Realistic Expectations

1. Cray, E. (1990). *Pick Up Your Socks.* Seattle: Parenting Press, Inc.

CHAPTER 9: Consider How Your Temperament "Fits" With Your Child

1. Thomas, A. and Chess, S. (1963). *Behavioral Individuality in Early Childhood* New York: New York University Press.

2. Turecki, S. (1985). *The Difficult Child.* New York: Bantam Books.

CHAPTER 10: Parent Proactively

1. Covey, S.R. (1989). *The Seven Habits of Highly Effective People: Restoring the Character Ethic.* New York: Simon & Schuster.

2. Lerner, H. (1985). *Dance of Anger: A Woman's Guide to Changing Patterns in Intimate Relationships.* New York: Harper & Row.

3. Kendall, P.C. and Braswell, L. (1985). *Cognitive-Behavioral Therapy for Impulsive Children.* New York: Guilford.

4. Braswell, L. and Bloomquist. (1991). *Cognitive-Behavioral Therapy with ADHD Children.* New York : Guilford Press.

CHAPTER 14: Structuring Your Home

1. Dinkmeyer, D. and McKay, G. D. (1982). *Systematic Training for Effective Parenting: The Parent's Handbook.* Circle Pines, Minnesota: American Guidance Service.

CHAPTER 17: Devising Behavior Modification Systems

1. Patterson, G.R., Reid, J.B., and Dishion, T.J. (1992). *Antisocial Boys.* Eugene Oregon: Castalia.

2. Forehand, R.L. and McMahon, R.J. (1981). *Helping the Noncompliant Child: A Clinician's Guide to Parent Training.* New York: Guilford Press.

3. Hinshaw, S.P. and Anderson, C.A. (1996). Conduct and Oppositional Defiant Disorders. In E.J. Mash and R.A. Barkley (Eds.), *Child Psychopathology* (pp. 113-152). New York: Guilford Press.

4. Snyder, J. and Patterson, G.R. (1995). Individual Differences in Social Aggression: A Test of the Reinforcement Model of Socialization in the Natural Environment. *Behavior Therapy, 26,* 371-391.

5. Patterson, G.R. (1982). *Coercive Family Process*. Eugene, Oregon: Castalia

6. Hinshaw, S.P. and Anderson, C.A., op. cit.

7. Barkley, R., Fischer, M., Edelbrock, C.S. and Smallish, L. (1990). The Adolescent Outcome of Hyperactive Children Diagnosed by Research Criteria: I. An 8 Year Prospective Follow-Up Study. *Journal of the American Academy of Child and Adolescent Psychiatry*, 29, 546-557.

8. Loeber, R. (1990). Development and Risk Factors of Juvenile Antisocial Behavior and Delinquency. *Clinical Psychology Review*, 10, 1-41.

9. Barkley, R. (1997). *Defiant Children: A Clinician's Manual for Assessment and Parent Training*. (2nd ed.). New York: Guilford Press.

10. Barkley, R. (1981). *Hyperactive Children: A Handbook for Diagnosis and Treatment*. New York: Guilford Press.

11. Phelan, T. (1984). *1-2-3: Magic.! Training Your Preschoolers and Preteens to do What You Want*. Child Management, 800 Roosevelt Rd., Glen Ellyn, Illinois 60137, 708-699-0848.

CHAPTER 18: Breaking the Cycle of Willful Noncompliance

1. Phelan, T. (1984). *1-2-3: Magic.! Training Your Preschoolers and Preteens to do What You Want*. Child Management, 800 Roosevelt Rd., Glen Ellyn, Illinois 60137, 708-699-0848.

CHAPTER 19: Using Active Listening

1. Gordon, T. (1975). *Parent Effectiveness Training: The Tested New Way to Raise Responsible Children*. New York: Penguin Books.

2. Ibid.

CHAPTER 20: Stimulants

1. Barkley, R.A. (1977). A Review of Stimulant Drug Research with Hyperactive Children. *Journal of Child Psychology and Psychiatry*, 18, 137-165.

2. Pelham, W.E., Sturges, J., Hoza, J., Schmidt, C., Bijlsma, J.J., Milich, R. and Moorer, S. (1987). Sustained Release and Standard Methylphenidate Effects on Cognitive and Social Behavior in Children with Attention Deficit Disorder. *Pediatrics*, 4, 491-501.

3. Barkley, R. (1990). *Attention Deficit Hyperactivity Disorder: A Handbook for Diagnosis and Treatment.* New York: Guilford Press.

4. Copeland, E. (1991). *Medications for Attention Disorders (ADHD/ADD) and Related Medical Problems.* Atlanta Georgia: SPI Press.

5. Barkley, R. (1995). Adderall—A New Drug for Managing ADHD? In R. Barkley & Associates (Eds.), *The ADHD Report* (Vol. 3, No. 2, p. 16). New York: Guilford Press.

6. Barkley, R., op.cit.

7. Barkley, R. A., McMurray, M.B., Edelbrock, C.S. and Robbins, K. (1990). The Side Effects of Ritalin: A Systematic Placebo Controlled Evaluation of Two Doses. *Pediatrics.,* 86, 184-192.

8. Ibid.

9. Denckla, M.B., Bemporad, J.R. and MacKay, M.C. (1976). Tics Following Methylphenidate Administration. *Journal of the American Medical Association,* 235, 1349-1351.

10. Johnston, C., Pelham, W.E., Hoza, J. and Sturges, J. (1988). Psychostimulant Rebound in Attention Deficit Disordered Boys. *Journal of the American Academy of Child and Adolescent Psychiatry,* 27, 806-810.

11. Barkley, R. (1988). Tic Disorders and Tourette's Syndrome. In E. Mash & Terdal (Eds.), *Behavioral Assessment of Childhood Disorders* (2nd ed., pp. 69-104). New York: Guilford Press.

12. Haerle, T. (1992). *Children with Tourette Syndrome: A Parents' Guide.* Rockville, Maryland: Woodbine Press.

13. Safer, D.J., Allen, R.P. and Barr, E. (1972). Depression in Growth in Hyperactive Children on Stimulant Drugs. *New England Journal of Medicine,* 287, 217-220.

14. Safer, D.J. and Allen, R.P. (1973). Factors Influencing the Suppressant Effects of Two Stimulant Drugs on the Growth of Hyperactive Children. *Pediatrics,* 51, 660-667.

15. Mattes, J.A. and Gittelman, R. (1983). Growth of Hyperactive Children on Maintenance Regimen of Methylphenidate. *Archives of General Psychiatry,* 40, 317-321.

16. Gadow, K.D. (1981). Prevalence of Drug Treatment for Hyperactivity and Other Childhood Behavior Disorders. In K.D. Gadow & J. Loney (Eds.), *Psychosocial Aspects of Drug Treatment for Hyperactivity* (pp. 13-70). Boulder, Colorado: Westview Press.

17. Barkley, R., op.cit.

18. Sprague, R. and Sleator, E. (1977). Methylphenidate in Hyperkinetic Children: Differences in Dose Effects on Learning and Social Behavior. *Science*, 198, 1274-1276.

CHAPTER 21: Other Medications Used to Manage ADHD

1. Biederman, J., Baldessarini, R.J., Wright, V., Knee, D. and Harmatz, J.S. (1989). A Double-Blind Placebo Controlled Study of Desipramine in the Treatment of ADD: I. Efficacy. *Journal of the American Academy of Child and Adolescent Psychiatry*, 28, 777-784.

CHAPTER 24: Knowing the Laws and Your Rights

1. Fowler, M. (1992). The Disability Named ADD. In M. Fowler (Ed.),*CH.A.D.D. Educators Manual*. (pp. 3-8). Fairfax, Virginia: CASET Associates, Ltd.

2. Aronofsky, D. (1992). ADD: A Brief Summary of School District Legal Obligations and Children's Educational Rights. In M. Fowler (Ed.),*CH.A.D.D. Educators Manual* (pp. 57-60). Fairfax, Virginia: CASET Associates, Ltd.

3. 20 U.S. C. 1400 et seq.; U.S. Education Department rules codified at 34 C.F.R. 300 et seq.

4. U.S. Public Law 101-476, Sec. 102.

CHAPTER 25: Keeping Records of Your Child

1. Learning Disabilities Council (1991). *Understanding Learning Disabilities: A Parent Guide and Workbook*. Richmond, Virginia: The Learning Disabilities Council.

CHAPTER 27: Providing Input Into The Selection of Your Child's Teacher

1. Campbell, S.B., Endman, M., and Bernfield, G. (1977). A Three Year Follow-Up of Hyperactive Preschoolers into Elementary School. *Journal of Child Psychology and Psychiatry*, 18, 239-249.

2. Weiss, G.. and Hechtman, L. (1986). *Hyperactive Children Grown Up*. New York: Guilford Press.

Index

A

Achievement 34, 37, 42, 44, 56, 251, 314
Active listening 219–220, 223–228, 238–241, 290
    twelve ways parents respond 228–241
Adderall 245, 249
ADHD
    Combined Type 21, 23, 28, 68, 72, 103
    Hyperactive-Impulsive Type 21, 23, 26, 53, 68, 77, 103, 189, 256
    Inattentive Type 21, 23, 26, 68, 196, 256
Adolescence
    behavioral symptoms 35–36
Adulthood
    behavioral symptoms 38–41
Aggression
    control with 135
    predictors of outcome 43, 255
    preschool 32
    turtle technique 293
Allowance 160
Anafranil (clomipramine) 261
Anger 91, 95, 96, 136–140, 142
    contamination 138
    control 137–140
    emotional overarousal and 65, 81–82
    expectations and 91
    in response to punishment 134
Antisocial Personality Disorder 41
Arguing. *See also* Noncompliance
    parent-child 102, 106, 138, 140, 162, 171, 208–214, 218, 221
Attention
    daydreaming 68, 83
    divided 68
    focused 68
    negative 158, 171–174, 183
    no attention problems 78
    positive 174–177
    selective 26, 68
    situations where no attention problems 69–70
    sustained 23, 68, 108
    vigilance 68
Attention tape 290–291, 329
Attentional capacity 70, 79, 125, 325, 338, 339
Attitude
    of superiority 235
    parenting and 345–347
Aventyl (nortriptyline) 261

B

Behavior management 13, 41, 80, 99, 129, 147–148, 169, 190, 197, 283, 328, 339, 346
Behavior modification 6, 60, 101, 129, 141, 179–205, 216, 337
Body cues 154, 167–168
Bonus points 161–162, 176, 188, 201–202, 286, 292, 300, 328
Brain damage 48
Brain stimulation
    curves 54–55, 272–274
    in the classroom 272–274
    relation to ADHD 55, 60, 73, 272–274
    understimulation 54, 55, 57, 60, 73, 272–274
Brain structure 50–53
"Bug list" 158, 183–184, 191, 197

C

Calming breath 138, 167
Catapres-TTS 265
Causes of ADHD 47, 50–53
CH.A.D.D. 95, 331, 345–346

Chart(s) 62, 93, 166, 180, 187, 193, 202, 204, 285, 339, 359
Child study team 309–310, 324
Chores 24, 34, 41, 60, 78–79, 82, 95, 160, 162, 209
Classroom adaptations/modifications 281–301
    for 504 or IEP 323–332
    suggested by federal mandate 308–309
    Classroom and ADHD 271–279
Classroom characteristics 338–339
Clonidine (Catapres) 265
Commands 57, 76, 101, 229, 333
    effective 125, 156, 176
Communication process 225
Communication with teacher 89, 270, 342–343
Conflict
    parent-child 107, 220
    poor parenting 47–48
    school and 316, 323
Conners, Dr. Keith 49
Consequences 4, 59, 147, 283. *See also*
  Behavior modification
    before the fact 25, 153
    big, medium, little deal 159
    consistent 75
    feedback and 181
    frequent 63
    immediate 59
    ineffective 74, 75, 179, 230,283
    interesting 60
    interesting and tangible 182
    logical 141
    powerful 75,182
    varied 76
Control Zone 118–120, 345
Curriculum modifications 272, 325, 327
Cylert (pemoline) 245, 248–249

D

Daily report card 285
Department of Education 305–306, 309, 315, 316
Depth of processing 70
Desipramine.*See* Norpramin; Petrofrane
Dexedrine (dextroamphetamine) 245, 248, 249
Dexedrine Elixir 248
Dexedrine Spansule 248, 254

Diagnostic guidelines 23–28
Directions
    following multi-step 124
    how to give 124–125, 287
    redirections 143
    simplified 326
    timer-managed 289
Dis-inhibition 4, 25, 28, 53
    executive functions and 52
    interferes with 53, 62, 72, 83–84, 157
Disorganization
    at home 126
    at school 34, 84–85
    homework and 34
    in adulthood 39
Distractibility 68–69
    classroom modifications for 293–295
Dopamine 53, 55, 245, 255, 261
DSM-IV 21, 23, 247
Due process 307, 316–317

E

Edison, Thomas 14–16
Educational disorder 271, 305
Elavil (amitriptyline) 261
Electroencephalogram (EEG) 52, 57
Emotional overarousal 65, 81–82
Emotional/behavior disorder (EBD) 306, 312, 330
Encephalitis 48
Executive functions 52
    homework and 55–56
Expectations 33, 91
    anger and 91
    before the fact 153
    realistic 91, 92, 95, 97, 168, 175, 198
    school 331, 343
    unrealistic 63, 91
External control 62–63, 110, 136, 157

F

Family meeting 155
Feedback 181
    consistent 181, 283
    frequent 181
    immediate 181, 283
    negative 100, 238
    positive 125, 144, 175, 233
    specific 143, 144, 157, 234
    spontaneous 175

Feingold, Dr. Ben
    diet 49
Food additives 49
Frequency monitoring 186, 189, 193, 200
Frontal lobes 71
Future outcome 42

G

Glucose
    metabolism 53
Goals
    appropriate 281
    daily 185, 192, 200–202, 286, 328
    end-of-the-week 185, 194, 196, 286
    long-term 72, 95, 282
    positive 183, 282
    short-term 184, 185, 282
    weekly 328
Goodness of fit
    parent and child 104
    teacher and child 269, 333–337
Gordon, Dr. Thomas 5, 224–225, 228, 291
Grading modifications 329
Gratification
    difficulty delaying 44, 80, 81, 95

H

Heredity 50
Homework
    low motivation and 37, 126
    reduced load 125, 129, 299, 342
    structure and 126–129
    understimulation 179
Hyperactive. See ADHD
Hyperactive-Impulsive. See ADHD

I

Impulsivity 25, 65, 72–73, 125, 138, 225,
    232, 277. See also Dis-inhibition
    ADHD diagnosis and 27, 44
    classroom modifications for 81, 291–
    293
    in adolescence 36
    in adulthood 40
    in preschool 23
    parents' 6
Inconsistency 272
    and brain stimulation 56

behavior pattern 55–56, 65, 77–80, 96
    conditions which contribute 78–80
    in feedback and reinforcement 181,
    283
    in school 272
Inconsistent
    parenting and 43, 204, 219
Individual educational plan (IEP) 311–
    313, 316, 320, 323–324, 342
    planning guide 325–332
Infancy
    difficult 29, 32
Insomnia 249, 252–253, 262–263
Interval monitoring 186, 189, 193

L

Language delay 31
Language of acceptance 238–241
Language of unacceptance 223–225,
    239, 241
Laws which protect students with ADHD
    Americans With Disabilities Act 309
    Individuals with Disabilities
        Education Act (IDEA) 306–307,
        309, 311
    Public Law 94-142, 306
    Rehabilitation Act of 1973 306–307
LDA 346
Learned avoidance 173
Learning disabilities 43, 271, 306, 346
    SLD 306
Let sleeping dogs lie 172
Levels of service 311–312
Levine, Dr. Mel 5, 71
Limbic system 51, 53

M

Meals 123
Medication. See also Catapres-TTS;
    Clonidine (Catapres); Medication
    chart; Prozac (fluoxetine); Stimulant
    medication; Tricyclic antidepressants
        appetite suppression 123, 248, 252–
        253, 263
        effect on parent-child relationship 48
        multi-modal treatment 244
Medication chart 266-267
Medication management 7, 243, 331, 342

Memory
    active working 71, 72
    limbic system and 52
    prospective 71
Methylphenidate. *See* Ritalin
Midbrain 51, 52
Modeling 43, 135, 137, 139, 149, 165,
    229, 239, 292
    other students and 294, 325
Motivation
    deficit 56–58, 59–60, 298
    in classroom 59–60, 272, 274, 298–301
Multi-modal 41, 42, 256

N

Negative alert 172
Negative behavior 79, 143, 158, 171–174,
    183–184, 191, 197. *See also* 1-2-3: Magic!
    response cost and 328
Neurobiological 53, 58, 60, 75, 83, 93,
    134, 179, 181, 272, 274, 296
Neurochemical imbalance 50
Neurologic soft signs 48–49
Noncompliance
    ADHD-related 65, 76–77, 102, 207–214
    cycle of 210–214
    examples of 100, 210
    excessive 76–77
    reasons to focus on 209–210
    types of 99
    willful 99–102
Norepinephrine 53, 245, 261
Norpramin (desipramine) 261–262

O

1-2-3: Magic! 190–191, 214–221
On-task behavior 282, 284, 287, 329
Organization
    achievement and 85
    ADHD and 84–85
    beginning of the day 296–297
    in the classroom 85, 272, 281, 296–
    298, 301
"other health impaired" (OHI) 306, 315
Outcome
    factors that predict 41–44

P

Pamelor (nortriptyline) 261
Parent deafness 141, 230, 232
Parenting. *See* Poor parenting; Proactive;
    Reactive
Persistence
    poor 55–56, 82–83, 103, 108, 185,
    251, 272, 282, 295
    stimulants and 251
Pervasive Developmental Disorder 28, 257
Petrofrane 261
Phelan, Dr. Tom 214–215
Placebo 247, 252
Poor parenting 4, 12, 47–48
Positive behavior 80, 140, 144, 157–158,
    161, 171–177, 180–181, 186–187, 191–
    192, 197, 284
Predictors of outcome 41–44
Prefrontal lobes 51–55
Prenatal factors 50
Preschool
    behavioral symptoms 23, 30–32
Proactive
    Control Zone 119, 345
    language 116–117
    parenting 4, 113–114, 117, 345
    solutions 116, 122–124, 126
Prozac (fluoxetine) 264
Public Law 94-142, 306
Punishment. *See also* Consequences;
    Response cost; Time-out
    abuse of power 136
    over-punishment 120, 134, 135
    permissable punishment 140
    problems with 4, 12, 74–75, 101,
    134–136
    removal of privileges 140–141
    verbal reprimands 141

R

Rating scales 247
    Academic Performance Rating
    Scale 247, 331
    ADHD Rating Scale 247
    Conners' Rating Scales 247
Reactive
    language 116–117, 119
    parenting 115–116, 119–122
    Worry Zone 117–120

Reframe thoughts 116–117
Reinforcement 59
    immediate 78, 80, 274
    intermittent 214
    negative 213, 215–216
    positive 158, 184, 213, 282–287
Relaxation 137, 138
Removal of privileges 140–141
Response cost 141, 188, 328
    modified 161, 188
Responsibility
    household 93
    maturity level 95
    response-ability 114
Reward menu 180, 186–187, 193, 202, 204, 285
Ritalin (methylphenidate) 12, 243, 245. *See also* Stimulant medication
    academic achievement 251
    administration 246–248
    anxiety and 253
    compared to generic 247
    compared to Ritalin SR 246–247
    dosage 246–247
    monitoring 247–248
    Tourette's syndrome and 254–255
Ritalin-SR 246, 254
Rules 58, 152–153. *See also* Dis-inhibition
    consequences and 62
    effective 63
    expectations and 63
    household 152
    internal control 62, 136
    no emotion 215
    no-talking 216
    noncompliance 61, 62, 72, 99
    regular review 296

S

S.T.E.P. 155
Schedules 126, 127, 149, 151, 190, 295, 308, 327
School age
    behavioral symptoms 32–35
School records
    of your child 319–321
    request for 314
Secondary behavior 101,147
Secret signal 162–163, 286, 328
Section 504 Plan 311–315, 320, 323–325, 342

Self-control
    ADHD a disorder of 4
    calendars 166
    defective 62, 95
    for parents 137, 142
    journal 166
    posters 167
    predict the day 166
    private contract 301, 328
    rate the day 166
    self-talk and 165
    the brain and 51
    tickets 160
Self-esteem 3, 35–38, 97, 100, 135, 139, 142, 208, 217, 220, 228–229, 234, 252, 262, 299, 314, 333, 337, 339
Self-monitor 143, 165, 175, 290–291, 330, 339
Self-rate 165
Self-regulation 51, 53, 55, 148, 199
Self-talk 165, 292
Shaping 161, 175, 184
Social cues 86, 96, 168
Social problems 85
    adolescence 35–38
    in school-age child 33–35
    preschool 30–32
Socioeconomic status 39, 42
Special education 13, 42, 45, 271, 306–317, 320, 323, 346
Special time 176–177, 226
Specific Learning Disability (SLD) 306
Start behaviors 191, 216
Stimulant medication 245. *See also* Adderall; Cylert; Dexedrine (dextro-amphetamine); Dexedrine Spansule; Ritalin (methylphenidate); Ritalin-SR
    addiction 256
    behavioral effects 250–251
    benefits 245, 249–252
    cognitive effects 250
    duration of use 257–259
    evaluation of effectiveness 258–259
    growth suppression 255
    long-term side effects 252
    misconceptions 254–256
    predictors of response 256–257
    rebound 84, 126, 254
    short-term side effects 252–254
    substance abuse 255–256
    Tourette's syndrome and 254–255
    when not to use 257

Stimulation curve 54–55, 272–274
Stimulus 113–114, 124. *See also* "Bug
    list"; Proactive; Reactive
Stop behaviors 177, 216, 223
Stress 81, 139–140, 167
    parental 38, 43, 81
Striatum 51, 52
Structure
    child 157–163
    classroom 295–296
    home 149–156
Substance abuse 255–256
    in adolescence 37
Sugar 49

T

Teacher characteristics 337–338
Temperament
    difficult 29, 32, 103–104
    dissimilarity between parent and
        child 107–109
    fit 103, 111
    infancy 29–30
    laid back parent 110–111
    preschool 30–32
    similarity between parent and child
        104
    traits 103–104
Testing 310
    individualized 295
    modifications 329–330
    one-to-one 69–70
    re-taking 300
Time-out. *See also* 1-2-3: Magic!
    for parents 138–139
    punishment 140
Tofranil (imipramine) 261
Token system 180, 186
    advantages 180, 284
    group 300, 328
    how to set up 183–187
    reasons for failure 181–182
Tourette's syndrome 12, 254–255, 257,
    262–263, 265
Transitions 83–84
    at home 29–30, 32, 65, 126, 153
    at school 295–297, 338
    with medication 84, 331

Tricyclic antidepressants 261. *See also*
    Norpramin (desipramine); Tofranil
    (imipramine)
    benefits 261
    dosage 262–263
    side effects 263–264
    when to prescribe 262
Trigger thoughts 140
Turtle technique 293
Two-column technique 158, 191

U

UADD 22, 26
Underachievement
    adolescence 37
    adulthood 39
    school-age 34–35, 45

W

When-then 156
Worry Zone 117–120

Z

Zametkin, Dr. Alan 53
Zentall, Dr. Sidney 73

About the Author

Janette Schaub is a noted psychologist who has treated more than 1000 children and adults with ADHD. She earned her Ph.D. from the University of Minnesota, where she conducted research on this disorder. In practice for more than 20 years, Dr. Schaub also teaches classes at area universities and consults with schools, clinics and other service agencies. She lectures extensively on ADHD, learning disorders, and child behavior management. She is a founding member of CHADD of the Twin Cities and serves on its professional advisory board. Dr. Schaub lives in Bloomington, Minnesota with her husband and three children.

Your Kid Has ADHD, Now What?

A Handbook for Parents, Educators and Practitioners